Football/Soccer

D1522288

Football / Soccer

History and Tactics

JAIME OREJAN

Foreword by ROBYN L. JONES

McFarland & Company, Inc., Publishers
Jefferson, North Carolina, and London

LIBRARY OF CONGRESS CATALOGUING-IN-PUBLICATION DATA

Orejan, Jaime, 1956–
    Football/soccer : history and tactics / Jaime Orejan ; foreword
by Robyn L. Jones.
      p.   cm.
    Includes bibliographical references and index.

    ISBN 978-0-7864-4784-8
    softcover : 50# alkaline paper

    1. Soccer — History.   I. Title.
    GV938.O74 2011
    796.33 — dc23   2011036053

BRITISH LIBRARY CATALOGUING DATA ARE AVAILABLE

© 2011 Jaime Orejan. All rights reserved

*No part of this book may be reproduced or transmitted in any form
or by any means, electronic or mechanical, including photocopying
or recording, or by any information storage and retrieval system,
without permission in writing from the publisher.*

On the cover: (top) English football team at the 1912 Olympics in Stockholm,
Sweden (Library of Congress); (bottom) Boudewijn Zenden (left) of Liverpool and Alexander Hleb of Arsenal in a Premier League match (Image Shack)

Manufactured in the United States of America

McFarland & Company, Inc., Publishers
  Box 611, Jefferson, North Carolina 28640
   www.mcfarlandpub.com

To my Elizabeth, for the countless times I left you alone with our two boys so I could travel and research for this book. You are the love of my life, my pretty woman, a wonderful mother, and I am grateful for your support and encouragement each and every day. You're still the one!

To my two boys James (Jay) and Joseph (Joey) ... you are my heroes. Thank you for the laughter and joy you bring to my life every day. Your insatiable appetite for learning, for having fun, and for enjoying life the way you do reminds me of the importance of always being a kid no matter what, and to just have fun. My life without the two of you would be empty and dull. You are a blessing!

To my biological parents, José Alfonso (RIP) and Elisa Valladares ... you nurtured me, loved me, and provided for me under difficult circumstances, and without asking. More importantly, thank you for providing for my education. You are irreplaceable jewels!

To my adopted parents Al and Margie Parish ... thank you for your encouragement, support, prayers, and always being there for me during my most difficult times. You have taught me so much about the value of life and love of God, and I am a better man because of you. Without the two of you, I would be a lost soul!

TABLE OF CONTENTS

ACKNOWLEDGMENTS

Special gratitude is afforded to Dr. Gerry Dillashaw, former dean of the School of Education during my tenure at Elon University, for his assistance in securing a grant for the research, and thus offsetting many of the expenses of this project.

To Mr. Peter Holmes and all the staff at the National Football Museum in Preston, England, for allowing me to research their archives, for allowing me to take and use pictures from their incredible collection, and for all the courtesies extended during my time at the museum. Thank you to Mr. Alexander Jackson, for taking the time to guide me through the archives. Without the assistance from the people at the museum, most of this project would not have been completed.

To Mr. David Barber, archivist at the English FA Headquarters in Soho Square, London, for his time and accommodation with the archives at the FA, and for his suggestion to visit the National Football Museum in Preston for more additional research.

To FIFA, for their permission to duplicate the Laws of the Game, and for their courtesies during my time at their headquarters in the summer of 2006.

To the archivists and personnel at the Olympic Museum in Lausanne, Switzerland.

To Mr. Alum Evans of the Welsh Football Association, for his candid conversation and time spent talking about football and tactics.

To Dr. Eirik Jensen in Denmark and Dr. Robyn Jones in Wales for their time, and willingness to help any way they could. Your friendship has been priceless over the last 20 years.

To all my friends and family for encouraging me to finish this book, and in particular to my good friend and neighbor Henry Korzekwinski for always picking me up when all seemed lost and I was ready to quit.

FOREWORD
BY ROBYN L. JONES

It is a pleasure for me to write this foreword; not least because of my longstanding relationship with the author. Jaime and I were graduate students together in the early 1990s at the University of Southern Mississippi where we shared a love and passion for the "beautiful game." Football is, however, also the global game (as witnessed by our immediate allegiance: he from El Salvador, me from Wales); but more importantly in this context it is "the people's game" (a point alluded to in Chapter 7). It is from this perspective that the book is constructed. Jaime's passion for the game, his numerous points of reference (from being a professional player, a coach and now an academic and researcher), come through in the text. In this respect, the book is much more than merely another history of football. Rather, Jaime brings a certain understanding to the analysis; not merely that of a passive observer, but of someone who cares enthusiastically about the sport, of someone who lives his words. This was reflected in the numerous trips he made to the UK to visit fellow historians, libraries, archives, and administrators to research his subject matter; as well as taking in as many games as he could! I believe Jaime has produced a very informative and interesting read related to the history of football tactics. By tracing them so, he also gives clues about how they may evolve in the future. I enjoyed my journey through the book; I hope it proves as stimulating for you.

Robyn L. Jones is a professor at the Cardiff School of Sport,
University of Wales Institute, Cardiff.

PREFACE

Over a large part of the planet, football[1] (soccer) is a way of life. There are an estimated 150 million professional and amateur registered players; fans and spectators can only be measured in the millions per season, per country; roughly two billion people from four to ninety years of age (some younger or older) practice kicking a ball on sand, on grass, and on hard or muddy play casts. However, many have wondered, What is football? Who invented it? Where does it come from? How did tactics and formations evolve?

The elements of present-day football are deeply rooted in antiquity. Nearly everyone, when speaking or hearing of football's origins, delights in the well-worn tale of ancient barbarians who allegedly contributed to the founding of the game by kicking around the skulls of their fallen adversaries.

To indulge in all sorts of speculation as to which ancient civilization through its kicking games invented football, really takes our eye off the ball, which is dangerous in searching for sources.

Purists of the game claim that the word *football* should really be applied only to the sport we call soccer. What else would anyone call a game played with the feet and with a ball? The word *football* came into use in England around the mid–fourteenth century to describe a game played *not* with the feet but on *foot*, in order to distinguish it from pastimes that were played on horseback.

Trying to work out and research who first played football, and where and when, is a fruitless but interesting occupation. Clearly, modern football is a sport that was devised by the British, refined by the Scottish players and coaches, and began to take a form recognizable to us in the England of the 1800s.

This book explores and explains the different cultures and civilizations throughout history that have played versions of the game, as well as the teams, players, and coaches that played a part in the development of tactics used over the years. An attempt is made to determine who invented the game.

The main objective of this book is to trace, analyze, and describe the historical development of football and team tactics used in Football Association from 1863, the year the English Football Association was founded, to the present.

In the book a brief history of the sport is presented, along with several reasons for the worldwide appeal of football as a spectator sport. There is a description of the Fédération Internationale de Football Association (FIFA), followed by an account of how football evolved from its crude and unorganized beginning to the modern version of the game. The most influential tactics or formations that have been used since 1863 are explained and, when possible, an attempt has been made to identify which countries, players, and coaches have been influential in making these changes possible, and for what purpose.

Additionally, the relationship between tactics and physical condition is explored, as well as the relations between tactics and other external factors such as the size of the pitch, the quality of the ground, the weather, the wind, the equipment, and the relation between tactics and the laws of the game.

The main areas addressed in the conclusion are the development of tactics in football, such as the importance of players, coaches, and environmental factors, which could determine the possible future of team tactics in football.

The historical research method has been used and data collected from books, journals, magazines, and films, including personal conversations, and from information retrieved from the headquarters of the English Football Association, FIFA, the International Olympic Committee (IOC), and other national FAs in Europe.

As more and more people are involved in the development of football programs in the United States as players, coaches, officials, or fans, there is an increasing demand for knowledge and better understanding of techniques and team tactics in particular. It is hoped that this book will be of assistance to coaches, players, and fans, helping them become more appreciative of the people's game and of its tactics. The book is significant because of the lack of resources and academic publications dealing with tactics in football.

Ultimately, my intent for writing this book was:

1. To provide a descriptive history of football from 1863 to the present

2. To trace the evolution and development of tactics from 1863 to the present

3. To describe the significant tactics, formations, and trends that have been beneficial to the development of football

4. To identify the most influential leaders in the development of football

5. To identify the major reasons or influences that effected tactical changes

6. To assist the coach, the player, and the fan to understand and appreciate the different aspects of team tactics in football

7. To consolidate and to preserve a history of team tactics in football.

INTRODUCTION

Am I so round with you as you with me,
That like a football do you spurn me thus?
William Shakespeare

Soccer, hereafter referred to as football, is the most popular sport in the world. It is the national sport of almost every country on earth except the United States, Australia, and South Asia, where baseball, rugby, and cricket, respectively, are more popular, and it attracts well over 2 billion spectators every year, according to *La Gazzeta dello Sport* (1994). The World Cup, the world's largest sporting event, is held every four years to determine world supremacy in football. It is estimated that the final game of the 2006 World Cup, played in Germany, was watched by over 2 billion people simultaneously (Goldblatt, 2007), and the most recent World Cup final, in the summer of 2010 in South Africa, was watched by well over 3 billion people (FIFA, 2010). In comparison, the annual American Super Bowl of the National Football League (NFL), the finals of the National Basketball League (NBA), and the "World Series" of Major League Baseball (MLB) are each watched by an average world audience of 300 million people. The universal appeal of football is evident in many countries, and to millions of people throughout the world it is the ultimate sport. There is no cultural practice more global than football. Right or wrong, there is no single religion that can truly match the geographical passion and scope of football. Is it not extraordinary that, at a time in human history characterized by unprecedented global interconnectedness, the most universal cultural phenomenon in the world is football? Cotrell (1970) writes that on Christmas Day, 1914, during the first year of World War I, British and

German soldiers opposing each other in France climbed from their static trenches into "no-man's land"—not to shoot at each other, but to play the people's game, an impromptu game of football.

Such is the powerful urge of this game, a phenomenon that can incite an uncontrollable passion, division, and yet at the same time close the gap of nationalistic, political, and religious differences. What other sport could halt a war just so people could watch a game? It happened during the Biafran war in Nigeria in 1968 when the great Pele was scheduled to play (Rote, 1978). The war resumed the next day. And what other sport could presumably start a war as in 1969 between El Salvador and Honduras? Although it has been called the "soccer war," the true motives were more political in nature, and the game was simply used as an excuse.[2]

Though the violence sometimes evoked by this sport cannot be explained simply in terms of the excitement of the game, there certainly exist many factors that can explain its appeal to fans all over the world. According to former FIFA president João Havelange, "The magical appeal of football is based above all on innate play instincts, on natural aspirations to measure one's abilities and on the pleasure that performance in the team unity brings" (*Soccer*, 1967, p. 13).

Football is a fast-moving game offering long periods of continuous action. While the total action of an American football game amounts to an average of 15 minutes of actual playing time, a football game has 90 minutes of continuous action (two 45-minute halves). Another major factor contributing to its appeal is the skill and accuracy it demands of the players, making the game a complete joy to watch. It is a game of precision and stamina rather than brute force. It appeals to people because it does not require unusual physical attributes. Finally, it does not require the purchase of expensive equipment, and is therefore affordable to all classes of society. Football is available to anyone who can make a rag ball and find another pair of feet to pass to, or a wall to kick the ball against. Football is not merely consumed by the societies of the world, it is embraced, it is embedded, and it is transformed by each culture into its own style. Nonetheless, the big question remains: How did it all begin? Where was football invented? Who invented it? How and where did tactics and formations originate?

A study of football history and its tactics in particular is appropriate at a time when enthusiasts are becoming increasingly aware of the importance of tactics in the game. At present there is a lack of written material

World War I photograph of players enjoying a game of football on Christmas Day, 1914.

on the serious aspects of football, in particular tactics. A few studies have been conducted on the development and history of tactics, but the majority of books, journals, and other pertinent information deals with drills, games, and training.

This book is a descriptive historical treatment of football and the development of tactics used from 1863, the year the English Football Association was founded, to the present.

More and more people are involved in the development of football programs in the United States as players, coaches, officials, or fans. According to SBRnet (2009), there are well over 800 colleges and universities that field teams for either men or women; moreover, high school and youth leagues are too numerous to count. No one really knows how many people play football worldwide; it is impossible to count them. FIFA has tried — and their estimate is that around a billion people play the game reasonably formally. That could very well be over 50 million referees, balls, and pitches, and 30 or more million kilometers of white lines, to mark each pitch — Therefore, there is an increasing demand for knowledge and better understanding of techniques and team tactics in particular. It is expected that this book will be of assistance to coaches, players, and fans in helping them become more appreciative of the people's game and of its tactics. The book and its contents are also significant because of the lack of resources and academic publications dealing with tactics in football.

This book is my attempt to write about the history of football, the history of its tactics, and the history of how humanity has played, watched, and has kept the "people's game" alive over the years in spite of the many setbacks it has encountered. Above all, it is a history of how coaches, players, and fans have somehow interacted in order to shape the way the game has evolved and how it is played.

1

EARLY BEGINNINGS

For kicking an object comes as easily as walking,
and how many of us have innocently kicked a pebble
until it was directed too far off course.
(Hollander, 1980, p. 13)

To propel a round ball with one's foot is so
natural a human activity that it is surely no
wonder that the practice was known to many
different civilizations.
(Glanville, 1979, p. 3)

Football is also written and pronounced in different languages as Fute-
ball, *foosball, voetbol,* as well as *futbol,* among others; the sport cannot be
traced to an exact beginning since it seems to have evolved from a variety
of games over a period of more than 2,000 years. Many people like to
claim that the word "football" should only be applied to "soccer," and not
to any other version of the sport. After all, what else would anyone call a
game played strictly with the feet and with a ball? Although this argument
is logical, the word "football" came into use in England around the early
fourteenth century to describe a game played not with the feet, but on
foot, it order to distinguish it from games or pastimes played on horseback.
Nonetheless, "football" is the widely accepted name to describe the most
popular game on the planet.

In the early forms of the game, the players kicked the ball, handled
it, ran with it, and moved it about in any way they could — and the most
notable feature in those early games was the absence of rules. As we will
discuss later, it was not until 1863 that a definite division was established

between a game played with the feet (football), and a game played primarily with the hands (rugby). Until that day in 1863, football was neither soccer nor rugby, but a brawling mixture of the two.

Researching the origins of football is somewhat confusing, to say the least. However, the basic elements — kicking, throwing, and running — have been part of man's natural urges since the world began. Many varieties of football have been invented at different times and in different cultures throughout history. Some of them we have records of, and others we do not. However, the modern version seems to have strictly British roots, though there are several records of football-like games in early times. According to Sepp Blatter (blogspot, 2009), current president of FIFA, football is as old as the world. People have always played some kind of football, from its very basic form of kicking a ball, to the sophisticated game we play today.

English folklore holds that when the English conquered the Danish around the 10th century, they found the skull of a Dane and proceeded to kick it in disgust, thus inventing the first "football" (Rote, 1978). Obviously, they would have needed several skulls in order to play a game, as each skull would have broken after a kick or two.

In China around 3000 B.C., a Chinese emperor named Huang-Ti is supposed to have invented a game called *tsu chu*, which means "to kick a ball of leather"— perhaps an early form of football. Apparently the players took turns at kicking a round ball, either over 30-foot-high posts or through a hole in a silk curtain (Gardiner, 1930). Hornby (2004) noted that the game may have been a part of a soldier's training, and was later included in ceremonies on the emperor's birthday. Around the same period the Japanese played a similar game by the name of *kemari*. According to Rosenthal (1981), the game is described as having goals made of colored ribbons and cloth. This is a type of circular football game, far less spectacular, but, for that reason, a more dignified and ceremonious experience, requiring certain skills, but not competitive in the way the Chinese game was, nor is there the slightest sign of struggle for possession of the ball. The players pass the ball to each other, in a relatively small space, trying not to let it touch the ground. Kemari was also known as "standing among trees." The playing space was six or seven meters square demarcated by four trees placed at its corners. These trees could have been cherry, willow, or maple, but pine trees we believed to have had higher status. Eight players would take the field, standing in pairs on either side of the trees. The ball

A game of *kemari* as played in Japan.

was presumably hollow, light, and made of deerskin, often coated white with albumen or dyed yellow by smoke from a pine needle fire. The courtiers with the highest social status would do the kick-off, and the players would simply try to keep the ball in the air (juggling) as long as possible. They used the trees to bounce the ball off. If a formal count of kicks and passes was carried out, the official responsible could award extra points for particularly impressive or stylish plays. Individuals were admired and respected for their ball skills and for their attention to the etiquette and traditions of the game. A day's kemari was best ended by a single high kick from the most senior player, the ball gracefully caught in the folds of his kimono (Gutmann, 1994).

Kemari became an important pastime of the elite, and even retired and active emperors became noted enthusiasts and participants. Several houses or schools of kemari emerged with their own unique styles of training, techniques, and rules. Emperor Gotoba first set down the regulations of the game, specifying the color and pattern of playing socks according to social rank and kemari skill. The game continued to flourish well into the nineteenth century, and lasted longer than the Chinese tsu chu. Yet neither game was able to capture the imagination of modern societies. Today, kemari has shrunk to a minority pastime of a minority social caste — aristocrats reduced to lobbying the emperor and government to preserve this small fragment of the country's feudal past (Guttmann & Thompson, 2001.)

What marks both tsu chu and kemari in the history of ball games is the fact that they were not primarily kicking games. Nonetheless, this preference to use the foot over the hands or any other part of the body to propel the ball, does not make either of these two sports unique or even the most venerable.

So, it could have been the Chinese or the Japanese who invented football. Unfortunately, their games appear to have all but died, and there is nothing to link them to the modern version.

Historical research shows that among the aboriginal Australians a game called *marn gook* has been played for millennia. Accounts written by other Australians in the 1840s suggest that it was predominantly a kicking game. Polynesians and Micronesians had their own kicking version using balls made from pandanus tree leaves. Native Americans played many team ball games and seemed to have had a general disdain to use their hands, preferring to use bats and feet.

Are these games the ancestors of football? Marn gook is probably as old if not older than tsu-chu and kemari. The American Indians played their games of football long after the Chinese and Japanese games disappeared. They also continued to play the ball horizontally, passing it towards a goal, as opposed to tsu-chu and kemari, which played the ball upwards.

If neither of these cultures were the inventors, then perhaps it was the ancient Egyptians, in whose tombs were placed balls that could have been used for football. Or perhaps it was the Berbers of the seventh century (the indigenous peoples of North Africa west of the Nile Valley) with their *koura*, a game that it seems to have served as a fertility rite to encourage abundant crops. Yet, again, koura seems to have died out as well.

In ancient Greece circa A.D. 200, the athletic-minded Greeks played a game by the name of *episkyros* or *episkiros* (Rote, Jr., 1978). Brasch (1970) notes that while the game was played within some boundary lines, it is not known whether the game involved kicking, throwing, or carrying the ball across a line defended by another team. However, it is possible that the game evolved from the ancient Chinese game of tsu chu after contact was made between the two countries. In contrast to the chaotic early forms of football in Europe, the Japanese and Chinese versions involved many rituals and were played as part of a ceremony. A similar game is still played today, and involves keeping the ball in the air inside a small court. The conquering Romans changed the name to *harpastun*, and Harris (1973), believes that some evidence points to both of these games consisting mostly of throwing the ball rather than kicking it. However, according to Goldblatt (2007), the rules of harpastun appear to be something akin to rugby, with kicking, catching, and physical contact. The theory is that the Romans, who were experts at borrowing Greek ideas and debasing them, took their game over and turned it into a much rougher affair. In the account of one of the games, Athenaeus writes, "He seized the ball and passed it on to a teammate while dodging another. Another fellow player he raised to his feet. All the while the crowd resounded with sounds of out of bounds. Too far. Right behind him. Over his head, on the ground, up in the air, too short, pass it back in the scrum." (Miller, 1991). The game was very popular with Roman legionaries, and like tsu-chu in China it may have been an element of military training. It is reasonable to assume that they took it to England during the years of Roman occupation between A.D. 40 and 43. According to Goldblatt (2007), there is a legend that in A.D. 276 the residents of the town of Derby beat a team of legionaries at a harpastun/football type game. As a game of social significance, and of mass spectator sport, harpastun can't be found anywhere, particularly at the Coliseum, where the Romans preferred the carnage of blood and guts.

According to Gardner (1978), in Mesoamerica the Aztecs as well as the Mayans played a game called *gomacari,* which consisted of kicking a ball with the knee through a vertically fixed ring attached to a wall. The winners were showered with prizes of money and jewelry, but the losers were sacrificed to the gods. (*La Gazzeta dello Sport,* 1994). The Aztecs, who called the game *tchatali,* added decorated stone rings.

Competitive ball games are present in nearly all cultures of the world, but only in Mesoamerica did the ball games take center stage. In the geographic area of what is now Mexico, Guatemala, Belize, El Salvador, and Honduras, ball games were the only game. For well over 3,000 years, between the Olmecs, the Aztecs, and the Mayans, every society in this region, every city from Teotihuacán in Mexico, to the scattered villages of

Central America played ball games. The archeological records left behind cannot quite match the splendor of the Coliseum or Olympia, but is grandiose is unparalleled. There have been well over 1,500 ball courts unearthed, from tiny, plain rectangular troughs in small villages, to the vast and elaborate constructions found in the great Mayan city of Chichén Itzá. Likely, many others have yet to be discovered, or were destroyed by the conquering Spaniards. Additionally, many of the ruined ball courts and tombs have provided us with an extraordinary trove of ceramic figurines, glyphs, carvings, reliefs, and statues that depict the games and their rituals (Scarborough & Wilcox, 1991; Wittington, 2001).

The mythological/religious books provide an even stronger record. The Popul Vuh is a written document of the Quiché Mayan cultures that ruled over what are now southern Mexico, Belize, and Guatemala from about 800 to 1400 B.C. The books consist of three parts. The first writes about the creation, and the third is an account of Mayan nobility. In the center of the document between the first and third parts, there is an account of the creation of the sun and the moon and along with it all the dualities in which Mesoamerican life was organized: light and dark, day and night, good and evil, life and death. The main characters of the written document are the hero twin brothers Hunahpu and Xbalanque. The story is that the twins' forefathers were the brothers Hun Hunahpu and Vucub Hunahpu. Both were exceptional ball players whose noisy game disturbed the lords of the underworld. It is written that the Dark Lords of Xibalba opened a portal to the brothers' court and tricked them into entering their world. Once in the Dark Lords' realm they were challenged to a game, which they lost, and were immediately sacrificed. Their bodies were buried in a subterranean court and the head of Hun Hunahpu was displayed on a calabash tree. Then one day when a goddess named Xquic passed by, the head spat in her hand, and she became impregnated. When the Dark Lords discovered her pregnancy she was banished to the upper world. Once there, she gave birth to the twins. The demigod brothers were now divine ball players and were eventually summoned to the underworld for the second leg of this generational encounter. The twins proved to be a match for their immortal foes and escaped back to earth with their father's and uncle's bodies, exhumed from the diabolical ball court. The corpses were placed in the sky to become the sun and the moon (Martir de Anglerría, 1964).

Opposite: Fixed ring on the wall for the game of *gomacari* in Mexico.

This story is at the core of their whole structure of belief, and likely the reason why ball games were so popular.

The precise form and meaning of their ball games changed over the next 3,000 years. In the smaller cities of the ancient Mexican civilization the game was played at the village level in small courts. In the city-state of Teotihuacán three centuries later, the game was restricted to the elite who played with bats and sticks. Among the Mayans, the game's ritual and religious dimension peaked. The game even spread east to what are now the island of Hispaniola and Puerto Rico.

The spread of the game was matched by its social depth. The large number of courts and objects found indicate that the game was played informally by commoners as well as the elite. Aztec and Mayan records point to highly skilled players from the lower classes competing against the nobility. The meaning of the game was linked to astronomy and the calendar of the time. The patron of the Aztec game was Xolotl, who appeared in the sky as Venus, and players appear in many murals as representatives of many cosmic bodies. Carvings show that often the games were part of exuberant and dramatic performances and that gambling was a big part of it. There are several records that point to the nobility wagering their land and show that the nobles held authority of the outcome of a game. Sometimes the game was substituted for war.

Today, modern football is at the center of the entire region's culture, and where once a magnificent court and city named Tenochtitlán once stood, now there is the metropolitan capital of Mexico — Mexico City, and the monumental Azteca stadium where the World Cup final has been played twice.

We know very little of the barbarian invaders such as the Visigoths and Vandals. Any sports they brought with them were soon lost once their kings embraced Christianity. The dominant sporting cultures and practices of medieval Christianity that these invasions produced were not amicable to ball games. Knights did not play ball games — they fought wars. The ruling classes of the day were more militarized than the nobilities of Mesoamerica or the Far East. The bourgeois cultures of Europe depended on the use of violence to maintain their social status, political power, and wealth. There was no time, no utility, and no glamour in such trivial pastimes as ball games; the joust, the hunt, and the tournament were the only sports fit for the mounted noble warrior caste. Yet despite this disdain for ball games, it is from this region that modern football did emerge. Unlike the development of basketball or volleyball — which were games invented specifically as new forms of exercise — football in what is now northwestern Europe did have traditional roots and practices to draw upon. It is astonishing that these practices survived despite the disdain of aristocrats for these types of ball games. They survived because they eluded the control of Rome even at its height, and absorbed Christianity without losing their traditional culture and customs. These were the Celtic cultures of western Europe. The Celtic-speaking cultures maintained a lot of their autonomy during the medieval era, and continued playing ball games in large open areas with large numbers of participants divided into two teams trying to get a ball to a particular place. Of course there were no rules or restrictions on how to accomplish this task.

Often, the games were played between two parishes or villages. Other times a village could be divided by age, geography, or between married and single men in a game linked to courting rituals. In Ireland the game was also well known. In 1527 the Statutes of Galway referred to the game by its English name, and it stated: "People should not play the hurlings of the little ball with hockie sticks or staves nor use no hands ball to play without the walls but only the great footballe" (Marples, 1954).

A game called *La Soule* was played in Brittany, Normandy, and Picardy and, like the Irish game, it was subjected to repeated bans by the clergy and secular authorities. In Cornwall the game was known as hurling and in Wales they played a game called knappen.

The only other team ball game of similar qualities played outside the Celtic and Anglo-Saxon areas is found in 16th century Florence, Italy. The game was known as *Calcio* and was generally played in the Piazza Santa Croce. Originally, calcio was reserved for rich aristocrats who played every night between Epiphany and Lent. In the Vatican, even popes, such as Clement VII, Leo XI, and Urban VIII, were known to play. Today calcio survives only as a tourist spectacle and is played in the central squares of Florence. The sport was not played for about 200 years, but it was revived in the twentieth century when organized games began again in 1930. Today, three matches are played each year in the Piazza Santa Croce in the third week of June. The modern version allows tactics such as head-butting, punching, elbowing, and choking, but forbids sucker punching and kicks to the head (Halpern, 2008).

It is probable that as the Romans expanded their empire into Britain around A.D. 217, they likely introduced their harpastun game, which was

changed somewhat with the passing of time according to the customs and
traditions of each conquered society toward what it is today. While the
Angles, Saxons, and Normans that made up much of the English mix may
have had their own ball games, it seems likely that they learned them in
the course of the long struggles with their Celtic neighbors. During the
Middle Ages, the adapted version, which prohibited the ball from being
thrown, became so popular and developed into such violent involvement
that many edicts were issued in the names of Edward II, Henry V, Edward
IV, Henry VII, and Henry VIII, which sought to ban, control, or restrict
it. It was indeed violent enough for deaths and injuries to be recorded. In
1314 Edward II issued the following public order:

> For as much as there is great noise in the city, caused by hustling over large
> balls from which many evils may arise which God forbid, we commend and
> forbid, on behalf of the King, on pain of imprisonment such game to be used
> in the city in future (Brasch, 1970, p. 215).

An observer described the rural version as a game "in which young
men, in country sport, propel a huge ball not by throwing it into the air,
but by string and rolling it along the ground, and not with their hands
but with their feet" (Walvin, 1994).

Things were not better in 1349, and Edward III tried to ban it yet
again because of his love for archery and the need for healthy individuals
to defend the kingdom. Additionally, he needed all the help he could get
in his war with France (Meisl, 1955).

In other legal documents the need for the people to focus on archery
was the rationale for banning or controlling the game. In 1477 Edward IV
issued the following statute:

> No person shall practice any unlawful games such as dice, quoits, football
> and such games, but that every strong and able-bodied person shall practice
> with the bow for the reason that the national defense depends upon such
> bowmen (Walvin, 1994, p. 78).

The wild version, characterized by brutal fighting and noise, was
played in the streets and involved hundreds of participants simultaneously
attempting to kick the ball into goals that were placed sometimes as far
apart as two miles (Keeton, 1972). Despite these bans, the game continued
to gain popularity; it was a game of the masses, not the aristocracy, and
it was banned several more times by the English monarchs over the next
four centuries before royal approval and encouragement was obtained. For
all the clear disapproval and repeated attempts to control it, football was

an established feature of rural and urban life. Even the efforts of the Puritans to purge all forms of entertainment, particularly games and gaming, failed. Football survived because it was preserved and nurtured in institutions that were beyond the reach of religion purists, artisans, and elite industrialists. British public schools were the keepers of play of the time. They provided a refuge and a nurturing ground for the wild games of that era. It is important to note that the sport was not only becoming a menace to public order, but it warranted its own name. It is around this time that the word "football" entered the English language.

There is no doubt that the modern version was devised by the British and refined by the Scots as the early innovators of the passing game. For over a thousand years before 1863 (the year the English FA was founded), an undeveloped and unstructured game with some rudiments of today's version was played in the British Isles. Although the rules varied from place to place, the game essentially involved two teams, each trying to force a roughly spherical ball to a target at opposite ends. It was violent, unruly, and anarchic, and repeatedly outlawed by English monarchs. Only in the early 19th century, when schools began to advocate muscular Christianity, was it decided that sport could be used for the moral edification of students, and it was then that anything approaching what we could recognize today as football emerged. Wilson (2009) noted that football did grow in popularity in the 19th century, but in those early days the rules varied from school to school, largely according to conditions. At schools with wide open fields such as Rugby and Cheltenham, the game differed little from the mob game, and players often were unscathed. In the close cloisters of Charterhouse and Westminster, such a rough-and-tumble game would have led to broken bones, and it was there that the dribbling game developed (Alcock, 1895; FIFA.com, 2008; Rote, Jr., 1978). However, before there were any tactics, there had to be a coherent and unanimous set of rules, and that led to the foundation of the English Football Association in 1863.

2

History of the English Football Association (FA)

Any treatise on football would not be complete without a sketch of the events that led to the foundation of the English FA. For all practical purposes, the revival and perhaps the birth of modern football dates back to the inception of that organization, probably one of the largest of the many organizations that direct the forces of football.

As the popularity of football increased, the sport was still not a game for gentlemen, and a unifying set of rules was needed to change that.[3] It was to assimilate these conflicting elements and to be united under one common set of laws that the FA first saw light. The men who gathered to form the Football Association had one aim: to formulate a set of rules by which all footballers, no matter which of the many sets of rules they were used to, could play without arguments. The biggest controversy in playing rules that existed at the time was between carrying the ball or kicking and passing it, and it was these differences which led to the split between what were to become football and rugby.

FA logo inside English FA Headquarters in Soho Square, London.

2. History of the English Football Association (FA)

William Web Ellis, a young student at Rugby, is believed to have single-handedly altered the evolution of football by his anarchic disregard for the rules during a game at Rugby, being played under the rules of kicking and passing the ball. Ellis picked up the ball and ran the length of the field. Even though he was reprimanded by players from both teams, Ellis is now considered the "father of rugby," and indirectly of "American football" as well. Rote Jr. (1978) notes that many fans of both of these sports travel to Rugby to read a historic marker erected there:

> This Stone
> Commemorates the Exploit of
> WILLIAM WEB ELLIS,
> Who with a fine disregard for the rules of
> Football,
> As played in his time,
> First took the ball in his arms and ran with it,
> Thus originating the distinctive feature of
> The Rugby game
> A.D. 1823

In those days the game was still somewhat rudimentary, and it was all about dribbling; passing, cooperation, and defending were perceived as being inferior and unnecessary skills. The controversy over carrying the ball highlighted the problems that existed in late 19th century football. Some schools permitted handling, others did not; offsides, throw-ins, and hacking (kicking below the knees), and even the number of players, were all part of the many sets of rules, and they depended upon which school was the opponent.

In 1848, H.C. Malden of Godalming, Surrey, convened a meeting at Cambridge with representatives from Harrow, Eton, Rugby, Winchester, and Shrewsbury, at which the first set of rules unified the game for the first time (Wilson, 2008). The new rules were printed as the "Cambridge Rules":

CAMBRIDGE RULES 1848

1. This Club shall be called the University Foot Ball Club.

2. At the commencement of play, the ball shall be kicked off from the middle of the ground; after every goal there shall be a kick-off in the same way or manner.

3. After a goal, the losing side shall kick off; the sides changing goals unless a previous arrangement be made to the contrary.

4. The ball is out when it has passed the line of the flag-post on either side of the ground, in which case it shall be thrown in straight.

5. The ball is "behind" when it has passed the goal on either side of it.

6. When the ball is behind, it shall be brought forward at the place where it left the ground not more than ten paces, and kicked off.

7. Goal is when the ball is kicked through the flag-posts and under the string.

8. When a player catches the ball directly from the foot, he may kick it as he can without running with it. In no other case may the ball be touched with the hands, except to stop it.

9. If the ball has passed a player and has come from the direction of his own goal, he may not touch it till the other s ide have kicked it, unless there are more than three of the other side before him. No player is allowed to loiter between the ball and the adversaries' goal.

10. In no case is holding a player, pushing with the hands or tripping up allowed. Any player may prevent another from getting to the ball by any means consistent with this rule.

11. Every match shall be decided by a majority of goals.

In 1857 the first club (as distinct from a school or university) was the Sheffield club, and it adopted a revised version of the Cambridge rules: pushing with the hands was allowed, but not hacking or tripping, nor was running with the ball as was practiced at Rugby. This new set of rules became known as the Sheffield rules:

SHEFFIELD RULES 1857

1. The kick from the middle must be a place kick.

2. Kick Out must not be more than 25 yards out of goal.

3. Fair Catch is a catch from any player provided the ball has not touched the ground or has not been thrown from touch and is entitled to a free-kick.

4. Charging is fair in case of a place kick (with the exception of a kick off as soon as a player offers to kick) but he may always draw back unless he has actually touched the ball with his foot.

5. Pushing with the hands is allowed but no hacking or tripping up is fair under any circumstances whatever.

6. No player may be held or pulled over.

7. It is not lawful to take the ball off the ground (except in touch) for any purpose whatever.

8. The ball may be pushed or hit with the hand, but holding the ball except in the case of a free kick is altogether disallowed.

9. A goal must be kicked but not from touch nor by a free kick from a catch.

10. A ball in touch is dead, consequently the side that touches it down must bring it to the edge of the touch and throw it straight out from touch.

11. Each player must provide himself with a red and dark blue flannel cap, one color to be worn by each side.

A third attempt at a unified set of rules took another step in 1862, when J.C. Thring — the younger brother of Edward, headmaster at

Uppingham — after the failure of the previous versions drew up a new set of ten laws entitled "The Simplest Game" (Wilson, 2008; Gardner, 1996). His second rule allowed the use of hands, but only to stop the ball and place it on the ground before the feet.

There was now a big division between those who liked the rugby version and those who preferred the dribbling game. Mr. Thring's third rule pinpointed part of the problem at the time: kicks must be aimed only at the ball. This rule angered the rugby enthusiasts, who believed that kicking at an opponent's legs was an essential part of the sport.

UPPINGHAM SCHOOL RULES 1862 (THE SIMPLEST GAME)

1. A goal is scored whenever the ball is forced through the goal and under the bar, except it be thrown by the hand.

2. Hands may be used only to stop a ball and place it on ground before the feet.

3. Kicks must be aimed only at the ball.

4. A player may not kick the ball whilst in the air.

5. No tripping up or heel kicking allowed.

6. Whenever a ball is kicked beyond the side flags, it must be returned by the player who kicked it, from the spot it passed the flag-line in a straight line towards the middle of the ground.

7. When a ball is kicked behind the line of goal, it shall be kicked off from that line by one of the side whose goal it is.

8. No player may stand within six places of the kicker when he is kicking off.

9. A player is out of play immediately he is in front of the ball and must return behind the ball as soon as possible. If the ball is kicked by his own side past a player, he may not touch it, or advance, until one of the other side has first kicked it, or one of his own side, having followed it up, has been able, when in front of him, to kick it.

10. No charging is allowed when a player is out of play — i.e. immediately the ball is behind him.

So there it was, the first steps in codifying the sport had been established. However, missing were such things as field dimensions, goal sizes, and the number of players to a side. Regardless of these temporary omissions, a more clear and orderly game was evolving. The dispute over rules came to a climax in 1863. The number of clubs was growing; there were now clubs being formed by young men who wanted to continue playing well after their college days were over. Finally, a meeting was held by the leading clubs in the London area on October 26, 1863, at the Freemasons Tavern in Great Queen Street. There they formed the Football Association (FA), which would regulate the game throughout the country.[4] It is hard

Top: Freemason's Arms. *Bottom:* Freemason's Arms logo.

John and Linda Annetts, current owners of Freemasons Arms, formerly known as Freemasons Tavern, where the English FA was founded in 1863.

to believe that in this little relic tavern of the past, football was born. Nowadays, the Freemasons Tavern looks no different than any other English pub. It is compact and dark-wooded with cozy intimate tables. Not many pub crawlers know the significance of this particular pub in all of London, but on closer inspection the answer leaps out. In a far corner of the pub, painted on the walls are the words: "The football association founded here 1963." Compared to London's other historical landmarks, the Freemasons Tavern gets few visitors, but one or two do find their way, and although it is not cluttered with mementos, there is a mini-shrine in the form of a small glass cabinet housing old boots and other memorabilia.[5]

The following clubs sent representatives to the meeting at the Freemasons Tavern on October 26: Forest (later to become the Wanderers, first winners of the FA Cup); NN Kilburn (NN stands for No Names but the club was always known by its initials, as was WBA); Barnes; War Office Football Club; Crusaders; Percival House, Blackheath; Crystal Palace; Kensington School; Surbiton; Blackheath Proprietary School. In addition, Charterhouse School sent an observer and some unattached footballers

Commemorative marker at Freemasons Arms of a football boot and a caption explaining the use of the word "soccer."

were present as well (Alcock, 1895). In a series of meetings over the next two months attempts were made to create a single set of rules or code from all the competing varieties of football represented around the table.

It was agreed that the clubs represented at this meeting would form an organization called the Football Association. It was clear that there was, at least by those who were present, an honest desire to prepare a set of rules which would unite all football players under one common association. Everything seemed favorable for the formation of a body which would unite football players of every sect. The first election of officers was conducted in a broad spirit. Mr. Arthur Pember of the N.N's, who had taken a prominent part in the organization, as well as in the successful conduct of the inaugural meeting, was appointed first president. Mr. E.C. Morley, of the Barnes club and a supporter of the dribbling game, had the distinction of being appointed the first honorable secretary. The adherents of the rugby game also had a share in the original management by selecting Mr. G. Campbell of the Blackheath to the post of treasurer. Although the 1862 rules provided a starting point, it was clear from the start that there were irreconcilable differences on two key issues: first, between those favoring the catch-and-run game and those who preferred the dribbling and passing game; second, between those who preferred "hacking"—where players deliberately targeted their opponents' shins as a way of stopping them in the tackle—and those who opposed the practice. Of course, the ordeal of adopting a common set of rules could not be carried out immediately because a minority of clubs led by Mr. Campbell of the Blackheath favored the inclusion of the Rugby School game—the ancestor of today's Rugby Union game. At that meeting, Mr. Campbell opposed to the plan of eliminating hacking, and he stated: "To do away with hacking you will do away with the courage and pluck of the game, and I will be bound to bring over a lot of Frenchmen who could beat you with a week's practice." Mr. Morley, the honorary secretary of the group — now referring to itself as the Football Association — responded, "If we have hacking, no one who has arrived at the age of discretion will play at football and it will be left entirely to schoolboys." (Green, 1953).

1860's Painting depicting a game of football in England.

At a further meeting on December 1 the rugby advocates (Blackheat, Kensington School, Surbiton, and Percival House), led by Mr. Campbell's delight in hacking, did not have an appreciable effect, and indeed a rule providing a penalty for its practice was carried. They were defeated by 13 votes to 4 and withdrew from the association (Goldblatt, 2007). The split was finally official, and from that moment on the two sports went their separate ways. The dribbling game was now called Association Football, and the handling game became known as rugby football, which eventually formed its own organization in 1871 called the Rugby Union.[6] It was at that meeting that the official announcement was made. Mr. Arthur Pember of the N.N.'s was appointed as its first president, and Mr. E.C. Morley of the Barnes club was chosen as the first honorary secretary of the association. Mr. Campbell consented to retain the post of treasurer until the next annual meeting: and his retirement a year later practically destroyed the last link between the followers of the two great schools of football (Alcock, 1895). If there is a date marking the official birthday of football then it can be said that it is December 8, 1863, when the proposed rules were formally accepted and published. That is the date on which the FA banned running with the ball and hacking.

For the record, these first FA laws were:

THE FOOTBALL ASSOCIATION 1863

1. The maximum length of the ground shall be 200 yards, the maximum breadth shall be 100 yards, the length and breadth shall be marked off with flags; and the goal shall be defined by two upright posts, eight yards apart, without any tape or bar across them.

2. A toss for goals shall take place, and the game shall be commenced by a place kick from the center of the ground by the side losing the toss for goals; the other side shall not approach within 10 yards of the ball until it is kicked off.

3. After a goal is won, the losing side shall be entitled to kick off, and the two sides shall change goals after each goal is won.

4. A goal shall be won when the ball passes between the goal-posts or over the space between the goal-posts (at whatever height), not being thrown, knocked on, or carried.

5. When the ball is in touch, the first player who touches it shall throw it from the point on the boundary line where it left the ground in a direction at right angles with the boundary line, and the ball shall not be in play until it has touched the ground.

6. When a player has kicked the ball, any one of the same side who is nearer to the opponent's goal line is out of play and may not touch the ball himself, nor in any way whatever prevent any other player from doing so, until he is in play; but no player is out of play when the ball is kicked off from behind the goal line.

7. In case the ball goes behind the goal line, if a player on the side to whom the goal belongs first touches the ball, one of his side shall be entitled to a free kick from the goal line at the point opposite the place where the ball shall be touched. If a player of the opposite side first touches the ball, one of his side shall be entitled to a free kick at the goal only from a point 15 yards outside the goal line, opposite the place where the ball is touched, the opposing side standing within their goal line until he has had his kick.

8. If a player makes a fair catch, he shall be entitled to a free kick, providing he claims it by making a mark with his heel at once; and in order to take such a kick he may go back as far as he pleases, and no player on the opposite side shall advance beyond his mark until he has kicked.

9. No player shall run with the ball.

10. Neither tripping nor hacking shall be allowed, and no player shall use his hands to hold or push his adversary.

11. A player shall not be allowed to throw the ball or pass it to another with his hands.

12. No player shall be allowed to take the ball from the ground with his hands under any pretext whatever while it is in play.

13. No player shall be allowed to wear projecting nails, iron plates, or gutta percha on the soles or heels of his boots.

The dribbling game prevailed, largely because of Law Six — the forerunner of the offside law: "When a player has kicked the ball, any one of the same side who is nearer to the opponent's goal line is out of play and may not touch the ball himself, nor in any way whatever prevent any other player from doing so, until he is in play...." In other words, passes had to be either lateral or backwards. It should be noted that dribbling was rather different to modern perceptions of the art. In *The Official History of the FA*, Green (1960), the late football correspondent of *The Times*, quotes an unnamed writer of the 1870s

"A really first class player ... will never lose sight of the ball, and at the same time keeping his attention employed in the spying out of any gaps in the enemy's ranks, or any weak points in the defense, which may give him a favorable chance of arriving at the coveted goal. To see some players guide and steer a ball through a circle of opposing legs, turning and twisting as the occasion requires, is a sight not to be forgotten ... skill in dribbling ... necessitates something more than a go-ahead, fearless, headlong onslaught of the enemy's citadel; it requires an eye quick at discovering a weak point, and *nous* to calculate and decide the changes of a successful passage." As far as shape is concerned, this comment reads pretty much like a modern form of rugby without any handling. Passing was considered as a last resort and indicated failure, even dishonor.

Tactics in those days were plain, simple, and basic, even after the number of players had been fixed at eleven. In those days, teams and players simply chased the ball. It was not until the 1870s that the goalkeeper became recognized as a universally accepted position; and not until 1909 did they begin to wear a different color shirt than the rest of the team. It was not until 1912 that the keeper was restricted to handling the ball only in his own box. This rule change was implemented to thwart the keeper from Sunderland — Leigh Richmond — his habit of carrying the ball to the halfway line. Players other than the keeper catching the ball in any circumstances had been ruled illegal in 1866, and in this respect the game was recognizable football. Other oddities remained: For example, teams would change end after every goal was scored. Beyond the goalkeeper, both the formation and practice of teams was a long way from the style of the modern game. If there was a formation in those days, it likely would have looked like two or three backs with nine or eight forwards. High crosses and heading the ball were absent as well. Therefore most of the action was concentrated around the main dribbling player where a huge scrum of other players would gather, often bundling and charging into each other like preschool boys of today (Mason, 1980).

The very first match to be played under the new "Football Association" rules took place on January 9, 1864, at Battersea Park, between London and Sheffield. The London team included the best-known footballers of the day, garnered from the Wanderers, a continuation of the Forest Football Club, Barnes, Crystal Palace, and N.N.'s (Alcock, 1895). Most of the Football Association's new rules — called "laws" — were very close to those of rugby. Just four rules, nine through twelve, gave football its unique nature.

Those skeptical of the chances of success noted there was no great clamor of clubs seeking to join the association, and there is little evidence that member clubs were keen to adopt the rules of the game specifically devised for their use. In spite of all the talk about the founding of the organization, local rules prevailed everywhere, and for years the growth of the association was rather slow and uneventful. As the association grew, there was increasing willingness among those who had preferred their own variation of the rules of the game, to eventually recognize the importance, if not the necessity, of a uniform set of rules.

Most of the Sheffield clubs showed interest, but continued to play football according to Sheffield rules nonetheless. However, the best of the London clubs, Forest FC, immediately adopted the FA rules; Lincoln FC preferred its own laws. At Louth, in Lincolnshire, they decided they could only accept the London Rules (as they were called). Association football was being played in some quarters, however, and mainly in London. Notable clubs using the FA rules in 1865 were Barnes, Crystal Palace, Forest, Forest School, No Names Kilburn, Civil Service, and Wanderers; they may not have kept to the new rules in every match, but they did sufficiently to keep the game alive in what was a difficult period for the FA. After some modifications were made in 1876, the rules of Sheffield were brought into complete agreement with those of the FA, and the last obstacle in the way of a universal code was removed (Alcock, 1895).

The new laws of the game made no provision for the numbers of players on each side, nor for the duration of play; these matters had to be agreed by the two captains concerned. Thus Barnes fielded only 9 men against 14 when they went to Penge to play Crystal Palace, and on the same day there was a nine-a-side match at Kilburn between No Names and Wanderers which lasted for one hour. Nobody minded. After all, it was only a game (Goldblatt, 2007).

The founding of the FA in 1863 opened the doors which resulted in an explosion of football enthusiasm that swept through England. Although the version of the game as we know it today had not emerged, teams from different places could at least play under the same set of rules. It was through the founding of the FA and its member clubs that tactics and strategies would develop. The corner kick became part of the game; referees were given control of the game, even to the point of cautioning and ejecting players for serious offenses. Additionally, free kicks were given for offside rule infringements. These represent a few examples of the progress being made, and the need for the development of new tactics to offset and/or bypass the new "laws of the game."

The FA remained the overall supervisor of the game, and the authority of the rules, as well as the organizer of international games — something that was to become its most glamorous function, if not the most important. Under the auspices of the FA, the first international game was held in 1872 between England and Scotland on a rain-soaked pitch on Saturday, November 30 (St. Andrew's Day), in Partick, Scotland. Both teams employed what could be considered attacking formations–Scotland (2-2-6), and England (1-1-8)[7] — however, the game in those days still had many of the mob-football characteristics of kicking, and rushing, and tactics more closely associated to modern-day rugby, not football. In spite of these seemingly attacking formations, the score was 0–0 (FIFA.com, 2009). The

"Mob football" as it was played in the 1900s.

game was well contested, and in fact the two teams were very evenly matched. The FA could not have had a better advertisement, and the vision of those who had been mainly responsible for the match was fully rewarded by the great impetus it gave to the diffusion of the FA rules throughout Scotland. A return match was brought at the end of the same season at Kennington Oval, where England won by 4–1.

The success of the first international match marked a new era in Association Football, and the effects were, as expected, far reaching. In Scotland the rugby game found itself faced by a formidable rival. New clubs were formed, and on every open space youngsters found amusement kicking a ball, to a point that there was constant accession of likely players to disseminate the game all over the country; and in the course of a few years the enthusiasm for the most famous

1874 Shin guards worn by English players.

Artist illustration of the First International — England v. Scotland.

INTERNATIONAL
FOOT-BALL MATCH,
(ASSOCIATION RULES,)
ENGLAND v. SCOTLAND,
WEST OF SCOTLAND CRICKET GROUND,
HAMILTON CRESCENT, PARTICK,
SATURDAY, 30th November, 1872, at 2 p.m.

ADMISSION—ONE SHILLING.

No. 806

Announcement of the very first international, England v. Scotland.

Scottish team at the time — Queen's Park — had developed an incredible effect, to a point that the rugby element, which had enjoyed a monopoly in Scotland, was now being enjoyed only by a minority. By this time the future of the association game was well assured. The union of the Sheffield rules with those of the parent body removed the last remaining obstacle in the way of a universal code for players. Since then, although the constitution of the FA has had several changes, the game has remained very much the same.

The selection of the English team was made by the FA, and included players from ten different clubs, with only Oxford University being represented by more than one player. This, of course, is still the method of selecting a national team, which for all practical

Logo used on England's jersey for First International v. Scotland.

purposes is an all-star team assembled only for international games. The players selected obviously must have the permission of their clubs to play, but because of the great honor involved this was never withheld — at least not in the early days. In England from 1886 on, the honor of being selected to play for the national team was and still is to date marked by the presentation to each player with a velvet cap complete with a tassel. [8] Wales played its first international game in 1876 against Scotland, and in 1882 Ireland was beaten by England 0–13 (Garner, 1996). The scope of international football at the end of the nineteenth century was not really international at all, for all four nations competing with each other were simply different parts of the same country: Great Britain.

What really put the FA on the map, and likely started the football explosion that would soon envelop the world, was its decision taken in the summer of 1871 to organize a cup tournament. At a meeting of the committee on July 20, it was resolved that a "Challenge Cup" should be established in connection with the association, for which all clubs should be

Football at Eton.

Depiction of football at Eton as it was played in 1870s.

invited to compete. The competition was to be conducted on a knockout basis, and was open to any team caring to enter. The idea was well received, and at a subsequent meeting attended by the committee representatives in addition to representatives of the Royal Engineers, Barnes, Wanderers, Harrow Chequers, Clapham Rovers, Hampstead Heathens, Civil Service, Crystal Palace, Upton Park, Windsor House Park, and Lausanne clubs, the resolution was carried. The Challenge Cup was established and open to all clubs belonging to the association. A silver cup was purchased for £20 and inscribed with the words "The Football Association Challenge Cup."

Fifty clubs were eligible to play in the first FA Cup, but only fifteen entered (Walvin, 1994). Many were deterred by the expense and the complexity of the travel, three never got further than registering their interest to participate, and only two came from the north: Queen's Park and Donnington

FA Charity Shield trophy — annual English club association football match contested between the Premier League champions and the FA Cup winners. It is now known as the FA Community Shield.

Grammar School. The others were: Hitchin, the Royal Engineers, Reigate Priory, Maidenhead, Great Marlow, Wanderers, Harrow Chequers, Barnes, Civil Service, Crystal Palace, Upton Park, the Clapham Rovers, and Hampstead Heathens (Alcock, 1895). Before the tournament started it drew criticism from those who felt that the competition would encourage excessive rivalry among clubs. It is important to remember that football at this stage was very much an amateur game for "gentlemen" amateurs. The top teams of the day were composed exclusively of former public school and university players, all highly educated men who gave their teams names like Wanderers, Old Etonians (alumni of Eton College), and Old Carthusians (alumni of Charterhouse School).

As it turned out, C.W. Alcock, the president of the FA and one of the prime movers in organizing the competition, was the first person to receive the cup when the team on which he was captain — The Wanderers — defeated the Royal Engineers in the final in 1872 by the score of 1–0. Amateurs and gentlemen continued to rule the FA both on and off the pitch for another ten years, and meanwhile the popularity of the FA and the FA Cup spread rapidly. Ten years later the number of teams was seventy-three, and for the first time one of the northern teams — Blackburn Rovers — reached the final where before a crowd of 7,000 they went down 0–1 to the Old Etonians. The 1882 final would be the last in which a predominantly dribbling side beat a predominantly passing side. Moreover, the Old Etonians were the last team to field a 2-1-7 formation. After this, almost every club assumed the new 2-3-5 formation in which the defense was allocated two more team members. Now the ball was moved across the pitch as well as up and down, and it was passed in the air as well as on the ground. Teams began to use the wings instead of bunching up in the center, and crossing and heading became part of the game. As a spectacle, football had been transformed, and so the players, fans, and organizers transformed as well.

Given the growing popularity that football was experiencing, there was not anything that could have prevented the rise of professionalism. It began in the industrial cities of the midlands and the north in a covert way. Many of the earliest managers/professors of the game were Scots who had come south in search of work and soon discovered that their football talents were much in demand. Soon, clubs from Blackburn and Preston were deliberately importing players, and providing them with jobs and paying them secretly after each game. The very idea of professionalism was something the gentlemen of the FA bitterly opposed. Any club that wanted to take part in the FA Cup competition had to be a member of the FA. In 1883 the FA expelled Accrington for offering inducements to a player, and the following year Preston, a team made up mostly of Scots, was banned from the competition for the same reasons.

Either way, professionalism was now widespread and becoming too successful for even the FA to stop it. At a meeting in 1885, the FA accepted the inevitable and professional football players became part of the association. They had to be registered annually with the FA, which was adamant on one point: The professionals would not be allowed to serve on any committees or attend any meetings of the FA. The gentlemen amateurs had given way to having professionals on the pitch, but were determined to retain administrative control of football nonetheless.

By the turn of the century, football had conquered Europe and South America. Its spread was not a country-by-country crawl but a sudden explosion, and within a decade football had sprung up all over the two continents. Football gained widespread popularity in England at a time when the nation was at the height of its maritime and commercial strength. English sailors were regular visitors to foreign ports, and English businessmen, engineers, and artisans often spent long periods living overseas. They took their sports with them, and the same pattern was repeated from country to country. The sailors or British expatriates would play cricket or football or rugby among themselves, and if there were not enough to play, they would invite locals to join in. Cricket never really made it, as it needed a lot of space, well-manicured grass, and lots of equipment, and games could last up to three days. Rugby caught on in only a few places, such as France and Argentina, but football on the other hand was widely accepted.

In no time, the clubs that the British had founded for their own amusement were flooded with local residents who liked what they saw and started to play, and they soon took over running the sport.

In Italy in 1887 Edoardo Bosio, an Italian businessman, returned from a trip to London and brought a football and enthusiasm for the FA Cup games that he had seen while in England. His attempts to get Italians excited were unsuccessful at first, but events in nearby Genoa changed that. There in 1892, a group of Brits founded a sport club called Genoa Cricket and Football Club. They played little cricket, but whenever they played football, large crowds gathered to watch. Soon Italians began to play and joined as members of the club.

The following year, the citizens of Turin started to play as well, and founded one of the most famous of Italian clubs — the Juventus Football Club. In Sicily, English expatriates founded the Palermo Football and Cricket Club. In 1898 the Federazione Italiana di Football, the equivalent of the English FA, was founded, and a championship was organized, which was first won by the Genoa club. The first 10 years of the 20th century saw clubs being founded all over Italy; Lazio in 1900, Verona in 1903, Naples 1904, Inter Milan 1908, Bologna 1909, and in 1910 an Italian national team competed for the first time with a victory of 6–2 over France. Professionalism was introduced in 1929.

Football found its way to the American continent and in particular South America pretty much the same way it did in Europe; it was being played in Argentina in 1889 by Brits working on the railroads. Alexander Hutton, an Englishman, founded the Argentine FA in 1893, and is thought of as the father of football in Argentina.

Uruguayan football started with the foundation of the Central Uruguayan Railway and Cricket Club by English railroad workers, who also founded the Uruguayan FA in 1900. The club changed its name to Peñarol in 1913, and is one of the most famous clubs in the world today.

Football made its appearance in Brazil sometime in the late 1800s in the streets of São Paulo when Charles Miller, born of English parents, returned to Brazil from England with two footballs, and took them to the São Paulo Cricket and Athletic Club run by Brits. Yet again, football killed cricket, and by 1902 several clubs formed the São Paulo League. Similar events were occurring in Rio de Janeiro, where the first football match was played in 1897 by the Rio Cricket Club. Unfortunately, the lack of communication between the two cities made the formation of a joint league difficult, and a separate Rio League was formed in 1906.

In the early days, of Brazilian football the game was reserved for high society; the players were generally sons of well-to-do Brazilians. All this changed when lowly clerks and factory workers formed the Corinthias Paulista Club, which admitted mixed-race players, who were accepted as whites. They were soon followed by a wave of brilliant black players. The national team played its first game in 1914 in Buenos Aires, losing 0–3 to Argentina. The cycle was completed in 1933 when professionalism was introduced.

Despite of the unification of the rules, the foundation of the FA in 1863, and the worldwide popularity of the sport, disputes persisted well into the 1880s, and this meant that an organization to protect and preserve the rules was a necessity. The International Football Association Board (IFAB) was thus created, made up of representatives from each of the United Kingdom's pioneering football associations — England's Football Association (FA), the Scottish Football Association (SFA), the Football Association of Wales (FAW), and Northern Ireland's Irish Football Association (IFA) (Rosenthal, 1981), and at the same time contributed to the rise and popularity of the game. The first meeting, made up of two representatives from each of the four associations, took place on June 2, 1886, to guard the "Laws of the Game." The FA, SFA, FAW, and IFA each had equal voting rights. Then, as it is today, a three-quarters majority was needed for a proposal to be passed.

The conference created the first international competition, the British Home Championship, and proposed the establishment of a permanent board to regulate the laws of the game throughout Great Britain and Ireland.

The Fédération Internationale de Football Association (FIFA), the

Statue of a football player at the entrance to the National Football Museum, Preston, England.

international organizing body for the sport, was formed in Paris in 1904 and declared that it would adhere to the rules laid down by IFAB. The growing international popularity of the game led to the admittance of FIFA representatives to IFAB in 1913. Initially, they only had two votes — the same number as each of the UK associations — and decisions required a four-fifths majority to pass, meaning that the UK could still change the laws against FIFA's wishes if they all voted together. In 1958, the board agreed on its current voting system, with each UK association having one vote, FIFA four, and six votes being required to carry any motion. IFAB deliberations must be approved by at least six votes. Thus, FIFA's approval is necessary for any IFAB decision, but FIFA alone cannot change the laws of the game; they need to be agreed upon by at least two of the UK members.

The board meets twice a year, once to decide on possible changes to the rules governing the game of football and once to deliberate on its internal affairs. The first meeting is called the Annual General Meeting (AGM) and the second is the Annual Business Meeting (ABM). Four weeks before the AGM, the member associations must send their written proposals to the secretary of the host association. FIFA then prints a list of suggestions that are distributed to all other associations for examination. The AGM is held either in February or March and the ABM is held between September and October.

The decisions of each year's Annual General Meeting of the board regarding changes to the Laws of the Game are binding for confederations and member associations from July 1, but confederations or member associations whose current season has not ended by July 1 may delay the introduction of the adopted alterations to the Laws of the Game in their competitions until the beginning of their next season (FIFA, 2010).

A boot from the 1950s.

3

THE FOUNDING OF FIFA

As previously stated, the term "soccer" is generally believed to have been derived from an abbreviation of association, "assoc," from the organization of the English Football Association in 1863. "Soccer," or Football Association Soccer, was used to distinguish the game from the American football version, hence the use of the acronym FIFA (Fabian, 1960).

Around the turn of the 20th century, football was making a big impact in other parts of the world as it was in the British Isles. British citizens were roaming and settling all over the world and the football contagion that swept through Great Britain proved to be just as contagious all over the world. Thus the game moved across borders and quickly spread throughout Europe. In the meantime, British sailors in their journeys around the world took the game to all corners of the globe, and soon thereafter, football associations (FAs), and federations began to be formed all over. One of the most fascinating aspects of the growth of football and its acceptance worldwide has been the ability of each nation to take the English game and adapt it to its own particular characteristics. The Brazilians play a technical and artistic style which rivals its music. The Germans play a well-disciplined and organized game with soundly executed tactics, while the Argentineans play a physical and determined style with lots of hustle and commitment, and most Africans take advantage of their speed and agility. Americans, though less skilled for the time being (but well respected), cover their lack of technical skill with hustle, determination, a never-say-die attitude, and "the old college try," which is very much a part of most of the culture of American sports.

However, the popularity of the game all over the world found the English only vaguely interested in what was happening. They accepted that foreigners could play the game, but could not accept that they could be as good as they were and so were not interested in any kind of international competitions. When a meeting was held in Paris to discuss the founding of an international organization to advance football throughout the world, the English did not bother to attend, as they considered the IFAB all that was needed to govern the sport.

In 1896 when the modern Olympics took place in Athens, most European nations had some kind of official football tournaments. Of course the best organized was in England, where the Football Association Challenge Cup, open to all clubs, was first contested in 1872. The first winner of the English League in 1889 was Preston North End[9] (personal communication). The FA Cup (the oldest trophy competition in the world) was established in 1871 and first awarded in 1872 to the Wanderers of London. The FA Cup is considered by the English to be their most important national competition, and is always presided over by a member of the royal family, who awards the trophy to the winning team.

The early football competitions were not limited to England. There have been cup competitions in Scotland since 1874, and a league competition since 1890. Wales has had a cup competition since 1878, and the Northern Irish cup was established in 1881 (Jones, 2004).

After the success of the inaugural Olympic competition in 1896 echoed around the world, the map of world football expanded considerably, and new tournaments emerged all over Europe. In 1900 Uruguay organized the first South American tournament, and that same year, the organizers of the second Olympic Games in Paris in 1900 allowed a limited football tournament with three teams (*La Gazzeta dello Sport*, 1994).

The worldwide appeal and popularity of the game brought about the need to unify and create a world governing body for football. In May 1904, the Fédération Internationale de Football Association (FIFA)[10] was founded in the rear of the headquarters of the Union des Sociétés Françaises de Sports Athlétiques at the rue Saint Honoré 229 in Paris on May 21, 1904 (FIFA.com, 2009). The foundation act was signed by the authorized representatives of the following associations:

France— Union des Sociétés Françaises de Sports Athlétiques (USFSA), represented by Robert Guerin and Andre Espir.

Belgium— Union Belge des Sociétés de Sports (UBSSA), represented by Louis Muhlinghaus and Max Kan.

Denmark— Dansk Boldspil Union (DBU), represented by Ludvig Sylow.

Netherlands— Nederlandsche Voetbal Bond (NVB), represented by Carl Anton Wilhem Hirschmann.

Spain— Madrid Football Club, represented by André Espir.

Sweden— Svenska Bollspells Forbundet (SBF), represented by Ludwyg Sylow.

Switzerland— Association Suisse de Football (ASF), represented by Victor E. Schneider.

The first FIFA Congress was held two days later on May 23, 1904, and Robert Guérin was elected as president. Victor E. Schneider of Switzerland and Carl Anton Wilhelm Hirschmann of the Netherlands were made vice presidents. Louis Muhlinghaus of Belgium was appointed secretary and treasurer, with the assistance of Ludvig Sylow of Denmark. These pioneers were faced with an incredible task because at the time FIFA existed only on paper. They had to give the organization shape and, at the same time, create organizations as true national representations and get new members. Of course, the English had to be convinced that their association with this brand new organization was indispensable (FIFA, 2010).

With well over 40 countries playing football at the time, FIFA was established as the world governing body for football. This organization introduced standardized rules which are to be used for all national and international competition (Fouls, 1979). The first official international match took place on the European continent between Belgium and France on May 1, 1904.

The second FIFA congress took place in Paris June 10 through 12, 1905. In the meantime the associations from Germany, Austria, Italy, and Hungary had joined FIFA; Scotland, Wales, and Ireland would follow the English example. By now there was already talk of creating an international competition to take place in 1906. The competition would consist of four groups and Switzerland would be the organizer. The first international competition was a failure. Many associations were still in their infancy and still working on their internal organizational issues. These difficulties were a heavy disappointment for FIFA and its president, who had set out about this competition with so much enthusiasm. Robert Guérin resigned from the presidency, and handed over his role to his vice president, Victor E. Schneider and to Andre Espir, his personal assistant.

Nonetheless, FIFA was able to exercise its strength. When the English clubs wanted to play games against teams from the continent without FIFA's authorization, FIFA forbade its members from playing against them. The English, who were beginning to develop a good association with FIFA, were particularly impressed by its strict and uncompromising procedure.

As previously stated, there was some apprehension in the United Kingdom to the idea of a world body for the sport they had created rules for, but this uncertainty was dismissed a few years later when at the third congress meeting held in Bern, Switzerland, Daniel Woolfall (former English FA president), replaced Frenchman Robert Guérin as FIFA president in 1906 — the year the FA joined FIFA. Daniel Woolfall was a pragmatist and had gathered a great deal of experience on the administrative board of the English FA. Under his guidance, English and continental football became more united. Moreover, he launched an inexorable battle for uniformity in the Laws of the Game. One of the conditions of the English FA for joining was that the IFAB would remain responsible for the rules of the game. Since its founding, FIFA has been very democratic in its structure. Each member nation is allowed one vote, except for Great Britain, which has had four votes, one for each of the IFAB members (Garner, 1996). The main objective of FIFA was to do on an international scale what the FA had done in England: to standardize the rules and to make sure everyone was playing the same game. By 1913 FIFA was allowed two votes on the IFAB, which represented a positive attitude by the British. Many more European associations joined FIFA, including South Africa in 1909, Argentina and Chile in 1912, and the USA in 1913, thus becoming the first non–European members.

The idea of having a major international competition began to be discussed, and FIFA assumed the responsibility for the administration and organization of a tournament that took place within the context of the Olympic Games in London in 1908. Many problems arose in the organization, which were still unresolved in 1912 when the tournament took place in Stockholm (FIFA.com, 2002). The new and not well known sport was not taken seriously at the Olympics and was basically considered a sideshow and not a competition. Although football was officially born in 1904 with the foundation of FIFA, it was not until 1924 and the Olympic tournament in Paris that the game really came into its own. It was there in Paris that for the first time, teams from other continents came over to take on the Europeans. The English continued to stay away from this tournament, but the Americans were there and the team from far-away Uruguay showed the world how football was played in South America. The competition was a success, and 50,000 spectators watched Uruguay beat Switzerland (3–0) on the final, becoming the world champions (www.France98.com/english/history/past). The South Americans' dominance was even more impressive at the Olympic tournament in Amsterdam in 1928. Uruguay did not disappoint, and defeated Argentina on the final. However, many nations abstained from the tournament, and FIFA saw that the time was ripe for a new independent football tournament free from the constraints of Olympic amateurism.

World War I had put a temporary end to the friendly atmosphere within FIFA and the IFAB. When the war ended, the British wanted Germany and its former allies banned from FIFA. It was not a popular decision, and the four British FAs, unable to gather enough support, resigned from FIFA in 1920, and in so doing took away the two votes FIFA had with the International Board. In 1928, with FIFA running the Olympic football tournament, the four British FAs walked out again, but FIFA was allowed to keep its votes on the IFAB. The British did not return to FIFA until after World War II. Twenty years had passed and the rest of the world had not only caught up with the British and their game but surpassed them in playing standards (Rote Jr., 1978).

As FIFA grew and gained stature among other countries, the concept of a world championship culminated in the first World Cup being played in 1930. [11] On May 26, 1928, in Amsterdam, the FIFA congress, presided over by Jules Rimet,[12] voted that a new tournament be organized in 1930 and be open to all member nations. On May 18, 1929, the FIFA congress met in Barcelona, and voted that the Olympic champions (Uruguay) be the first nation to host a World Cup. There were other candidates, including Hungary, Italy, Spain, Sweden, and the Netherlands, but from the start Uruguay was the favorite for important reasons: They had won the two previous Olympic tournaments (1924 and 1928), and they would be celebrating in 1930 the 100th anniversary of their independence (www.France 98.com/english/history/past, 1998).

The World Cup in 1930 in Uruguay was a remarkable success, both in sport and financial terms. However, the organizers were disappointed that only four teams from Europe participated: France, Belgium, Yugopslavia, and Romania. Their anger was so intense that four years later the world champions refused to defend their title, and did not send a team to Italy for the 1934 competition nor the 1938 competition in France.

3. The Founding of FIFA

Although the English refused to take part in the first three World Cups, they retained their arrogance and an extraordinary aura of invincibility that was not dispelled until the 1950s when they traveled to Brazil to participate in the World Cup for the first time. There the greatest football shock of all time beset the English. After a 2–0 victory over Chile, the game against the American team, which had only played two games together before arriving in Brazil, seemed a mere formality. But the score that came over the wires on June 29, 1950, was England 0, USA 1. It provoked worldwide disbelief, but the score was correct. Mighty England, the masters and assumed inventors of the game, had been humbled by the American part-timers. England now had to beat Spain in order to remain in the competition, something that proved beyond them. They went down 0–1 and returned home, their first World Cup adventure an ignominious failure.

The founding of FIFA in 1904 was predicted on the goal of providing football with an international body to ensure its unity, development, and control. Today, FIFA membership totals over 200 countries (FIFA, 2009). Elimination play for the World Cup tournament begins two years prior to the final 32-team tournament, which was expanded from 24 in 1998 in France. Football is the most popular sport in the world, practiced by millions of people, and the number of spectators in stadiums and television viewers amounts to billions (www.France98.com/english/history/past, 1998).

The role of FIFA covers the application of the rules of the game, the international transfers of players, the organization of competitions (World Cup, under-17 and under-20 World Cups, Women's World Cup, Olympic Games Tournament 5-a-side, Beach World Cup), and the organization of courses on administration, training, refereeing, and sports medicine, with the goal of developing football throughout the world (FIFA.com, 2009).

Presently, FIFA is an association governed by Swiss law and based in Zurich. It has 208 member associations and its goal, enshrined in its statutes, is the constant improvement of football. FIFA employs some 310 people from over 35 nations and is composed of a congress (legislative body), executive committee (executive body), general secretariat (administrative body) and committees (assisting the executive committee).

Over the past 25 years football has enhanced its status as the world's leading game, reaching into other branches of society, commerce, and politics. Football, more than any other factor, has enveloped whole regions, people, and nations. With approximately 200 million active players it now constitutes a substantial chunk of the leisure industry, having opened up new markets for itself and for the rest of the business world.

The potential has yet to be exhausted, especially in Asia and North America. As of mid–2007, FIFA has grown to include 208 member associations, thus making it one of the biggest sports federations in the world. On June 8, 1998, Joseph S. Blatter, a Swiss, was elected as successor to Dr. João Havelange and became the eighth FIFA president. This victory at the 51st FIFA Ordinary Congress in Paris elevated the Swiss, who had already served FIFA in various positions for 23 years, to the highest rank in international football. Blatter is one of the most versatile and an experienced exponent of international sport diplomacy and is totally committed to serving football, FIFA, and the world's youth (FIFA, 2010).

4

FOOTBALL IN THE
UNITED STATES

The original inhabitants of North America, the American Indians, may have played a kicking game similar to football; however, most authorities give credit to the European immigrants for having brought the game to the United States (Chyzowych, 1982).

Not even the most ardent supporters can claim that the United States of America had any influence in the development of football worldwide. In fact, for 130 years the history of football was written in Europe and Latin America, not in the USA. Once or twice in the developmental stages of football the Americans were noticed, for relatively modest achievements like reaching the semifinals of the first World Cup in 1930, and the victory over England in 1950 in Brazil. Of course these achievements were remarkable because the USA was regarded as a minnow in world football.

The lack of impact on the international scene was a reflection of the sport's minor-league status within the United States. However, that does not mean that there was no football activity at all. In fact, there was plenty. Football had crossed the Atlantic with the New England settlers, and was soon giving the Puritans the same sort of problems that it had caused in the homeland.

Football was being played quite a lot in the United States by the late 1860s, and the pattern of its development in the United States was similar to the patterns of its development in England. The game in the USA received a lot of the same treatment it received in England. Because the game was rough and violent, it was forbidden, and actually outlawed. The Boston town authorities struck a familiar note in 1657: "Forasmuch as sundry complaints are made that several persons have received hurt by boys and young men playing at foot-ball in the streets ..." and went on to impose a fine of twenty shillings on anyone who should be caught playing the sport. It was not the first ban, nor the last but, as in Britain it was a waste of words (Garner, 1996).

Football found its way to several schools and colleges, and by the 1800s it was played at several Ivy League schools, notably Harvard, Princeton, and Yale. The game developed much as it had in England, with college and prep school students playing the game according to local rules. Harvard and Yale used the game as part of the ritual of welcoming incoming freshmen to college; this welcoming was known as "Bloody Monday," that name describing the quality of play (Rosenthal, 1980). Play in these games was so violent that the administration and faculty banned the game in 1860, but students still participated and the game continued to flourish.

Brasch (1970) writes that on November 6, 1869, the first intercollegiate match was played at New Brunswick, New Jersey, between Rutgers and Princeton, following the rules set forth in 1863 by the London Football Association. In 1873, the American Intercollegiate Football Association was formed with such prestigious universities as Columbia, Princeton, Rutgers, and Yale as charter members. This association adopted rules similar to those of the English FA. With this accomplishment, football in the USA should have flourished as it did in Great Britain, but unfortunately, that was not the case. As it turned out, Harvard preferred its own version of football, in which players could pick up the ball and run with it. When other colleges refused to play Harvard under such rules, the college turned to Canada and in 1874 scheduled two games with McGill University in Montreal. The second of these games was played with an egg-shaped ball under rugby rules, and proved pleasing to Harvard players. They adopted rugby, and induced Yale to follow suit.

In November 1875, Yale and Harvard played a match under what was termed "concessionary rules." However, most of the rules supported picking up the ball instead of kicking it. In fact, most of the rules for that game were very similar to those set forth by the Rugby Union Board. This choice of rules influenced other colleges, and the American Intercollegiate Football Association rules were now organized along those lines. Princeton players, who were present at the game, returned to their campus and called a meeting to propose that their brand of football should now be rugby instead. By a narrow margin they voted in favor of rugby, and as far as the colleges were concerned, football took a backseat. This changed the destiny of football in the USA, and it went into a dormant stage until early in the 20th century (*Soccer for Parents,* 2010). Even if the vote had gone in favor of football, the sport would not have lasted very long either way. This was a time when America was beginning to assert its own nationality, and was more than ready to demonstrate that it was not a nation built on the traditions of other people, particularly the English. The American sportsmen did not want to be labeled as imitators of the English originals. At one point in the USA, cricket, the most English of games, was very popular, but it was condemned as effete and slow, and this gave way to baseball, which, it was claimed, was a 100 percent American invention.[13]

In the colleges rugby was soon overtaken by the Americanization process, and within a few years that process and several rule changes produced a new version of the sport — American football — which bore the slightest resemblance to rugby.

In spite of the virtual end of collegiate football, enthusiasts kept the game alive, albeit far away from college campuses. Most enthusiasts were immigrants who came to the USA in search of new lives. Most were working class and settled around the industrialized cities of the Northeast and Midwest. As in Britain, football in the USA belonged to the poor, hardworking immigrants who regained their ethnic identity through the familiar sport from home, while those who preferred the adaptation of rugby rules were generally the affluent and well-to-do.

Despite the setback, amateur football was widely played throughout the eastern United States, particularly New York, New Jersey, and Philadelphia. The *New York Times* of the day covered many matches featuring teams such as Brooklyn Celtics, Anglo-Saxons FC, Clan McKenzie FC, Spanish-American FC, and Overseas FC. The team names tell the story. Teams were largely composed of immigrants who feverishly kept up the games and traditions of the old country. Ethnic football provided the necessary means for the game's survival in the USA for the next several decades. The first games played were of the pick-up and choose-up-sides variety. However, following the pattern set in the industrial areas of Britain, factories, mills, and corporations began to sponsor local teams, and as they became successful, leagues were formed (Allen, 1967). To the many ethnic players the word "soccer" meant "football," and in 1884 they formed a league called the American Football Association (AFA). This was something notable for the Americans; it was the first FA formed outside of Britain.

However, within five years, it was in trouble, plagued by internal squab-
bling, an activity that has always been part of the history of football in
the USA.

The New York clubs complained that the league's schedule was dis-
advantageous to them, and therefore withdrew from the league. They
formed their own league called the American Amateur Football Association
(AAFA). It distinguished itself from the AFA, which by the 1900s had
become a semiprofessional league.

In 1912 both organizations turned up at the FIFA congress in Stockholm, and both requested recognition as the controlling body of American
football. FIFA asked them to go back and to form one single national
body. A year later the AAFA had gathered enough support from almost
every club and organization, and formed another organization called the
United States Football Association (USFA). They returned to FIFA rep-
resenting everyone except the semipro clubs of the AFA, but they, too,
joined the USSF when FIFA announced recognition of the new organization.

The sport was not fully organized until 1913 when the USFA was
formed and was recognized by FIFA as the governing body in the United
States (USSF Administrative Book, 1992). This group soon changed its
name to United States Soccer Federation (USSF) in an effort to prevent
confusion with the game of American football (Rote Jr., 1978). Although
its membership included leagues in Chicago, Pittsburgh, and St. Louis,
the USFA was mainly an East Coast affair. The organization was run by
amateurs, and most of them were not American by birth. It was run by
men like Randolph Manning, an English-born and German-educated
medical doctor who was elected as the first president, and soon declared
that the USFA's goal was to make football the national pastime of the winter in the USA.

The founding of the USSF in 1913 revived football interest in the
USA, and it sparked the administrative work that had to be done in order
to accomplish the objectives of unifying football in the United States.
FIFA's recognition gave the USFA/USSF jurisdiction over all amateur and
professional football in the USA. The new association controlled and reg-
ulated players in terms of amateur and professional status, as well as a
player's eligibility to compete in international matches (Rosenthal, 1981).
Football in the USA now had a governing body, but it was not heading in
the direction outlined by Dr. Manning. The growing pains of the USFA

exposed many mistakes made by the football community, and these mistakes were repeated over and over for the next fifty years.

The USFA went through a series of name changes, and it could never move beyond what it was — an amateur organization managed by immigrants. Their attempts to promote football as a major sport were always undermined by their own internal bickering and lack of vision. The fact that they were immigrants or amateurs has nothing to do with their internal issues. The problem was that the USFA was simply a gathering organization for foreigners whose love and passion for football was nothing but a measure of their reluctance to become full-fledged Americans. Sadly, their attitude took place during the formative years of the USA as a nation, which fueled xenophobic sentiment towards football — a foreign sport for foreigners.

In 1921 a pro league called American Soccer League (ASL) was formed. It included teams backed by major companies such as Bethlehem Steel, and several international players — mostly from Scotland — joined the league. It flourished for a decade, and most of the players on the U.S. team that made it to the semi finals of the 1930 World Cup came from the ASL.

Unfortunately, the league was weakened, not by baseball or American football, but by an ongoing struggle with the USFA over whether ASL teams could be forced to play in the USFA's Cup competition. At that time the ASL operated outside the control of the USFA, and by the time the dispute was settled on October 9, 1929, the Wall Street crash and the beginning of the depression were only a few weeks away. With all the unemployment and factory closings, the ASL shut down operations and ceased to exist.

There is no need to dwell on what the USSF did for the next 50 years, as very little was accomplished. For 50 years football in the USA remained an immigrant sport outside the mainstream of American life, and although the organization expanded its membership throughout the country, it was withdrawn farther into an ethnic cocoon. Most Americans were right to think of football as a foreign sport because even within the USA, it was practiced mainly by foreigners, who often used non–English words in the names of their leagues and teams. The organization ignored colleges and high schools, and attempts to upgrade the professional side always ended in failure.

Competitions were played at the amateur and semiprofessional levels until 1967 when two rival leagues, the United Soccer Association (USA) and the National Professional Soccer League (NPSL) merged to form the North American Soccer League (NASL) in 1968 with seventeen clubs. Sadly, by the time the 1969 season started, the NASL was down to just five clubs.

This was another debacle due to the mistaken notion of the club owners that football in the USA was just another commodity that could be marketed by public relations alone. They all talked about being in it for the long haul, but the moment the profits failed to materialize, they bolted. Nonetheless, the disappointment had a good side to it. The NASL had taken football to parts of the USA where it had never been seen before — places such as Atlanta, Dallas, and Kansas City — where it had actually been well received. In fact, these three cities were among the survivors in 1969.

The NASL barely survived, and managed to slowly rebuild its strength. With the leadership of Phil Woosnam as commissioner and Lamar Hunt, owner of the league's Dallas Tornado in particular, nobody could afford to write off the NASL. If Lamar Hunt thought that there was a future in professional football in the USA, people believed, then there would be plenty of investors willing to hear what he had to say. Many did, and by 1978 the NASL included 24 clubs, some in major television markets, and even teams in Vancouver and Toronto, Canada.

The league got a boost when the New York Cosmos signed Edson Arentes Do Nascimento — known worldwide as Pele. Clive Toye and Phil Woosnam, the only executives of the NASL at the time, both agreed that the NASL could not survive without its own superstars. Unfortunately there were no American players that could be classified as such. They believed that there was only one player who could fill that void: Pele.

Little by little the NASL began to rebuild its strength, and it started to attract several wealthy backers. Among them was Warner Communications, which owned the New York Cosmos, and they did not need much convincing to sign Pele, whose popularity was proved many times when his Brazilian club Santos had toured the USA, always drawing crowds far above average. He was well known not only for his name and for his brilliant skills as a footballer, but also for the fact that he was at the time the highest-paid athlete in the world.

Pele played his last game for Santos in October 1974. Eight months later he signed a three-year, $4.5 million contract to play for the New York Cosmos. His arrival proved to be a success, and it brought football to the limelight in the USA. At the time the Cosmos was playing at the dilapidated Randall's Island Stadium, where the press box was always filled like never before for any football game. Articles on Pele began to appear in major magazines: Pele was on the Johnny Carson show: Pele was at the White House with President Ford. Everywhere he went, the crowds followed. Soon other famous players began to arrive — Johan Cruyff, George Best, Giorgio Chinaglia, and Franz Beckenbauer, among others.

In 1977 the New York Cosmos moved to Giants Stadium in New Jersey, and all of a sudden the crowds got bigger. The playoff game between the Cosmos and Fort Lauderdale saw a crowd of 78,000 fans. Celebrities such as Mick Jagger, Rod Stewart, and Henry Kissinger were regular attendees. ABC signed a television contract in 1979, and everything seemed to be in place for football to take its place alongside baseball and American football. However, in 1981 the NASL lost three clubs, and the following year, despite some huge crowds and big-time players such as Pele, Gerd Muller, Franz Beckenbauer, Carlos Alberto, Eusébio, George Best, Gordon Banks, and Kyle Rote Jr., poor attendance, along with several legal and financial problems, caused ABC not to renew its contract. That same year the NASL lost seven more clubs; among them, the Dallas Tornado — Lamar Hunt's team. The most faithful football entrepreneur in the USA could no longer deal with the financial losses. Everyone in the league was losing money. The league was down to twelve clubs in 1983, and to nine in 1984, which resulted in the announcement in March of 1984 that the league was closing its doors and would no longer operate (Harris, 1976).

This FIFA-sanctioned league with teams from Canada and the United States had a history of financial trouble resulting mainly from a consistent lack of planning and dwindling spectator support (Gardner, 1976). The collapse of the NASL meant the end of professional football in the USA. There was now only a six-a-side indoor league played by clubs in the Major Indoor Soccer League (MISL). Indoor football had been played in Europe and South America since the 1930s. It was not a new sport, but it appealed to the NASL owners since they could get more out of their players. To the short twenty-four-game summer session they could add a winter season as well. The indoor game also allowed the owners to do something that FIFA would not permit with the outdoor game. They could tinker with the rules, and proceed with the Americanization of the sport. Suddenly indoor football had penalty boxes, massive substitutions, and offside lines as in ice hockey. As the MISL gained strength, the NASL weakened even more, and soon the MISL began to lure some of the best NASL players with higher offers. Football in the USA had found yet another division within its ranks — the outdoor game versus the indoor version. After the collapse of the MISL in 1992, and in spite of the relative success of the indoor game, which attracted large crowds, some teams formed new leagues, but still struggled for survival.

A new league, named Major League Soccer (MLS), with full financial backing and seemingly more fan support, began play with ten teams in April 1996. The ten teams started with a roster of 18 players, all under a single-entity[14] arrangement and with a strictly enforced player salary budget of only $1.3 million. Soon stars such as Mexican goalkeeper Jorge Campos, Bolivia's Marco Etcheverry, Colombia's Carlos Valderrama and Italy's Roberto Donadoni signed on. Of course these stars could not fit into the stingy salary cap, but that problem was solved by sponsors paying most, if not all, of their salaries. After 14 years the new league has continued to flourish by providing some high quality and entertaining football, plus it has the continued support of investors with a long-term commitment to the growth of the sport — including faithful supporter Lamar Hunt. The signing of new world stars, including David Beckham, in 2007 has given the league much-needed publicity and credibility worldwide. It is up to the new league to continue improving its product and to prove itself with positive results at the international level.

As of 2011 Major League Soccer, had 18 teams in the U.S. and one in Canada, with expansion planned by the 2012 season. The United Soccer Leagues (USL) are a collection of five leagues, with four currently in operation, spanning the lower divisions of men's professional football, as well as women's and youth football. The USL First Division, previously the second-level professional league in the USA, did not operate in 2010. When Nike sold its stake in the overall USL organization, a group of disgruntled First Division owners announced plans to launch a new incarnation of the North American Soccer League in 2010. The USSF refused to sanction either the First Division or the new NASL for 2010, and the two groups eventually agreed to unite for 2010 only under the banner of USSF Division 2, run directly by the USSF and including teams from both leagues. USSF Division 2 features nine U.S. teams, two Canadian teams, and one Puerto Rican team. The USL Second Division is the professional third-division league and features six U.S. teams for 2010. The semiprofessional fourth-division league in the United States is the USL Premier Development

League (PDL), which has 59 teams in the U.S., seven in Canada, and one in Bermuda. Though the PDL does have some paid players, it also has many teams that are made up entirely or almost entirely of college football players who use the league as an opportunity to play competitively in front of professional scouts during the summer, while retaining amateur status and NCAA eligibility. In addition to MLS and the USL, the United States Adult Soccer Association (USASA) governs amateur soccer competition for adults throughout the United States. It is effectively the amateur fifth division of football in the United States. The USASA sanctions regional tournaments that allow entry into the Lamar Hunt U.S. Open Cup, the oldest continuous football competition in the United States. This annual competition pits teams from all five levels of the American football pyramid against each other, similar to England's FA Cup.

Unlike the professional organization, amateur football has enjoyed tremendous growth and success in the United States since its early days. The last official estimate includes over 6,000 high schools and over 800 colleges that field teams for either men or women (sbrnet.com, 2009). In fact, there has always been college football in all the years the USSF has controlled the sport. Ironically, it was strongest with the same Ivy League schools that rejected the sport in the 1870s. Harvard took football in 1905, and when the Intercollegiate Soccer Association (ISA), was formed in 1926, it included Princeton and Yale among its twelve members.

Unfortunately the USSF and the colleges couldn't care less about each other's activities. That was fine with the colleges as they, too, proceeded to Americanize the sport. They played four quarters instead of two halves, they used two referees instead of one, they replaced the throw-in with a kick-in, and of course they permitted liberal use of substitutes.

College football grew slowly at first, but by the 1960s when college basketball and American football became increasingly specialized, football was seen as an ideal sport for the average-size athlete, and of course it was also an inexpensive team sport to organize and finance.

In 1959 the National Collegiate Athletic Association (NCAA), introduced a national championship, and by 1972 the colleges had a ranking system and a Senior Bowl game as well. Scholarships became available, and that added to the growth of the game at the high school level. At the beginning of the 1970s there were over 70,000 boys playing high school football, and by the 1980s that figure had increased to 180,000.

With the passage of Title IX[15] the women's game also started to explode, and by the mid–1980s there were over 165 colleges sponsoring women's football. Unlike in most soccer-playing nations, the growth of the women's game in the USA has helped increase overall interest in football in the United States. Both the 1999 and 2003 FIFA Women's World Cups were held in the United States, and the United States has emerged as one of the best national teams in the world. They are currently ranked first in the FIFA Women's World Rankings, have won two of the five FIFA Women's World Cups held thus far, and have also won gold medals in three of the four Olympic women's football tournaments held to date The crowd of over 90,000 at the Rose Bowl for the 1999 FIFA Women's World Cup remains the largest crowd in the world ever to witness any women's sporting event.

Women's football in the United States is also played at the professional level. The professional first-division women's soccer league (WSL) in the U.S. is Women's Professional Soccer, which has operated exclusively in the United States since its launch in 2009 with seven teams. One of the charter teams folded after that season, two joined the league for 2010, and another charter team folded during the 2010 season, bringing the number of competing teams back to its original number of seven. The USL's W-League is currently the women's semiprofessional second-division league, which contains 22 U.S.–based teams and seven Canadian-based teams. This league serves roughly the same purpose for women's football as the United Soccer League's (USL) Professional Developmental League (PDL) serves for men's football, in that it allows collegiate players to maintain NCAA eligibility while continuing to develop their game against quality opponents. There is no equivalent to the U.S. Open Cup in the women's game currently.

The future existence of MLS is not going to be easy, but there is more reason for optimism now than in years past. The league has football-specific stadiums, TV contracts, and several major sponsors. There are more and more Americans playing, and playing better, and the relative success of the men's national team in recent World Cup competitions has sparked added interest. The football atmosphere in the USA is now more favorable than ever for a professional league to succeed. It is up to MLS and its administrators to provide the missing ingredients of the past: high quality product, entertaining games, quality management, wealthy owners with long-term commitment, and more importantly to avoid Americanizing the sport. To find a style for the American player is one thing, but to change the principles on which the game is played worldwide will only lead to disaster yet again.

Yes, football is indeed the world's game, because of the number of countries that play it. Football crosses racial, cultural, age, and socioeconomic barriers, and it can be played by people of all sizes and body shapes. It can be played almost anywhere and with little equipment but a round ball. Bill Shankley, former manager of Liverpool FC, summed up his enthusiasm for football: "The way some people talk about football, you'd think the result of one game was a matter of life and death. They don't understand; it is much more than that" (cited in *Soccer*, 1967, p. 1).

Pele in his autobiography (1977) called it "The Beautiful Game," a game of love, passion, and fans. That and much more is what football is all about.

5

THE FIELD AND THE PLAYERS

The Field of Play

Traditionally called "the Pitch," it shall be rectangular, its length being not more than 130 yards (120 meters) nor less than 100 yards (90 meters) and its breadth not more than 100 yards (90 meters) nor less than 50 yards (45 meters). For any international competition the field shall be no more than 120 yards (110 meters) nor less than 110 yards (100 meters) and the breadth not more than 80 yards (75 meters) nor less than 70 yards (64 meters). The length in all cases should exceed the breadth (FIFA, 2009).

Other details of the field are shown in Figure 1.

The Goals

The goals shall be placed on the center of each goal line and shall consist of two upright posts, equidistant from the corner flags and 8 yards (97.32 meters) apart, joined by a horizontal crossbar the lower edge of which shall be 8 feet (2.44 meters) from the ground. The width and depth of the crossbars shall not exceed 5 inches (12 centimeters). The goalposts and the crossbars shall have the same width (FIFA, 2009).

The Players

A full team consists of 11 players on the field, one of which is the goalkeeper. In the modern game of football the positions of the field players are no longer strictly defined. Players can move back and forth all over the

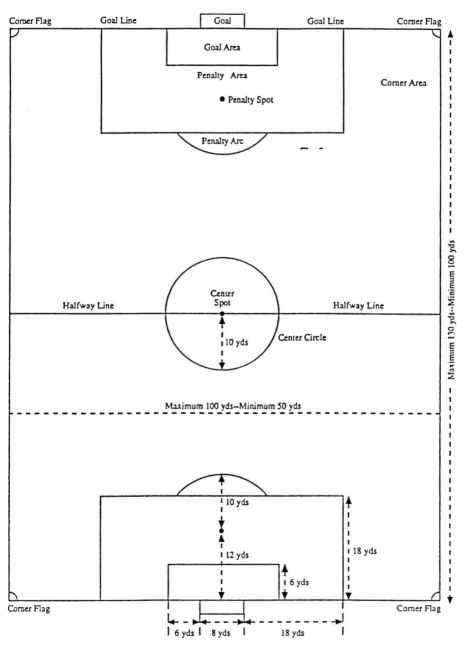

Figure 1. The field of play.

field and are able to play defensively and offensively at all times. They must be able to switch positions instantly as different situations develop in a game. Thus the responsibilities of all players except the goalkeeper are constantly shifting and positional names serve less and less to define the players' roles. The traditional lineup included fullbacks/defenders, halfbacks/midfielders, and forwards, with the outside forwards also known as wingers. The number of fullbacks, halfbacks, and forwards depends on the formation used and the system that a coach desires. Rounding out the 11 players is the goalkeeper or keeper, responsible for preventing goals. As responsibilities have changed through the years the traditional names of field positions have become less meaningful, and, in addition to fullback and forward, other terms used today are sweeper, stopper, and striker.

Goalkeeper

The goalkeeper's priority is to prevent the ball from going into the goal. The keeper is also responsible for organizing and assisting the last line of defense. But the moment the goalkeeper gains possession of the ball, the keeper must start the attack by putting the ball back into play in such a way that the opponents will not immediately regain possession. The goalkeeper is the only player allowed to use the hands, but only within the penalty area, as shown in Figure 1. Thus, the skills required for this position include agility, speed, quickness, concentration, and the ability to catch, punch, throw, and kick the ball.

The goalkeeper is responsible for what should be considered the most sensitive area on the pitch. While the rest of the field players can rectify a mistake, the keeper's is final. A team with a good goalkeeper gains confidence and is likely to be more successful.

Through the years this position has changed drastically. In the beginning the keeper's role was purely defensive. He was merely an acrobat who waited around his box to prevent the ball from going into the net. Over the years the keeper has had to adapt to the changes in the game, and has taken a more active role offensively.

The modern keeper is an integral part of the team, both offensively and defensively. The keeper role is to be aware of everything his teammates are doing, and to instruct them with voice commands of their positional playing both on defense and offense. The keeper and his positional responsibilities are now so diversified that he has become an additional fullback acting oftentimes as a sweeper or libero.

The ideal height for a goalkeeper is between 5'9" and 6'1", with proportional weight and strength. Speed and quickness are essential, and once the decision has been made to go for the ball the keeper must let his teammates know of his intentions, so they can cover the area he is vacating. A keeper must have quick reaction and agility. The keeper can't afford to be indecisive. He must come out when required, and must be ready to jump, dive, or fling himself through the air to make a save. This requires great skill and a well coordinated, supple body.

Concentration is particularly important as keepers may have long periods of inactivity, yet they must always be ready for a sudden counterattack. The smallest lapse of concentration could prove disastrous. A good keeper must stay calm and not allow the tension or a mistake to get him down.

Anticipation, positioning and imagination are probably a keeper's greatest assets. His ability to be able to anticipate and to predict what an opponent will do and react to it are crowning qualities of a good keeper. He must be a student of the game and be able to anticipate/predict what will happen through knowledge rather than on instinct alone.

Confidence and courage are two ingredients that any keeper must possess. The slightest bit of uncertainty can be exploited by the opposition. If a keeper makes a mistake, he should not stop and dwell on it. He must maintain his concentration, keep cool, and transmit the confidence to his teammates. It takes courage to launch oneself at the feet of a huge forward bearing down on goal, and he must be prepared to move anyone out of the way by the strength and determination of his jumps or dives. The keeper must have the nerves to expose himself to hard physical contact where he will have little or no chance of protection. The keeper who thinks twice about doing something is generally the one that gets injured.

Defenders/Fullbacks

The primary role of the defenders is to prevent the opposition from scoring by delaying the penetration of the attacking forwards inside scoring territory; they must also be ready and able to launch a counterattack once they come into possession of the ball. They also serve to protect the goalkeeper from an overwhelming attack by the opposition. The sweeper, whose main role is to provide defensive coverage and to defend against an unguarded attacker who has broken through the defense, is the last defensive hope except for the goalkeeper. The stopper's chief job is to mark, or guard tightly, the opposing striker or the most dangerous player on the field, usually the top scorer. Both the sweeper and stopper can move up occasionally to support an attack and to take shots on goal.

The role of the fullback has changed a great deal over the years. Traditionally the fullback has always had be strong, quick, and decisive — a good diagnostician who knows exactly what is expected. The modern game has imposed new demands — great ball control, heading ability (offensively and defensively), and dribbling skills, among others. He must be able to initiate a counterattack, and be able to join in with the midfield. When necessary, he must be ready to move up-field and be part of the attack.

Midfielders/Halfbacks

There are three to four midfielders or more, sometimes called halfbacks, on a team. They are usually referred to according to their positions on the field — right, left, center, and defensive and offensive wingers. The coach must decide the kind of midfielders needed and what positions they must play. These players act as a link between the defense and the offense, and should be very adept at initiating attacks as well as breaking up the opposition attacks. The midfield area is crucial in tactics, and it is often said that the team that controls the midfield has a very good chance of winning the game.

The defensive midfielder usually plays back in the area between the last line of defense and the other midfielders. The job of the defensive midfielder is to mark the opponent with the ball, acting as a defensive screen, and, when attacking as a link player, to receive passes from the fullbacks or the goalkeeper and pass to the forwards.

The playmaking midfielders (right or left) are the organizers of the team in the midfield area. Here is where the buildup for an attack begins, and the pace is set by making penetrating passes into the opponent's defensive third. The attacking or offensive midfielder plays an important role in the scoring. These players' main responsibility is to provide close support for the forward line when the team is on attack, thus acting as link between the forwards and the midfield area. On defense, the offensive midfielder is the first to challenge attacking opponents in the midfield area, stalling an attack by cutting passing opportunities.

The halfbacks of yesteryear would be astonished to see the modern halfback at work. Today's halfbacks are highly skilled all-around players, and their contributions, be they offensive or defensive, play a key role in the success or failure of a team.

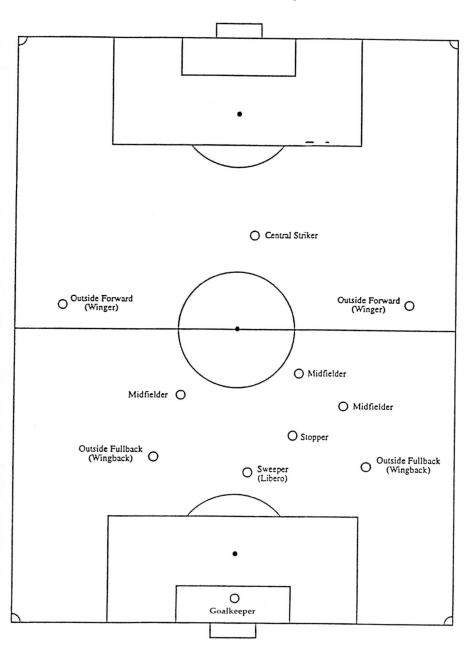

Figure 2. Basic alignment of players on the field.

Their main defensive responsibility is to destroy an attack by the opposition. A good halfback must be resourceful in covering for his teammates and determined in his challenges. Physical strength, stamina, and quick recovery are utterly essential skills.

Their main offensive responsibility is to initiate and support attacks, and they must be industrious and imaginative with the ball. The halfback certainly has to have a flair for spotting and/or creating an opening during an attack.

Forwards

The main responsibility of forwards is to score goals and to create opportunities for others to score goals, but they also should be able to switch to a defensive posture when the other team has the ball. The outside forwards, also called wingers (right or left), usually play close to the touchlines, forcing the opponents to spread out and thus opening more space for the attack. They often make cross passes from the side to teammates in position to score. On defense the forwards must challenge their opposing player, and if necessary, even chase the player all the way back to the defense. The central forward or striker (right or left) scores most of a team's goals. This player must be able to outmaneuver the last defender and to create space and scoring opportunities. On defense, the forward must immediately challenge any player with the ball and provide support to the midfield. Refer to Figure 2, for a basic alignment of players' positions.

Whether we call them forwards, strikers, or wingers, they must have the prerequisites to spearhead and attack. They must have an innate attacking sense, positional sense, improvisation sense, and a flair for the unpredictable.

6

HISTORY OF TACTICS
AND STRATEGIES

For the purpose of this book, the words "strategy" and "tactics" are interchangeable. Strategy and tactics deal with what the whole team can do to win a game. The coach or manager decides what strategy the team will use, and the manager decides what strategy is best for the team to beat its opponents. However, once on the pitch it is up to the players to evaluate the situation and decide, depending on their own ability and theoretical knowledge, how to achieve the best results. While it is the players who must go out and try to win the game, is the manager's responsibility to decide on the formations and what strategy to use for each game. The manager must also decide which players, according to their tactical ability, will be used to carry out that strategy.

Beginning of the Modern Game

On Monday, October 26, 1863, a group of men met in Freemasons Tavern in London, England, to form the first Football Association (Gardner, 1976). This was probably the single most important development in the history of football, because at that meeting the first real laws of the game were written down. Since that date most countries have created their own football associations, and more than 200 countries now belong to FIFA (FIFA.org, 2009).

The early laws of the game were similar to the present laws of the Rugby Football League. For example, a player could catch the ball with his hands. There was no provision for a goalkeeper; the pitch was 200 yards long maximum, but there was no minimum; and the goalposts were eight yards apart, but had no crossbar on the top (Beim, 1977).

Before 1866 the offside rule in football was the same as in rugby. A player was considered offside if he was ahead of the ball (Beim, 1977; Bernard, 1956; Eastman, 1966). In 1866, however, the law was changed: a player was considered offside if he was ahead of the ball and near his opponent's goal with fewer than three opponents between him and the ball (Greaves, 1966; Wade, 1967).

Because of the offside law, the game was dominated by dribbling. Player positioning was virtually nonexistent, and players tended to bunch around the ball. By the early 1870s the laws of the game had changed considerably. Field players were now prohibited from using their hands, and a goalkeeper appeared who could use his hands to stop the ball (Hughes, 1975). The length of the pitch remained the same, but a tape was stretched across the goal acting as a crossbar (Beim, 1977). Later, in 1882, the tape was replaced by a real crossbar (Bernard, 1956).

The throw-in from the touchline appeared during the 1870s (Hughes, 1975). The players were allowed to throw the ball with one hand, and the throw was awarded to the player who first touched the ball after it had gone over the touch line (Eastman, 1966). According to Beim (1977), the throw-in rule was later changed to give possession of the ball to the opponent of the team that last played it before going out of bounds. In 1882 the two-handed throw-in we know today replaced the one handed throw-in from the touchline (Vogelsinger, 1982). In 1891, according to Vogelsinger (1982), goal nets were introduced and the penalty kick was added, and in 1902 the penalty and goal areas were marked, as are enforced today.

The passing game and combination play began to develop out of the necessity to avoid bunching around the ball. This in turn changed the shape of team formations, and gave more balance to attack and defense (Rosenthal, 1980). As attackers found weaknesses in the opposition's defense, defenders began to change their tactics to eliminate those weaknesses.

Birth of Passing

Tactics in football are very simple. The two main areas are to score and to prevent the opposition from scoring. Because of the simple set of rules governing the game's principal objectives, the sequence of play is easy to understand even for a novice to the sport (*Soccer Magazine*, 1983). This is not to imply that football is a crude or predictable game. Football's simple tactics are very flexible and variable and, when executed properly, can be infinitely exciting.

In football, a player has very few options as to what to do with the ball. The best chance a player has to score is to be right in front of the goal. This happens very infrequently, but when it happens a player must be ready to shoot with speed (Rote Jr., 1978). Any hesitation on a player's part could result in a missed opportunity for a sure goal. It is amazing how many players become mesmerized by the open goal mouth and yet waste precious moments to avoid the oncoming defenders (Gardner, 1976).

A player does not always have ample opportunity to get close enough to the goal to score. A player must, therefore, find a way to the goal. If a player receives the ball where there is no chance for a shot, the most positive reaction is to run forward with the ball while dribbling, until close enough for a score or at least a shot on goal.

Prior to the postwar period, this method of dribbling was very popular and produced many graceful players with the ability to move past opponents in succession until the chance for a shot was possible (*Eleven*, 1983). Nowadays passing is more widely used to get close to the goal for a shot. With the emphasis on individuality, football in the early days was not a "team" sport, and there was neither place nor any need for team tactics, much less passing. The idea of the game was simple: score goals. Heading and shooting from long range were still unknown. The player in possession of the ball simply attempted to break through by dribbling, with all his teammates close by in support to pick the ball in case he lost control, and to continue dribbling past the opposition towards the goal. Of course the opposition massed in front of the player with the ball — much the same as a group of elementary school children playing today.

The Scots have been credited with bringing the pass into use for the first time. The famous amateur Scottish team Queen's Park of Glasgow was the first team to introduce any real tactics, and brought the first true passes into the game (Batty, 1969; Beim, 1977; & Rote, 1978). Realizing that the opposing players were bunched around the person with the ball, the Scots began to pass the ball. By inter-passing they were able to show how the whole field should be used, thus forcing many defenders out of position and unable to prevent the attackers from penetrating the defense. Queen's Park remained unbeaten for the first nine years of its existence, and not a goal was scored against them on the first three, (Rote, 1978). This tactic forced everyone to think about redistributing the players on the pitch. No longer was it sufficient to mass directly in the path of the player with the ball, as that would allow the new weapon to be used against them. With the introduction of passing, team formations moved quite rapidly in order to prevent the opposition from scoring.

When a player is unable to move the ball by dribbling, either because of lack of skill or because his path is blocked by defending players, the player must attempt a pass to an open teammate. A long pass to an open teammate gives the receiving player more chance to move forward and advance. Even so, the shorter the pass, the more precise it will be.

Longer passes are more threatening to the opponents' goal, but shorter passes are safer. Critics feel that the game is too dominated by the pass style of play; a series of well-executed passes has a much quicker ability to advance towards the opponent's goal (Beim, 1977). Triangular passing, wall passing, swerved passing, overlap passing, reverse passing, through passing, and one-touch passing are different methods of passing employed to outwit and confuse opposing defenders while on attack. With the exception of the through pass and the wall pass, all passes are aimed at the position the teammate now occupies. The through pass and the wall pass are aimed at the position the teammate has not yet reached but is speeding towards. This type of pass is a necessity in defeating the offside trap, which is becoming a widely used tactic among many teams (*La Gazzeta dello Sport*, 1994).

To trap an offensive player into being offside (see definition of terms in Chapter 1), the tactic by the fullbacks of moving forward, leaving the attacker alone, was developed, hence the effectiveness of the through pass in this situation.

Credit for developing and refining the technique of the offside trap is given to Bill McCracken and Frank Hudspeth of Newcastle United (Csanadi, 1963). Both were fullbacks who, by virtue of their strategic positions on the pitch (their view of the action taking place in front of them), were able to stop an attack with a well timed, sneaky move upwards so as to trap the attackers offside.

The effectiveness of the offside trap led to its implementation all over England. However, this tactic, coupled with all the defensive tactics of the time, resulted in staunching the flow of the game (Clues, 1980). Goals were scored, but the game had deteriorated to a dull and slow affair. Spectators were being turned off, and the game had somewhat returned to its original dribbling form (Morita, 1984).

It was soon realized that if something was not done to change this dreadful situation, football would continue to lose its appeal. So, in 1925, as Vogelsinger (1982) tells us, the authorities changed the rule to reduce from three to two the number of players necessary to put a player onside. This new rule allowed the attackers a greater chance to score more goals and allowed for fewer stoppages. What was decided in 1925 remains in effect today!

Although accurate passing and dribbling are some ways to advance the ball, the hit-and-hope method is frequently used. As an alternative to advancing with the ball, or passing it accurately, it is hit as hard as possible upfield, and the hitter hopes for the best. No specific aiming is involved other than aiming the ball into enemy territory, and the usual outcome is the loss of the ball to the opposing team. English teams use to use this tactic a great deal — the reason has been attributed to the wet weather in the United Kingdom, which forces the ball to be played in the air quite a lot rather than on the ground, as opposed to most Latin American teams' style (Rosenthal, 1980). For teams lacking ball skills, it is a common and boring technique.

The long pass, when used sparingly, can become a valuable tool in moments of panic and near disaster. A defender who wildly kicks the ball out from in front of the goal mouth is performing a valuable service to the team regardless of how tactless it might seem. Where the ball lands or who gets it is irrelevant so long as a goal or the near goal opportunity is avoided.

According to Vogelsinger (1982), the goalkeeper also has a version of hit and hope. A long kick upfield has a 50-50 chance for a teammate to actually receive the long pass. In upper levels of the game, the keeper will roll or throw the ball to a teammate who then passes or carries the ball upfield. A long kick from the keeper is used when time is running out and a goal is needed to either tie, win the game, or waste time. (Rote Jr., 1978).

There are times in a match when a player, regardless of skill, must play for safety or risk giving a goal. Glanville (1979) indicated that there are three play-it-safe tactics, also known as "wasting time tactics," available to a player. Although they are widely used by lower-level teams and are justified in extreme conditions, most of these methods are extremely unpopular with the spectators. The techniques are the kick to touch, the conceding a corner, and the back pass.

Kick to touch is accomplished by clearing the ball to the far end of the pitch — the other touchline. By doing this the defending players have succeeded in getting the ball out of their end and have stalled for time while the opponents retrieve the ball.

Conceding a corner occurs when a defender feels that is too risky to dribble or pass the ball out of the defensive end or to the sideline and kicks the ball over the goal line, thus conceding a corner. This tactic could prove to be dangerous at times as it is possible to score goals from a corner kick (Cottrel, 1970).

The back pass takes place when, instead of passing the ball forward, the player with the ball passes the ball to the goalkeeper to waste time. The back pass can also take place when teammates pass the ball back and forth to each other with no intention of moving the ball forward.

All these techniques make no attempt at forward advancement and settle for security. The back pass is the most disliked by knowledgeable spectators, but can be effective when wasting time.

Other Tactics

Pressure is a key tactic of football. When the ball is far down the pitch, players without the ball still serve an important role in the execution of plays. They must constantly move around, adjusting to the flow of the attack, and attempt to confuse and harass the opposition (Hollander, 1980). The simplest and most basic maneuver is to run in the direction that will block a run or a pass.

Fast sprinting ability is necessary for the modern football player, who must both be quick and have great endurance (Lodziak, 1966). In the earlier years, quicker players usually played forward and stockier players usually played defense (Kane, 1970). Today, more abilities are required of each player, as athletes have become more powerful and more intelligent in regard to tactics.

Man-to-man marking has also become an important part of the game. An opposing player known to be a great scorer may sometimes have one player assigned to mark him. However, if this task is not fulfilled properly, then the defending team can find itself at a major disadvantage.

Special Tactics

Special tactics employed during the game are "set plays." These set plays can take place during kick-offs, dropped balls, throw-ins, goal kicks, free kicks, penalty kicks, and corner kicks. The most dangerous of all is the free kick, whether indirect or direct (see definition of terms). All these kicks cover a wide range of situations in which a player might be involved during a match. This type of tactics in set plays are simple to learn and easy to teach. Unfortunately, novice managers have books full of intricate diagrams with dotted lines, arrows, and symbols all designed to enhance the game, but rendered impossible to execute if the manager lacks knowledge and technique. Many players, however, choose to ignore these complex and sometimes ill-advised tactics and rely on their instincts, intuition, and general experience on the field. The overburdened player with a mass of technical, theoretical, and complex information may well become too clever for his own good and lose the spontaneous inventiveness that sets the game of football apart from others (*Soccer Magazine*, 1983).

Movement

Harris (1976) mentioned that movement is an important part of a team's tactics. Movement refers to what a player does or where a player goes when not in possession of the ball. While a teammate has the ball, the other teammates must be positioned in a supporting way or distracting way. In a supporting way, the player without the ball moves to an area where he can become a scoring threat when receiving the ball, or can merely assist the teammate with the ball by becoming an outlet pass if the ball carrier is going to lose the ball or just needs a passing opportunity. The player without the ball can assist a teammate by distracting the defense. This can be accomplished by preoccupying the opposition, making decoy runs and certain swift moves aimed at confusing opponents and thus drawing attention away from the player with the ball (Batty, 1969). Whenever an attacking teammate makes a move, the defense should react to it. When the defense does not react, goals are usually the result.

Plan of Attack

A team's plan of attack usually is created or developed by the manager just prior to the match. The manager may feel that one strategy will work better than another. Thus, scouting reports or past experiences against a particular team assist the manager in making a plan of attack in order to try to defeat the opposition.

The plan of attack may be for a team to maintain ball possession, which is accomplished by the short pass as used by most Latin American teams (Rote Jr., 1978) or the long pass, in order to beat a slow defense, as used by a few English teams and a good portion of northern European teams (Beim, 1977). The manager may also suggest different styles of attack, such as going straight up a manager may ask the players to use the "offside trap," or may insist on zonal marking versus man-to-man (Batty, 1969; Fouls, 1979). The plan of attack also refers to the formation the team uses during a match. Zonal marking is used when each defender is given a particular area to guard (Vogelsinger, 1982). This may become very effective with a team that has limited experience defending.

Tactical Formations

On November 30, 1872, in Glasgow as reported by Rote Jr. (1978), Rosenthal (1981), and Gardner (1976), the English fielded eight forwards in the first English-Scottish match. They also noted that when the same two teams met May 27, 1972, only two players were forwards. Yet in 1974 during the World Cup, the Dutch were playing total football with eight forwards again — at least, so it appeared at times. Such is the changing pattern of tactics and formations in football.

The actual changes in the game seem almost to have been planned out when examined in a historical perspective (Brasch, 1970). That examination of changes revealed a regular increase in the number of fullbacks used over the years as indicated by Harris (1973). The changes happened spontaneously, with some made during the career of each succeeding coach. These formations were considered major innovations at the time they took place. Over the course of the years these innovations substantially changed the game (Gardner, 1976).

The earlier games in the 19th century used one defender. This game was very different from the game played today (Morita, 1984). This was the time of the single fullback who was stationed back near the goalkeeper and nine men playing up front acting as forwards. Passing had not yet been utilized. Today passing is a key ingredient of the game, and without it, the game would likely be ruined.

In the earlier games teams did well without passing. At the time the object of the game was for a player to dribble the ball past the opposition until it was lost. Teammates were not involved in play until the ball was lost; they would simply follow the player with the ball, and if one of them was to somehow gain possession of the ball he would attempt to do the same thing (Batty, 1969; Morita, 1984).

The game board was used by coaches in the early 1900s to explain tactical formations.

The first games were set up with a keeper, a fullback, and nine players up front to try to score. Hollander (1980) indicated that the formation was commonly known as 1-0-9, meaning a keeper, a fullback, no midfield, and nine forwards, as seen in Figure 3

In 1863, when the English Football Association was founded (Young, 1968), one of the nine forwards was brought back to assist the lone fullback. This move, according to Morita (1984) and Csanadi (1963), marked the beginning of the changes that were to come. As a result of this move a new formation was developed, as well as a new field position: the halfback or midfielder (Batty,1969). The new formation was known as 1-1-8. See Figure 4 for details.

During the 1870s a second midfielder was added as a result of weaker teams needing defensive help (Morita, 1984). Thus the formation 1-2-7, as detailed in Figure 5, became widely accepted. At the time this seemed the best lineup for the dribbling game.

Until now the idea of passing the ball was totally nonexistent. A football club known as Queen's Park from Scotland came up with the idea of

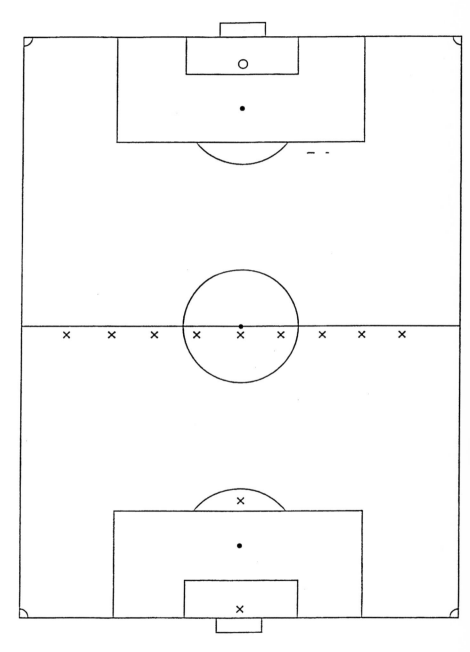

Figure 3. The 1-9.

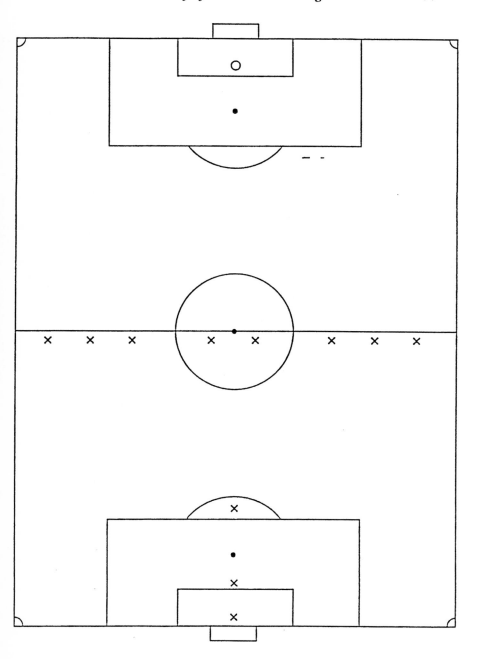

Figure 4. The 1-1-8.

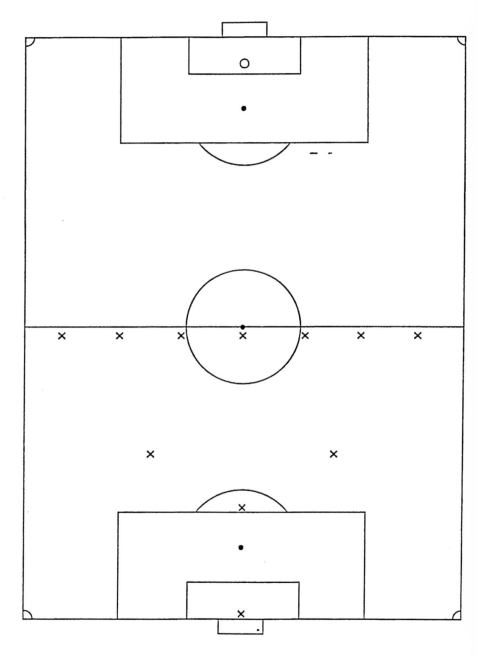

Figure 5. The 1-2-7.

moving the ball by passing it to other teammates (Lodziak, 1966). This bright new idea confused the opponents who were not used to having players pass the ball. As a defender tried to get near the ball, it was soon passed to another player. This caused confusion for defenders and great success for attackers. Soon thereafter, passing was adopted by other clubs in the league (Batty, 1969; Glanville, 1979; Kane, 1978; Rote Jr., 1978). Now the game of dribbling had been abruptly halted in exchange for the more successful and exciting passing game.

Immediately after the addition of the passing game came the addition of a spread game. Now able to pass the ball effectively, players no longer had to run in clusters (Csanadi, 1963). Passing made the game dramatically faster with the ball moving much farther in so little a span of time (Morita, 1984). The addition of passes to the game made the job of the lone defender too much to handle; thus another defender was added (Kane, 1978). The new formation became known as 2-2-6, as demonstrated in Figure 6. .

As passing skills improved, the formation once again had to be changed in order to compensate for the newest addition. The new formation called for the addition of another midfielder. Batty (1969) mentions that one club in England, known as Preston North End, imported a number of Scottish players who were exceptionally skilled in the short-pass game. Thus, with an excess of passing players, they developed the center-half back or center-midfielder around 1880. The new format was a 2-3-5, as shown in Figure 7. This pyramid-like formation of two defenders, three midfielders, and five forwards was used for nearly 50 years with much success.[16] According to Lodziak (1966), the center-half back was the key. This particular position required great stamina and skill, and was responsible for both offensive and defensive maneuvers. The new formation also allowed the defense to face an equal number of offensive players, thus allowing for better man-to-man marking (Rote Jr., 1978).

Another change was due to the fact that teams did not want to give up goals. So the center-half back, who at one time assisted in the attack, was brought back to play a more defensive role, and became solely a defensive player (Kane, 1978). The new formation thus became a 3-2-5, as seen in Figure 8. According to Morita (1984), this new formation became so successful that new improvisations had to be made; thus the inside forward was moved back to create the WM formation, as seen in Figure 9. When viewed from above, the positions of the five forwards resembled the letter W and the positions of the combined fullbacks and halfbacks resembled

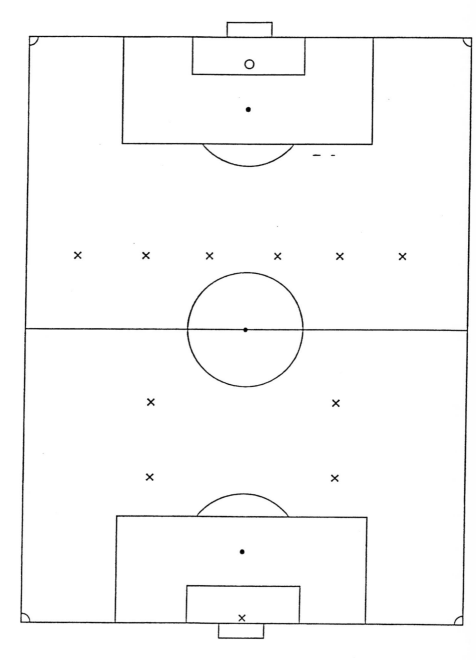

Figure 6. The 2-2-6.

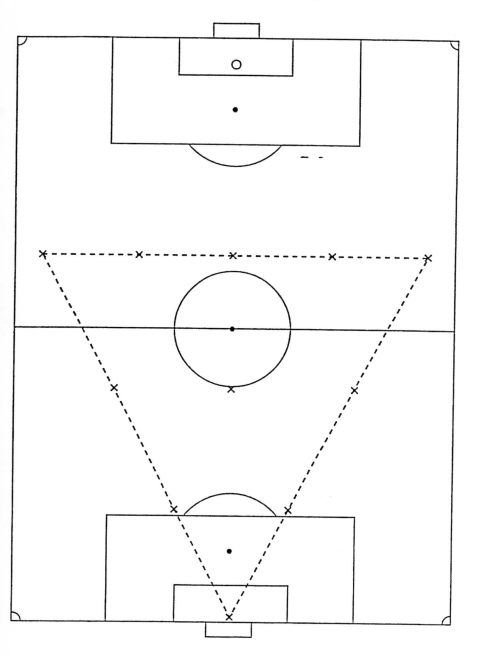

Figure 7. The Pyramid or 2-3-5.

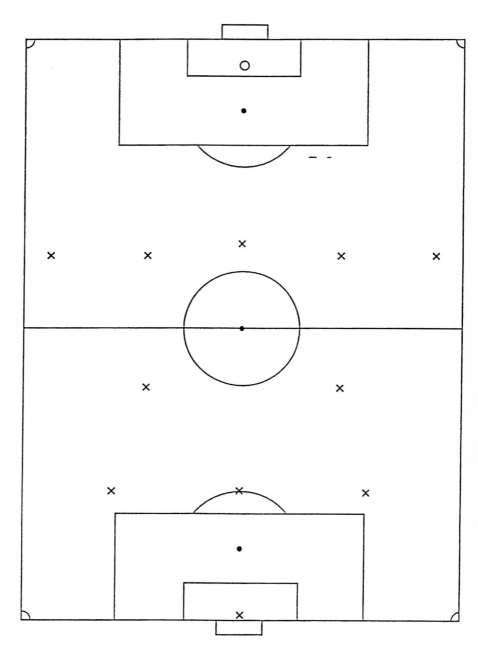

Figure 8. The 3-2-5.

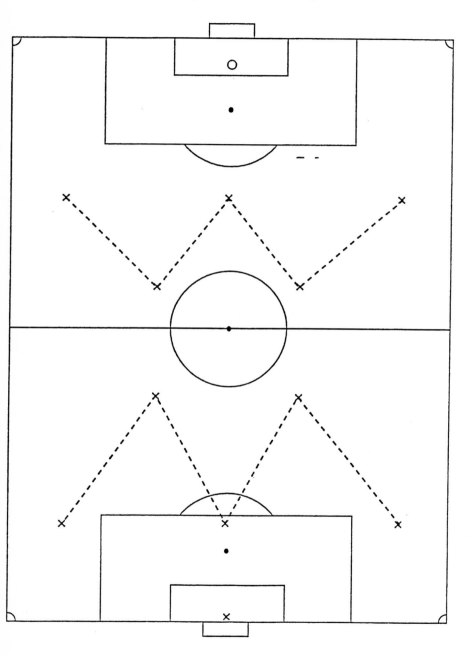

Figure 9. The WM.

the letter M. In the lapse of eight years with this formation the English club Arsenal won the league championship five years and the Football Association (FA) Cup twice (Rosenthal, 1980).

This style, which resembled the modern-day fast-break, was revolutionary for the English clubs. But European and Latin American teams continued to play the pyramid-style formation for quite some time after the WM innovation was made (Morita, 1984).

The spearhead formation was brought about to try to top the WM formation. Vogelsinger (1982) states that one central attacker/forward was brought back to replace the lost center-halfback, giving the pattern of a formation known as 3-3-4, as shown in Figure 10. He also indicates that this formation enabled the two central attackers to attack as a pair (double spearhead) and, if executed properly, the formation could do a great deal of damage to the grouped defenses attempting to stop them. The center forward in the role of the spearhead was assisted by the two outside forwards. The two outside forwards remained in a fairly central position, thus allowing the center forward to move across the pitch in search of an opening behind the defenders and becoming a target for passes from the two outside forwards. This formation is considered very natural as the forward line is likely to find itself in this shape without being aware of it (Vogelsinger, 1982).

A variation of the spearhead was the echelon, which deployed one wing forward in a very deep position and was used effectively against a three back defense, by allowing the attack to flood one side of the pitch while retaining wide position on the other side — a formation that was used with considerable success by Brazil's 1950 World Cup team.

In order to stop the twin attack of the spearhead, the double stopper was developed. Beim (1977) writes of how the Brazilians brought four fullbacks into the game to provide the team with a much-needed defensive boost. They now had a six-man attack and a six-man defense. Having four attackers, two halfbacks, and four defenders provided them with the ability to outnumber the opposition in attack and in defense, as seen in Figure 11. The new formation was now a 4-2-4 system.

Many other teams copied this strategy because they could gain the ability to quickly change from a strong attack to a strong defensive posture. The one setback to this new technique was the difficulty in finding players with the required ability and stamina needed for this new system (Csanadi, 1963; Kane, 1978). In order to alleviate some of the pressure imposed on

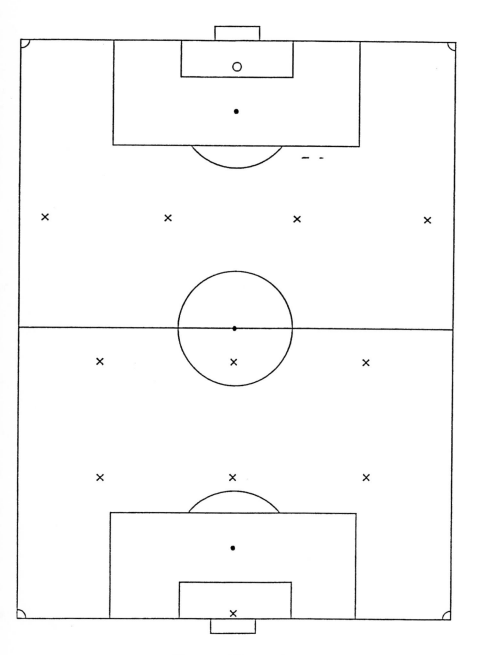

Figure 10. The 3-3-4.

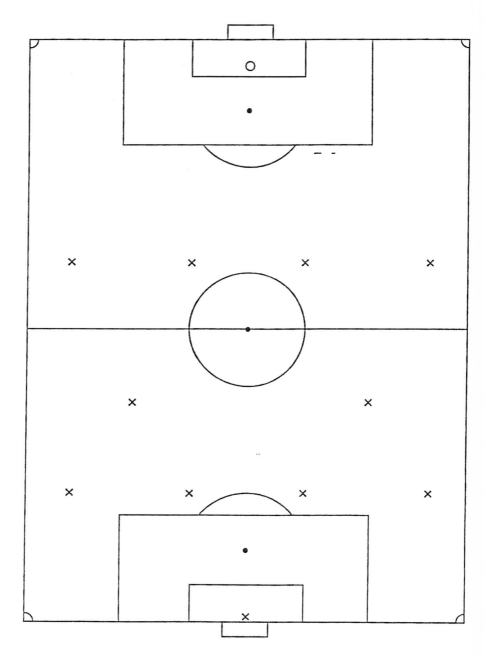

Figure 11. The 4-2-4.

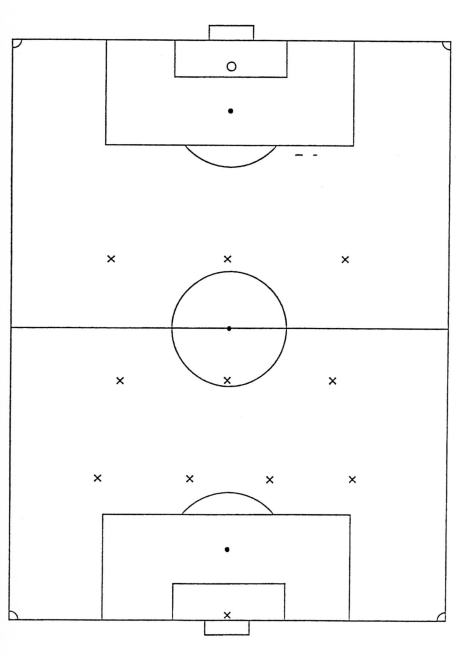

Figure 12. The 4-3-3.

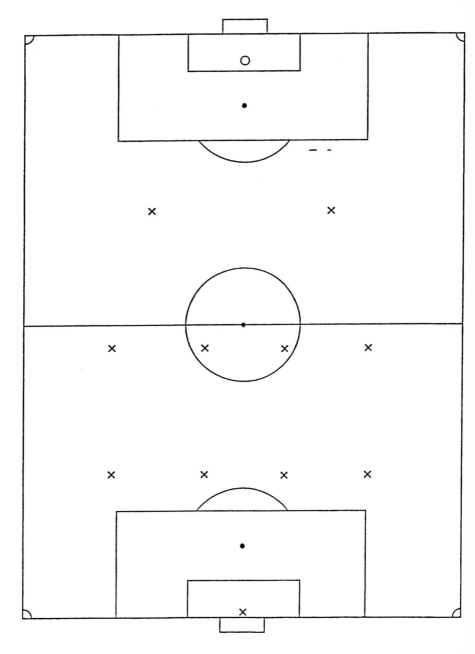

Figure 13. The 4-4-2.

these halfbacks, another attacker was moved back. The game now had more defensive players than offensive and it had a formation known as a 4-3-3, which is still widely used today, as shown in Figure 12 (Beim, 1977).

In the 1960s another solution to advance the defensive game was developed. One more attacker was moved back in order to have four midfielders. This helped teams a great deal defensively, but left only two attackers to face the vast number of defensive players on the opposing team (Rote Jr., 1978). The new formation was now a 4-4-2, as can be seen in Figure 13.

In the past 20 years, coaches in fear of losing have incorporated a fifth defender known as sweeper (Chyzowich, 1982). The sweeper, according to Chyzowich (1982), has the liberty to move around at leisure to pick unmarked attackers. The sweeper acts as a safety to pick up what teammates cannot contain, and has the freedom to play either in front or behind the defensive players. The "Swiss bolt" was the original name given to this position when it first originated in Switzerland, but the word "sweeper" is more widely known and accepted.

The pattern of football has been outlined. The game began as an explosive, highly offensive game. Through the years and with the emergence of the manager and the pressures imposed on him to win, the game has taken a turn to the more defensive style of play and formations. The formations most widely used today are the 4-3-3, the 4-4-2, and the formation which includes the sweeper. Other styles have become inadequate, obsolete, inappropriate, or simply too difficult to compete against other formations. Nevertheless, other formations should be taken into consideration and studied in more detail, such as the libero, the cattenaccio, total football, the irregular W, and yet again the original WM formation. All these formations, among others, will be discussed in Chapter 8 in great detail, as will the managers, the teams, and the players that made them famous and worthy of studying.

7

Major Tactical Formations

The first traces of tactical formations began to take place when players and managers realized the importance of teamwork in order to make better use of their strength. They noticed that it was more useful to pass the ball to teammates positioned in various parts of the pitch than to kick it at random. These new changes and formations were meant to save considerable time and effort since the players were no longer required to run after the ball without purpose.

Tactical formations are a recognizable pattern of play resulting from the use of certain players in fairly clearly defined functions on the pitch. Tactical formations should be sufficiently flexible to allow the individual strengths of players to be used to the maximum, and to allow temporary changes according to the problems which may be posed by the opposition (Csanadi, 1963).

In football, the starting lineup gives the impression of being somewhat fixed. However, as the game progresses, each player attempts to fulfill the tasks set by the system/formation that the team and the manager have adopted. At this point it is important to mention that the job of each individual player cannot be laid down in detail by any system. The wide variety of players' styles and the unlimited possibilities offered to an individual during the course of a game make it impossible to fully describe what a player is expected to do. All that a tactical formation can do is to give a general direction as to whether a player is supposed to act as a defender while another is entrusted with an attacking role, or both.

Descriptions of football formations always start with the defense. That should mean that the goalkeeper comes first, but as this is the one position in football that has remained unchanged over the years, it is assumed that everyone knows where he plays. Thus, the formations in football always start with the fullbacks on up to the forwards (e.g., 2-3-5 means two fullbacks, three halfbacks, and five forwards).

At this point it is important to acquire a clear understanding of the difference between tactics and formations.

Systems or formations[17] are based on the game as a whole and the needs of a particular team. They develop when a team adopts one method of formation over a certain period of time. Formations should be flexible in order to enable the different strengths of each player to be used to the maximum effect, and at the same time to allow temporary changes to take place according to the problems posed by the opposition and their formation (Wade, 1967).

Tactics are the means of carrying the objectives of the formation — the movement of players under certain circumstances and the different situations in attack and defense. Tactics also deal with the manner in which individual teams perform during a match and they could be affected by a variety of reasons such as climate, the type of ground, the demands of the officials, the laws of the game, and, of course, the manager.

One school of thought believes that the game should be played on a man-to-man basis in all phases of the game. This may be unrealistic, as it is almost impossible to mark a player all over the pitch for ninety minutes. If an opponent breaks free from the ball, the system or formation is destroyed. The opponent could exploit the advantage gained, and basically run through the opposition unopposed.

The other school is not concerned with restraining individual opponents by marking them for ninety minutes. This group contends that if the spaces are filled, opposing players sooner or later must come into these spaces, and if they gain control of the ball, a counter-attack can be mounted better and faster.

Let it be understood that there is no formation which will cover poor passing and poor shooting. There is no system that will cover for players who will not support each other, and there certainly is no formation at all for players who are not willing to run. Formations are simply concerned with the arrangement of players on the pitch. When a team loses a game, is not necessarily because of the formation they used. Oftentimes it is because the team failed to perform one or more key factors of teamwork. In fact, two teams can play with the same formation, and still play a completely different way, and achieve different results. Why? Because the players are different, and are generally given different instructions for each game they play. One manager might instruct his fullbacks to move forward on attack whenever possible, while the other may tell his fullbacks never to move forward. A manager may elect to use wingers, while the other one may not. There is altogether too much fluidity in football for it to be a game of rigid formations and position play.

Modern formation and tactics really started in 1925, when the offside law was changed. Before 1925 the law stated:

A player is off-side if he is nearer his opponent's goal-line than the ball at the moment the ball is played unless —

a. He is in his own half of the pitch

b. There are THREE of his opponents nearer to their own goal-line than he is

c. The ball last touched an opponent or was played by him

d. He receives the ball direct from a goal-kick, a corner kick, a throw-in or when it was dropped by the referee

What made a difference in 1925 was to change the one word in "b" from THREE to TWO (Alcock, 1895, Hughes, 1975). The aim of this change was to make goals easier to score because attacking players could now score goals from positions where before they would have been declared offside.

Let us now look at different formations and tactics, and learn how they evolved over the years.

The 2-3-5 or Pyramid

Because this was the first widely applied team formation and remained in wide use for well over fifty years, the 2-3-5 is often called the classic formation, and hence also known as the pyramid (Gardner, 1976). As noted in the previous chapter, the Scottish were the first to see the benefits of the passing game. Their style soon spread to England where a club named Preston North End built a memorable team based upon the Scottish short pass, which became more effective after Preston withdrew one of the forwards to form a 2-3-5 or pyramid lineup as seen in Figure 7. (This is the type of alignment used in the popular foosball tables in game rooms around the world.) This extra halfback became a center-half, who now was primarily an attacking halfback, but was expected to help in defense when needed.

In this system, the two fullbacks guarded the penalty area (Rote Jr.,

1978), and the fullbacks also marked the opposing inside forward and the wingers or outside forwards. The half backs helped out in defense, permitting the center-half back to move into the attack, while the five forwards were spread across the field (Lodziak, 1966). From an attacking point of view the main advantage is that the team could attack with six players. With five forwards and the center-half, the 2-3-5 stresses attacking football, and basically only three players — the keeper and the fullbacks — where defenders. The job of the fullbacks was to protect the area in front of the goal. The three half backs were expected to attack and defend, with the main job of the outside half backs or wingers being that of containing the opposition's wingers. However, the center half was considered to be primarily an attacking player and the brain of the team as well. From his key position, he was the leader, and he could see whether to pass left or right, long or short, dribble, or surge forward for an opportunity to score (Wilson, 2008).

The main drawback of this formation was that if the opposing center-forward beat the defending center-half, one of the fullbacks had to mark the center-forward, leaving a gap in the defensive area as described by Gardner (1976). Although the 2-3-5 formation was stronger defensively than earlier arrangements, it still gave the advantage to the forwards who outnumbered the defenders.

With the offside rule change in 1925, the number of goals in the English first division rose by 40 percent, from 1,192 in 1925 to 1,703 in 1926. With the goals that resulted from the change, center forwards of the day broke all kinds of scoring records: Dixie Dean scored 60 goals in 39 games in the English first division; George Camsell of Middleborough broke the second division record with 59 in 37 games; and in Scotland J. Smith of Ayr United made 66 goals in 38 games (Rote Jr., 1978). The emergence of the "stopper" soon put an end to this avalanche of goals. Reaction to this gluttony of goals was effective, and tactical. Defenses had to be strengthened, and while this tactical formation allowed for the creation of the offside trap as explained before, it in turn brought about the development of the WM formation.

The WM Tactical Formation

As noted before, the change in the offside rule in 1925 had an immediate effect on goal scoring. Something had to be done to stop the high-scoring center-forward of the classic pyramid formation. According to Batty (1969),

Beim (1977), Kane (1970), Lodziak (1966), Rosenthal (1980), and Vogelsinger (1982), credit for developing the tactics to stop the center-forward goes to Herbert Chapman, manager of the North London football team Arsenal, although many others made the claim as well.

The alignment employed by Chapman at Arsenal was named the WM formation because of the on–paper configuration of the players, as demonstrated in Figure 9. Wade (1967) notes that Chapman recognized with this system all the basic principles of play, and, at the same time, splendidly analyzed the difficulties which most teams experienced in adapting their play to the new offside law.

Chapman believed that to play the WM system properly, players had to be specialists with strictly defined responsibilities (Beim, 1977). Thus, he went out and signed players who could play the positions of the WM system to his liking (Rosenthal, 1980).

In order to develop a winning attack, Chapman looked for wingers with speed and the ability to move towards the goal and score. He filled these positions with Joe Hulme and Cliff Bastin. Between the two they managed to score 53 goals during one season. The center forward of the WM formation was developed to counterattack the stopper. Chapman employed the skills of Dixie Dean, who had 37 hat tricks during his 18 seasons of top-class football (Wilson, 2006).

He moved the fullbacks of the middle to the outside, where they now marked the opponent's wingers and played in a diagonal around the center-half so that each back had cover when necessary. The center-half was withdrawn from his old attacking position to fill the gap in the middle between the two fullbacks, thus marking the opponent's center forward. The halfbacks, in the meantime, were given the responsibility of marking the attacking inside forwards, making an M formation in defense.

The key to the WM defense was the stopper. He had to be tall, strong, and an especially good header. Chapman found this player in Herbie Roberts, who was satisfied with a totally defensive role, and his outstanding heading and sure tackling enabled him to limit the opponent's center forward (Beim, 1977). He became the prototype of all stoppers — the tall heavy backs who for years dominated English defenses.

In the WM formation the center-forward and the outside forwards are the bulk of the attack. Support and depth are provided for these attackers by the inside forwards, who are dropped back toward midfield (Csanadi, 1966).

In order to cope with the attack, defensive alignments match defenders with attackers on a man-to-man basis. The center-forward is marked by the center-halfback; the wings are marked by the fullbacks, and the inside forwards are marked by the wing halfbacks, resulting in an inverted W or M.

The W system also requires an exceptionally gifted center-forward who is fast, powerful, able to shoot and pass with both feet, and a good header (Gardner, 1976). The tight defensive coverage given to this position made it necessary for the center-forward to be aggressive and physically tough. The inside forwards in this system are the brain of the attack. They have to be talented in the skills of football, particularly in their passing and ball handling (Lodziak, 1966). They have to be able to feed passes and move intelligently to positions were they can receive passes or take shots on goal.

Another major function of the inside forwards, as indicated by Hughes (1966), is to work with the wing halfbacks in controlling the midfield area. This is crucial, since even to this day attacks are initiated there. It is often said in football that the team that controls the midfield likely will win the game.

The wings, or outside forwards, must be fast, talented ball handlers, able to take the ball down the sidelines and pass the ball accurately while on the run to their teammates attacking the goal (Wade, 1967). The wings are expected to come inside when the situation presents itself and shoot on goal, as all forwards must. The wing halfbacks are the liaison between the deep defenders and the attacking forwards. Their first duty is to defend, particularly since they operate in the midfield where the opposition is trying to build an attack. Thus, they must be good tacklers and aggressive defenders (Eastram, 1966).

The wing halfbacks function offensively when they move up the field behind and in support of their forwards. In this role they must be able to feed clearances out of the defense back u p to the forwards, thus sustaining the attack on goal and maintaining pressure (Greaves, 1966).

The center-halfback by necessity is concerned with staying close to his defensive assignment: the center-forward (Rote Jr., 1978). His role diverts him sometimes from taking part in the attack for fear of leaving the center-forward in a dangerous position (Batty, 1969;Csanadi, 1963). In this system the most that can be expected from the center-halfback, in terms of attack, is that he could join the wing halfbacks in trying to sustain the pressure of the attack on goal by moving up to midfield and trying to prevent clearances out of the opponent's defense (Joy, 1956).

Chapman's WM formation was used to shine the limelight on Arsenal. When he took over the team in 1925, Arsenal was a mediocre team, but under his managerial skill Arsenal went on to achieve great success. In 1927 Arsenal lost the final of the FA Cup to Cardiff City, but in 1930 they defeated Huddersfield Town to claim the prize (Beim, 1977). Arsenal won the league in 1931 having lost only 4 of their 42 league matches. They were finalists in the FA Cup in 1932 and won two more league titles in 1933 and 1934. Chapman died in 1934, but his Arsenal team became known as the elite of football during that time. Such success did not go unnoticed, and by the late 1930s the WM was the standard formation of every English club (Garner, 1996).

Several coaches believe that this style of play is good to use when dealing with inexperienced players. It is commonly taught as the formation that must be mastered before anything else. However, what must be mastered is skill and ball control; thus the system chosen will be successful regardless of the style of play chosen.

The M-W System of Play

The M pattern evolved from the W system. When the defenses caught up to the tactics of the W, it became necessary to change the attack yet again. This was accomplished by utilizing the inside forwards as the spearheads of the attack, with the center-forward dropping back toward the middle of the pitch to gather balls and to start the attack (Greaves, 1966). The wings also dropped back, thus giving the shape of an M to the attack, as seen in Figure 14. The idea of the M system was to place two talented and skillful forwards into the spaces created as the result of moving the wings and center-forward back. This tactic asked for the fullbacks and the center-half back to be out of the penalty area, with the wing half backs covering the attacker's inside, providing more individual maneuvering in the penalty area (Rosenthal, 1980). This formation provided greater control in midfield by having the center-forward and the wingers moved into the area, thus enhancing the defense. However, this formation lacked enough attackers upfield, thus lowering the opportunities to score.

The Swiss Bolt

The pyramid system was still flourishing when the Swiss reorganized their defense to provide greater safety.

While many teams were converting to the WM system during the 1930s, Karl Rappan, an Austrian, developed the Swiss bolt or verrou

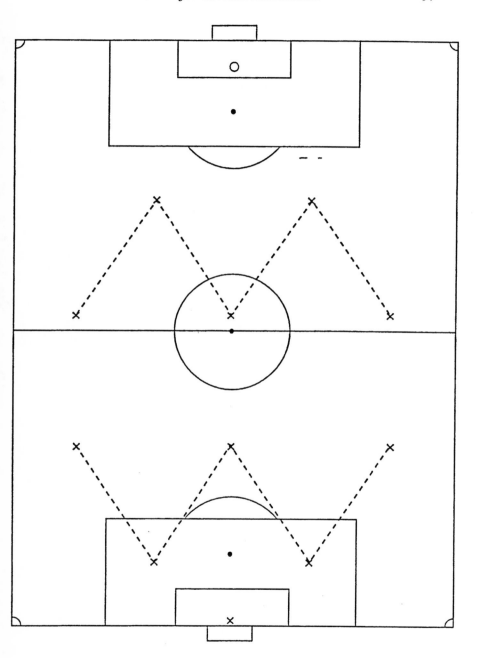

Figure 14. The MW.

system (Goldman, 1969). This system was a forerunner of the English sweeper and the libero of the Italian cattenaccio. The system provided a team with an equal number of defenders to the opponent's attackers, and gave the defenders an extra back (the bolt), to provide the necessary coverage in defense and to protect the open space in front of the goal as shown in Figure 15. According to Rosenthal (1979), Rappan believed that if a team was weaker than its opposition, then it had to concentrate on defense, and that even a strong team could benefit from a "free" back. When using this system, Rappan used three backs, as was the trend of the times, but he added a man behind the last line of defense to provide cover and pick up any attacker who had beaten any one of the defenders (Batty, 1966).

In the Swiss bolt system, the wing halfbacks marked the opponent's wingers, one defender played in the middle, and the other fullback became the free back or bolt. The three spearhead forwards were now marked by the two wing halves and one of the fullbacks, with the other fullback patrolling the penalty area as a reserve defender. The center-half as well as one of the inside forwards marked the opponent's inside-forwards and contained them in their building up of attacks.

The bolt system was based on the reserve defender. This added man to the defense was expected to move back and forth in the penalty area, ready to tackle any opponent that may have beaten the outer line of defense; When the extra defender moved into action, the player beaten by the opposing forward had to move back to act as the reserve or extra defender (Csanadi, 1966).

In attack, the Swiss bolt system relied most on counterattacking strategy. As soon as possession of the ball was regained, the defending forwards and defending halfbacks went on attack. Once they lost possession of the ball again, all the defensive players had to sprint back to their positions (Rosenthal, 1979). This system was extremely demanding physically since it required players to work very hard and cover great areas of the pitch. Additionally, players had to be intelligent and able to adapt to a variety of roles if the system was not successful (Batty, 1966). The formation's main shortcoming was that it placed incredible demands on the center-half, because the two wingers operated exclusively as forwards and stayed up at all times rather than dropping back to help the midfield when possession was lost. That meant that when the "bolt" faced a W-M formation, the front three matched up against the three defenders, and the inside forwards to the opposition's wing halves, leaving the center-half to deal with two

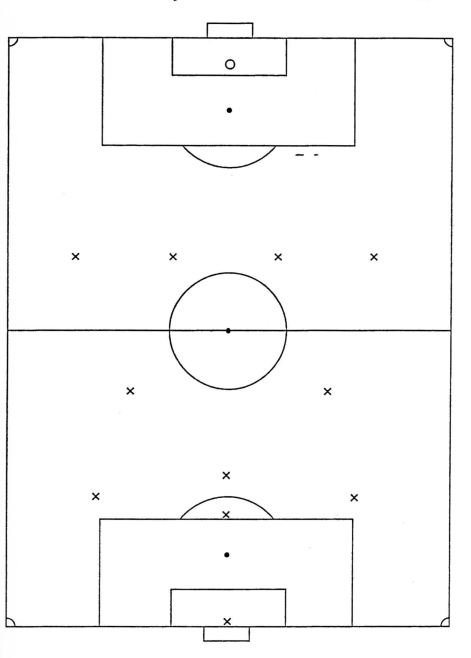

Figure 15. The Bolt.

inside forwards. This was a shortcoming faced by teams playing with a free man on the back; a spare man in one part of the pitch meant there was a shortage of a player elsewhere.

Against a 2-3-5 formation, the situation was worse. The team playing with the bolt had a man at both ends of the pitch, but that meant that the center-half had to deal not only with the opposing forwards, but with their center-half as well. Rappan won two league titles with Sevette and five more with Grasshoppers, but it was his success with the Swiss national team that showed the efficiency of his system.

Rappan spent almost his entire managerial career — which extended from 1932 to 1963 — coaching Swiss teams and the Swiss national team. After his role as player-coach at Servette, Rappan became a full-time coach and joined the Grasshopper Club, managing the Zurich club from 1935 to 1948 and winning five domestic league titles and seven cups. In 1948, he returned to Servette for a second period at the club, now as coach only. He remained there until 1957, adding one more league title and one cup to his record.

After Servette, Rappan had a one-season spell at FC Zurich. From 1960 to 1963, he coached the Swiss national team exclusively, and after this last period in charge of the national squad, he joined the club Lausanne Sports, being their coach from 1964 to 1968, and winning one league title in 1965. After almost four decades of service in Swiss football, he returned to Austria to be the technical director of Rapid Wien — his former club as a player — for the 1969–70 season.

Rappan had four different tenures as head coach of the Switzerland national team: 1937 to 1938, 1942 to 1949, 1953 to 1954, and 1960 to 1963. He managed Switzerland in 77 international matches, the most ever by any Swiss team coach. He won 29 matches, also a record, and lost 36 times, secondmost all-time (Sports, 2006). With Rappan as its coach, Switzerland qualified for the World Cup in 1938, 1954 (where they beat Italy and lost 5–7 to Austria in quarterfinals), and 1962. Rappan recorded 3 wins, 1 draw, and 6 losses as a coach in World Cup finals tournaments, and his last match as Switzerland's coach was on November 11, 1963, against France in Paris, a 2–2 draw.

Origins of the 4-2-4

Although the Brazilians are frequently given credit for introducing about 1958 the 4-2-4 system as seen in Figure 11, it actually originated in

Hungary in the early 1950s (Rosenthal, 1979). The Hungarians initiated the tactical revolution with a concealed version of the 4-2-4. The system was introduced by Gustav Sebes, the Hungarian national team coach, and by his assistant, Marton Bokovi of the MTK club in Budapest (Lodziak, 1966). Their idea was born when they failed to find a good center-forward for their WM system, so they looked for two goal-minded forwards to combine with two wing forwards (Gardner, 1976). He found Zoltan Czibor, Sandor Kocsis, the incredible Ferenc Puskas, and Laslo Budai, known around the world as the Magic Magyars. They played 47 matches for the national team, of which they won 40, tied 6, and lost 1— the World Cup final to Germany in 1954 (Rosenthal, 1979). Budai and Czibor operated as wingers close to the touchlines, thus spreading the opposition. Puskas and Kocsis operated as the inside forwards, with ample space to penetrate the opponent's defensive territory (Gardner, 1976).

At first it was a revolutionary change to have the center-forward withdrawn in order to become the initiator of attacks, instead of acting as a spearhead forward. In the Hungarians' victory (6–3) at Wembley over England in 1953, the pundits were surprised to see the Hungarian wingers moving into the attack from behind their inside forwards. In the return match in Budapest in 1954, the Hungarians were once again superior and defeated the English 7–1.

Many modifications were made to this formation over the years until every part of the system was affected. However, despite all the tactical variations adopted with the 4-2-4, the role of the defensive center-half remained intact.

The 1958 World Cup in Sweden revealed a new stage in the development of this formation, particularly on defense, and the Brazilians were cast in the role of innovators. The Brazilian national team, under coach Vicente Feola, used a 4-2-4 to win the World Cup in Sweden in 1958. The reason many attribute the invention of the 4-2-4 to Brazil is that by 1958 it was easily recognizable, and the Brazilians played it more rigidly than the Hungarians, who were more flexible in the formation (Gardner, 1966). Some people thought that the Hungarians were still playing the WM, while the 1958 Brazilians played in a rigid 4-2-4 formation, which made their positions easily identifiable. The four Brazilian players included Zagalo and Garrincha as the two wingers, with Vava and the great Pele as the inside forwards. Opposing defenses could not contain both Vava and Pele effectively since they always had a two-against-one situation (Lodziak,

1966). After the 1958 World Cup, most teams around the world adopted the 4-2-4 system. This system has been very popular around the world for some time and its main objective is to give the team six or seven forwards when the team is on the attack. On defense one of the wing forwards and the midfield players retreat to give additional support to the four defenders. When on attack the two midfielders and the two wing fullbacks assist the four forwards (Beim, 1977).

The Brazilian 4-2-4 was the outcome in which Hungarian football played a major role between 1950 and 1956. In the back of Brazil's 4-2-4, the two defenders on the wings are expected to mark the opposing wingers, while the two fullbacks in the middle cover the spearhead forwards. In opposite contrast to the Hungarian team of the 50s, the Brazilians' back four stood almost in line, and seldom ventured over the halfway area even when their forwards were pounding the other goal. The wall of the four-man defense gave the two halfbacks much better freedom to part in attacks.

In the Brazilian formation, the four-man defense is expected to insure against any surprise move by the opposition, as it is assumed that four defenders should be enough to outnumber the opposing forwards. This numerical superiority can be increased with the two halfbacks dropping back to aid in defense.

The Brazilians introduced new elements to the team formation, and succeeded in making innovations to known methods of defense and attack. While on defense, they used a zonal method, especially on midfield, thus allowing for a more relaxed man-to-man marking. While on attack, they used a combination of quick short passes or fast, deep-penetrating long passes. It would seem that their formation was rather defensive minded, but switching from attack to defense was actually safer, smoother, and certainly more effective.

The basic theory behind the 4-2-4 system is to allow a team to have a minimum of seven defenders covering the opposition's attack, and when they are on attack, to have a minimum of six attackers moving forward toward the opponent's goal.

The attacking role of the two midfield players is practically the same as the attacking role of the inside forwards in any football system. These two players move up in support of their forwards, thus providing depth, penetration, and breadth to the attack. It is important to understand that these two players must be versatile forwards and sure, strong defenders. They should be able to carry all of the functions required of midfielders and fullbacks for the entire game. The advantage of this system rests in the ability of getting extra attackers into the offense, and to get additional help to the defense, often without any specific defensive responsibility.

The success of the 4-2-4 is dependent upon the talent, strength, and endurance of the two midfielders. At the same time, this can also be the biggest disadvantage of this system. If these two players are weak and unable to keep up with the fluidity and pace of the game, both the defense and offense will suffer, as they are likely to create gaps that the opposition could utilize to build its attack. If this is the case, the defense will be under constant pressure, which would create an inability to strike back at the opposition. A coach wanting to use this system must truly evaluate his personnel, as his two midfielders will have to be two of the best players on the team.

The Italian Catenaccio

According to Lodziak (1966), this formation, as seen in Figure 16, has caused more controversy than any other formation in football history. It has many variations, but all variations have one thing in common: a definite emphasis on defense. During the 1950s, while most teams around the world were busy learning or transforming the old WM system to the new 4-2-4, the Italians were devising the "super defense" known as catenaccio (Italian for "chain") (Beim, 1977). Initially, this defensive system took the form of the old Swiss bolt, but by the late 1950s the modern catenaccio defense was well established.

Nereo Rocco, manager of the small Italian club Triestina, revised the verrou system developed by Rappan. Rocco stationed a fullback permanently behind the other three defenders of the W, not to mark any particular opponent, but rather to provide cover for teammates and to protect the vital area in front of the goal (Beim, 1977; Gardner, 1976; Lodziak, 1966). The new fullback was known as libero, "the free man"—though the English, when they finally acknowledged the position over a decade later (Gardner, 1976), called him sweeper.

During the 1948 Olympic Games in England, it was quite evident that there were several quality players in the Scandinavian Peninsula, and as a result the wealthier Italian clubs started to sign many of these players. It was a brilliant idea as most of these players were amateurs and a club did not have to pay any transfer fee. Italian clubs such as Juventus, A.C.

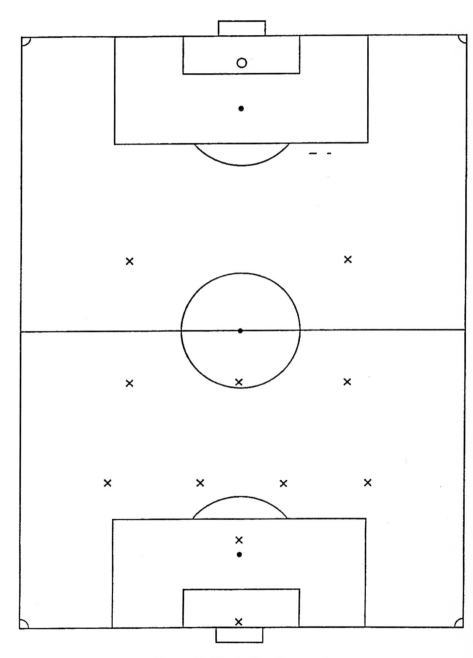

Figure 16. The Italian Catenaccio.

Milan, and Inter Milan were able to bolster their sides with Scandinavian players.

Juventus won the 1949–50 season with John Hansen and Karl Praest of Denmark. In the 1950–51 season, A.C. Milan had signed three players from Sweden, Nils Liedholm, Gunnar Gren, and Gunnar Nordahl. Nordhal went on to become one of the high goal scorers of the Italian league for many seasons. With these three players, A.C. Milan was able to win the 1950–51 season. The following season Juventus added Karl Hansen of Denmark and regained the title. Finally, in the 1952–53 and 1953–54 season Inter Milan won the title with the assistance of Lennart Skoglund of Sweden and a Hungarian named Stefan Nyers.

As these three clubs strengthened their teams by "buying" top players from around the world, the managers of the lesser clubs realized that something had to be done, and the development of a tight defense began.

In the beginning, managers simply opted to double-mark the opposition's top forward, letting the center-back play the role of stopper. Usually, this relieved the center-back from having to mark a particular player, and allowed him to concentrate on covering the danger area in front of the goal. As the weaker teams adopted defensive tactics, they now were losing by fewer goals. Often the game ended in a draw, or, rarely, a win against a top team.

The trend towards the defensive game was noted in Italian football during the 1950s when the number of goals scored by the league champions decreased. Between the seasons of 1949 and 1951, the winning team had scored over 100 goals, but by the 1952–54 seasons that number had decreased to 60 goals. By this time the Swiss bolt was fully developed into a true catenaccio, the ultra-defensive system that now allowed a weaker team to draw, and to win an occasional game. Sadly, even the stronger teams began to adopt the stronger defensive formation.

Helenio Herrera, a native of Buenos Aires, Argentina, is generally given credit for perfecting the catenaccio while manager of Inter Milan in the early 1960s. Herrera came to Inter Milan from after managing teams in France and Spain, where he led Barcelona to back-to-back championships during the 1958–59 and 1959–60 seasons. He was at the time the only coach who had the distinction of managing the national teams of three different countries, and although he was not an instant success at Inter, he eventually led them to several league championships, two European Cups, and one World Club Championship. His system was by no means a wholly defensive affair, as his teams were able to attack from the defense by getting the ball as quickly as possible to the forwards, and then counterattack quickly against the opposition (Beim, 1977).

One of Herrera's initial moves at Inter was to place the left wing Mario Corso into the midfield, where he felt his talents could be better used. This move left Inter without a winger and created more space for the left back, Giacinto Faccetti, to be able to make overlapping runs and to score more goals. There is no doubt that Herrera's managerial ability was responsible for much of Inter's success, but there is also no doubt that without his outstanding players, Inter would not have been as successful. These included players like Corso, Faccetti, Mazzola, Peiro, midfielder Suarez, and libero Picchi, who was the main stay of Inter's catenaccio (Wilson, 2006).

There are various forms of this system, but the principle behind the catenaccio is that defenders will mark opponents man-to-man and then leave one player to act as the free man behind the defense (Chyzowych, 1982). When a team using a catenaccio matches up against a team playing 4-2-4, the catenaccio formation becomes 1-4-2-3. However, when the opponent is playing a 4-3-3, then the catenaccio formation is a 1-3-3-3. Everything depends on the opponent's strength and the aim of a particular match (Gardner, 1976). For example, if a team playing catenaccio is looking for a draw, they increase the numbers in midfield; if they feel they can win, they increase the numbers in the front line (Beim, 1977). The one disadvantage of the catenaccio is that with its ultradefensive mentality, the game can degenerate into an incredibly boring game, particularly if both teams employ the same system.

The history of catenaccio says a lot about the development of football tactics, and there was nothing positive about its origin. It was designed not to win games but to avoid losing games, or at the very least to avoid losing by high scores. The Italian Serie A had for years been rather unbalanced, with a few rich clubs always taking top honors. It was Rocco's catenaccio at Triestina that put the formation in the front pages, as Triestina soon climbed to second place in the league in 1948. Soon thereafter, other teams began to copy Triestina.

The trend of clubs adopting this formation accelerated in the 1950s, when rich Italian clubs began to buy players from Argentina and Uruguay. Almost all of the new signings were brilliant attacking players. In order to counter them, the smaller clubs sank deeper into the grips of catenaccio, and the defense was padded even more, by adding a "libero" play behind a line of four fullbacks, rather than three, which left only two forwards to deal as best as possible up front. The results of catenaccio cannot be ignored. It did make scoring difficult, but there was always the possibility that the defending team could break away suddenly and score an unexpected goal. Watching two teams play the same formation, both packing their penalty area and hoping to snatch a goal from a counterattack, degenerated into a colossal bore, which thankfully was largely confined to Italian football. This was the evolution from catenaccio to what became known as "il giocco Italiano" — "the Italian game."

Brazil's 4-3-3 Formation

During the 1962 World Cup, the Brazilians displayed a new system that the whole world would later copy, the 4-3-3, as seen in Figure 12. This system is great for a team that desires the defensive strength of the 4-2-4, but is not blessed with the midfield personnel (Rosenthal, 1980).

The most important reason why Brazil, managed by Aymore Moreira, went to a 4-3-3 system in the 1962 World Cup was the loss to injury in the second match of competition of superstar Pele (Beim, 1977). Amarildo, who replaced Pele at the inside left position, performed well and scored several goals. However, Amarildo was no Pele! Thus, it became necessary for Brazil to use its other superstar Mario Zagalo more as a midfield player, rather than as a forward, to provide more support in the middle (Beim, 1977; Rote Jr., 1978). Zagalo still frequently ended up as a striker, thus fulfilling a dual role for his team.

Teams and coaches around the world saw and realized the importance of the 4-3-3 system and hurried to adopt it. Unfortunately, few teams had a player like Zagalo, and most began to play with three midfielders at the expense of one of their wingers. The worldwide adoption of the 4-3-3 changed the type of players that managers now looked for. Because the 4-3-3 requires constant fluid and position interchanging, players now needed to be adept at both attacking and defending. With this move, modern football started to lose the great specialist wingers such as Sir Stanley Matthews of England.

In defense the 4-3-3 used seven defenders in addition to the keeper. Since most teams have at least four men as defenders and six as their main attacking force, a team playing 4-3-3 can technically have one extra defender than the other team has attackers. As a result one fullback can be used as a free (libero) man.

The major reason this system is so widely adopted is that coaches have found it extremely difficult for two men to handle effectively the midfield role, which was necessary in the 4-4-2 system (Gardner, 1976). By adding a third midfielder, the other team's attack could often be stopped by the midfield rather than the back line of defenders (Glanville, 1979). The 4-3-3, according to Csanadi (1963), also forces the use of midfielders on attack, because three lone forwards cannot adequately sustain a strong attack. Coaches realized that three midfielders could provide more control and better fluidity to the game by bridging the gap between the defense and the attackers.

The key to success in the 4-3-3 system is that players coming from behind can easily utilize the space created by the front-running players (Beim, 1977). Such moves, as described by Harris (1976), give the defenders an element of surprise and bring a very positive attitude to the game. As a result many goals are now being scored by midfielders and even defenders coming through the back line (Beim, 1977). The 4-3-3 system provides for good balance over the entire field and for continuity among the defense, the midfield, and the front line. The worldwide adoption of the 4-3-3 greatly changed the type of players that coaches wanted and needed. They no longer looked for players who could play only one position; they now needed players who could do a good job both offensively and defensively (Thompson, 1977).

The 4-3-3 system also forces midfielders into the attack because the three lone forwards cannot adequately sustain a strong attack. Overlapping runs by modern midfielders and defenders can make use of the space created by the forwards, and as a result score goals as well. A perfect example of this was the 1970 World Cup in Mexico, where fullbacks and midfielders scored over 60 percent of the goals (Beim, 1977).

The 4-3-3 reflects the tendency to regard midfield as essential in order to assure a carefully built-up attack. The system is equally important for a well prepared defense, but that can be difficult to achieve when outnumbered. In the 4-3-3 the defense must have two skillful fullbacks, who need to be able to attack like wingers. If faced with an equal number of attackers to defenders, the defense can apply man-to-man coverage on the ball and zone coverage when off the ball. The two key players are the two center fullbacks who must cover for each other and their wing fullbacks.

If they are confronted by three attackers, the defense can adopt a catenaccio-type defense. In this situation the fullbacks mark the wing forwards, one of the center fullbacks plays the role of stopper, and the other that of a free or nonpermanent sweeper/libero by covering the vital space behind the defenders. At the same time, he can provide cover for his teammates who may be under pressure.

The advantage of having this nonpermanent sweeper/libero is that he can be used as a playmaker in midfield, and from time to time can join into a full attack. This can be effective because by coming out of the back of the defense, he does not have a permanent opponent. Thus, he can add to the numerical superiority in midfield and create chaos for the opposing defense. This allows for greater flexibility, and enables the defense to remain compact.

This particular formation, however, can be very defensive minded, and that is one of its greatest advantages, especially when playing against powerful attacking teams. However, a team playing this formation could be content with playing defense and keeping the opposition from scoring, even if they don't score either. A good time when this type of formation could be of value is late in a game when the team is trying to protect a lead. Of course this means that the team must abandon any possibility of scoring, unless it is fortunate to start a quick counterattack. Oftentimes this is not a good strategy since defensive-minded teams will crowd their penalty area, and in times like this anything can happen — including an own goal. This defensive style of play can become boring to players and spectators alike, as it stunts the creative play that can be a part of good, balanced attacking and defensive game. Without this balance, the game can become dull.

England's 4-4-2

Sir Alf Ramsey, who left his post as manager of Ipswich Town to become England's manager of the 1966 and 1970 World Cup teams, is generally regarded as the innovator of England's 4-4-2 system, as seen in Figure 13, (Hughes, 1975).

England, once hostile to the idea and science of coaching, had now taken it in with a vengeance and had produced a generation of coaches trained and licensed by the English FA. They now had introduced a methodical approach to the game, but since they all came from the same "school" they were rather orthodox in their style, and included words that were not so welcomed. Their vocabulary included quasi-technical words such as "work rate" which loomed large. This was the key to Sir Alf Ramsey's 1966 England squad.

The 1966 World Cup was the first major football event to be covered by television, and was an enormous popular success. On the pitch the host nation ran out the winner, leaving its opponents feeling hard done by.

With fifteen African nations declaring forfeit even before a single match had been played, the 1966 World Cup did not get off to a good start. The African protest was due to a new FIFA rule stipulating that the winner of the African zone must then beat the winner of either Asia or Oceania to reach the finals. This ruling was overturned four years later in Africa's favor.

Nonetheless, this was England's moment. Thus far it had not fulfilled its potential as a football power. This time, as the host nation and in the spotlight, it could no longer put off its worldly destiny. One hundred and three years after the London Football Association drew up the rules that laid the foundation for the people's game, the World Football Championship had arrived in England, back where the game began, where the first professionals had played, and where the idea of international competition had been born in 1872.

The organizers could be certain that there would be no problems with unfinished stadiums. The English had not built a new stadium since Wembley was opened back in 1923. They felt that whatever was good enough every Saturday for the English league clubs was good enough for foreigners, and thus chose to play all the World Cup games on six club grounds. England, of course, would play all its games at Wembley.

No new stadiums were built, but for the first time in the history of the World Cup, there would be a mascot. The traditional English lion was turned into a cuddly boylike creature, complete with football boots, and dubbed World Cup Willie. Willie was placed on thousands of posters and advertisements, the first of a line of increasingly commercialized World Cup symbols.

Another significant event of the 1966 World Cup was the disappearance of the Jules Rimet Trophy. The cup was brought to England and placed on display at London's Central Hall; and despite the presence of six security guards assigned to protect it, the cup was stolen. Nothing like this had ever happened in World Cup history, and although the cup was insured for over $80,000, FIFA and the English FA were stunned. The theft was keenly felt by Dr. Barasi of the Italian Football Federation, who during World War II had buried it to prevent the occupying German army from taking it along with other booty stolen from Italy.

England's embarrassment was relieved when a man named Corbett and his dog Pickles went for a walk in a suburb of South London. With some fortuitous digging in a garbage heap, Pickles unearthed the trophy. Thanks to Pickles, there would be no need to have another cup made until the Brazilians won the Jules Rimet outright in 1970.

Sir Alf Ramsey was appointed manager of the England team in October 1962. His appointment caused a stir immediately when he predicted that England would win the next World Cup, which was to be held in England in 1966. This was a bold statement to make, as England's performance on the international stage had been poor up to that point. Nonetheless, managers often make such predictions — none will say that their teams will stand no chance. The World Cup started in 1930, but England refused to participate until 1950, when it suffered an embarrassing 1-0 defeat at the hands of the USA, a game in which Ramsey played at right-back. When Ramsey took over, he demanded complete control over squad selections. Before Alf Ramsey, Walter Winterbottom had been manager, but selections and other decisions were often carried out by board committees from the English FA. When Sir Alf Ramsey took over all of these duties, it led to him being referred to as "England's first proper manager."

Alf Ramsey was a firm but fair manager and was often regarded as difficult by the press. He ran a strict regime with his players and made sure that no-one felt that they enjoyed special status, star player or not. In May 1964, a number of players failed to show up for a meeting in a hotel about an upcoming tour, among them Jimmy Greaves, Bobby Moore, and Bobby Charlton. When they returned to their rooms, they discovered their passports left on their beds. They knew what that meant. His strict regime didn't suit everyone, but the players with real talent and respect for the game responded well to them and had great respect for Ramsey. Very few of those who played for Ramsey spoke badly about him. In the preparations for the 1966 World Cup, Ramsey made sure that no player was confident of a place in the final 22, which resulted in players performing at their highest level. His decision to appoint a young Bobby Moore as captain also showed Ramsey's ability to see great potential in young players. He was also a master tactician, a quality that he had first shown with his reading of the game as a player. When it came to tactics, Ramsey indeed had revolutionary ideas.

During his tenure at Ipswich, Ramsey began experimenting with a new style of play that would eventually lead to success in the World Cup and which eventually led to his England squad becoming known as "The Wingless Wonders" and, later, as "Ramsey's Robots." As natural wingers were not always known for their defensive qualities, Ramsey started dropping them in favor of attacking midfielders who could also drop back into defensive roles. This system proved revolutionary as it often baffled opposing fullbacks, who would naturally expect to see a winger coming down the flank at them once the ball was kicked off. Instead, the attacking midfielders and strikers were taking the ball through the middle of the defense and scoring. This style of play proved successful at Ipswich, but really showed its worth when England traveled to Spain to play a friendly match with the Spaniards before the World Cup. Bobby Charlton later commented, "The Spanish fullbacks were just looking at each other while we were going in droves through the middle" (Wilson, 2009). To go to Spain (who at the time were the reigning European champions) and win easily was a rare achievement for an English national team. It was clear evidence that Ramsey's techniques were working.

According to Beim (1977), Ramsey was planning to use Brazil's 4-3-3 formation, and when the World Cup began he started with that formation, which included an orthodox winger and individualistic player in Jimmy Greaves, unmatched as a goal snatcher but not noted for his "work rate." In fact he tried three different wingers in the first three games, and by the time the fourth game arrived, there was no winger on the team, and certainly no Jimmy Graves. Ramsey did not feel that there were any legitimate wingers available on the English national team, so he wound up playing without any "true" wingers during the rest of the 1966 World Cup. What Ramsey did was to withdraw the wingers to a midfield position; his strategy had the fullbacks and midfielders making repeated attacks by overlapping the runs in the outside and forcing the ball into the penalty area (Fouls, 1979).

With his final squad chosen, Ramsey set about to win the World Cup for England. The 1966 World Cup got off to a slow start. The first group game was against Uruguay. Despite an array of attacking talent, including Jimmy Greaves and Roger Hunt, England was held to a 0–0 draw. Alf

Ramsey's statement made three years earlier was in serious doubt now, but he remained calm and continued experimenting when his side faced Mexico in the next game. As noted earlier, Ramsey was using the 4-3-3 system and for each of the group games he used a different winger; John Connelly against Uruguay, Terry Paine against Mexico, and Ian Callaghan against France.

Ramsey dropped Alan Ball and John Connelly and brought in Terry Paine and Martin Peters, whose advanced style of play as a midfielder matched the qualities Ramsey looked for in his system. England beat Mexico 2–0. Ramsey replaced Terry Paine with Ian Callaghan for their final group match, against France, which England won 2–0, thus securing qualification to the knockout rounds. Two problems resulted from the final group match against France. After making a vicious tackle and being cautioned, midfielder Nobby Stiles came under fire from senior FIFA officials, who called for Alf Ramsey to drop Stiles from the team. Alf Ramsey would have none of it, and firmly told the FA to inform FIFA that either Stiles would remain in his team or Ramsey himself would resign (Wilson, 2008). Another bad tackle was committed during that match, which resulted in Tottenham striker (and one of England's most prolific goal-scorers) Jimmy Greaves being injured and sidelined for the next few matches. Despite having more experienced strikers in his squad, Ramsey selected young Geoff Hurst as Greaves's replacement, once again seeing potential in the young West Ham forward. The France match also marked Ramsey's final game playing with a winger. After that, he dropped Ian Callaghan from his side and brought back Alan Ball to strengthen the midfield.

For the knockout stages round, England's first opponents were a rather difficult and rough Argentina side. Alf Ramsey once again showed his tactical awareness, and now he choose to play without any classical wingers. He decided to switch from a 4-3-3 formation to a 4-4-2. This tactical system did nothing to arrest the spread of defensive football, but it proved effective for Ramsey and his English squad. England had won its three games in Group 1 without conceding a goal, but it was uninspiring football, and it was only the nationalistic fervor of the home crowd that enabled England to leave the pitch at the end of each game to cheers.

With Ball and Peters operating on the flanks, the midfield now boasted Nobby Stiles and Bobby Charlton in the center.

In the quarter-finals the English met the Argentineans, and West Germany met Uruguay. Both were Europe vs. South America matches, and both were refereed by Europeans. To make matters worse, an Englishman refereed the German game, while a German refereed the English game. It was not a sensible arrangement!

The English referee sent off two Uruguayans, and the Germans won easily 4–0. At Wembley, the German referee ejected the Argentine captain Antonio Rattin, and the English won 1–0, though not so easily. At first, Rattin, professing bewilderment, refused to leave the pitch. What had he done, he wanted to know? At one point it even looked as if the entire Argentine team was going to walk off. After ten minutes of discussions, arguments, and gesticulations, Rattin slowly departed. Referee Rudolf Kreitlein was later quoted as saying he dismissed Rattin for misconduct: "I do not speak Spanish, but the look on his face was enough."

The elimination of both the Argentina and Uruguay teams brought immediate protest from the South Americans. The Brazilians with substantial justification were already complaining about the lax European refereeing standards that had allowed Pele to be so maltreated. Now the Argentines and Uruguayans decried an Anglo-German "plot" that had maneuvered their teams out of the tournament.

After the violent quarter-final against Argentina, England scraped the 1–0 win thanks to Geoff Hurst latching onto a beautiful cross from Martin Peters and heading home a goal. Ramsey came under criticism when he stopped his players from swapping jerseys with the Argentineans in protest at their dirty play, and was reported to have described Argentinean players as "animals." The remark probably helped to lose him his job after England failed to qualify for the 1974 tournament. The 1978 World Cup was to be played in Argentina where, because of his outburst, Ramsey was barred as a football official. The FA could have appealed but with Ramsey's methods failing they decided against it.

In the semifinal, England faced a fluent and skillful Portuguese side containing the tournament's top goal-scorer, Eusébio. Nonetheless, England won a 2–1 victory in a memorable match which saw them give up their first goal of the competition from the penalty spot. Ramsey had found the perfect defensive formula, which went unchanged throughout the entire tournament. England and Portugal played a delightful and pulsating game of rare football and sportsmanship. England won because Bobby Charlton scored twice, while Eusébio scored once. England was now in the World Cup Final for the first time ever; at last it looked as though it had a team capable of winning the trophy. Only West Germany, victors over the Soviet Union in the other semifinal, stood in their way.

Since 1936 England had played Germany seven times; England had won seven and tied one.

The final game was viewed by 100,000 fans at Wembley and by another 400 million via satellite TV. The game was superb, exciting, fast, and open in style. It was a pleasant contrast to the negative football displayed in most of the other matches. England was a goal down within 13 minutes when Ramon Wilson — usually the safest of backs — headed an incoming ball straight to the feet of Helmut Haller, who put it past a screened Gordon Banks. For the first time in the tournament England was behind, 1–0. Within six minutes the score was 6–1. Bobby Moore's long free kick seemed to be dropping harmlessly ahead of the English forwards, when suddenly an unguarded George Hurst headed the ball past Hans Tilkowski.

The second half swayed one way then another, with both teams playing beautiful attacking football. Martin Peters made it 2–1 in England's favor with 12 minutes to go, and then Charlton missed a golden opportunity to add another goal. With the deafening roar of the triumphant English fans ringing in their ears, the Germans pushed everyone for a final assault. With only seconds remaining in regular time the Germans were awarded a free kick near the English goal. It rebounded off the human wall of English defenders to Wolfgang Weber's foot, sending it to the net past a disheartened Banks and all of England.

For the first time since 1934, the final went into extra time. Hurst received a long center pass from Allan Ball and drove it viciously past Tilkowski. The ball smashed against the underside of the crossbar, then bounced down to the ground and seemingly back into play. England appealed for a goal. Referee Gottfried Dienst from Switzerland was not sure, and with 100,000 fans holding their breath, he consulted with his Soviet linesman, who confirmed the goal. To this day it seems unlikely that the ball actually crossed the line. Nonetheless, the sporting Germans did not press their protests. They attacked desperately, but England, boosted by the goal, was clearly the better team now. Hurst added another goal before the end — his third, making him the first player to score a hat trick in a final.

On July 30, 1966, Sir Alf Ramsey's promise was fulfilled, as England became the world champions by defeating West Germany in a thrilling final. A lot of Ramsey's tactics and decisions proved their worth in this final. Alf Ramsey came under pressure to restore the fit-again Jimmy Greaves to the squad: but he stuck to his guns and kept faith with Greaves's replacement, Geoff Hurst, who was able to completely vindicate Ramsey's decision by scoring a hat-trick. Filling his side with a good balance of experience and youth proved vital when the grueling final went to extra time. The youth in the team powered England through extra time. A particular example of this was Alan Ball who, at 21 years old, was the youngest player in the England squad. Even during the extra time, Ball never showed signs of tiredness and never stopped running — famously setting up Hurst's controversial second goal, and creating a few chances for himself as well. Even as the match ended with Geoff Hurst scoring England's fourth goal, Ball was still running down the pitch.

Ramsey remained his usual self during the celebrations: not joining in, but rather opting to let his players soak up their achievement. With his bold promise now fulfilled, Ramsey had proved that the 4-4-2 system could work and had assembled an England team that could compete on the highest level due to physical fitness and good tactics. He remains an example to this day and is the only England manager ever to have won the World Cup.

Ramsey who had acquired an English FA coaching license, wanted players with all-around ability and stamina to run all day long, players prepared for ninety minutes of constant action (substitutions were still not permitted in World Cup games). He wanted players with a high "work rate." A good example of this kind of player was Alan Ball, whose "work rate" tireless play and stamina showed during the extra time of the 1966 final game (Gardner, 1976; Wagg, 1984). England's wingless wonders won the championship game because they were the best of a substandard crop, a solid no-nonsense team that kept errors to a minimum.

The nationalistic passion that engulfed all of England after winning the World Cup obscured the fact that, by any other standards, this was not a very attractive style of play. "Workmanlike" and "high work rate" best described them. They were simply a highly trained group of men doing a job of work, rather than enjoying the game. However, many people thought that they had done it with a 4-3-3. Both the 4-3-3 and the 4-4-2 require so much position interchanging that is often very difficult to determine a player's assigned position (Beim, 1977).

Total Football

The monotony of defensive systems and in particular the catenaccio, was relieved by the appearance of total football, which was popularized by the West Germans and the Dutch in particular (Chyzowych, 1982). This style reached its peak in the 1974 World Cup in Germany and evolved during the 1978 World Cup in Argentina. The attacking style of the Brazilians was taken up in Europe, notably by the Germans who won the 1972 European championship with a team that attacked, if not with the brilliance of the Brazilians, then certainly with a flair that eliminated the myth of the stoic German temperament. This style of play reached its zenith with the Holland national team in the 1974 World Cup dubbed "The Clockwork Orange," referring to the national team colors (Gardner, 1976).

The Dutch seemed to arrive from nowhere. A small country with a long but remarkable football record, Holland was in the 1960s a mecca for youth culture — a swinging country with very liberal ideas. Out of this atmosphere cane a generation of free-spirited footballers who made Feyenoord and Ajax two of the strongest football clubs in Europe. Feyenoord took the European Cup in 1970, and Ajax were the winners in 1971, '72, and '73 — the first team to win three in a row since Real Madrid's heyday of the 1950s. The 1974 team, coached by Rinus Michels and made up mostly of players from Ajax and Feyenoord, was in terms of time spent together one of the least prepared teams of the competition. Yet such was their ability and mutual understanding to be able to play any position on the pitch that it was not necessary to work out any complicated system of play (Gardner, 1996).

The foundations for total football were laid by Jack Reynolds (BBC.co.uk, 2008), who was the manager of Ajax from 1915 to 1925, 1928 to 1940, and 1945 to 1947. Rinus Michels, who played under Reynolds, later went on to become manager of Ajax himself and refined the concept into what is known today as "total football" (*totaalvoetbal* in Dutch). He used it in his training for the Ajax squad and the Netherlands national team in the 1970s. This style was later refined by Stefan Kovacs after Michels left to manage Barcelona. The great Dutch forward Johan Cruyff was the system's most famous exponent both as a player and coach (FIFA, 2009).

Although Cruyff was fielded as a center forward, he wandered all over the pitch, popping up wherever he could do most damage to the opposing team. This resulted in a need for a dynamic system like total football. Johan Cruyff's teammates adapted themselves flexibly around his movements, regularly switching positions so that the tactical roles in the team were always filled.

Space and the creation of it were central to the concept of total football. Ajax defender Barry Hulshoff explained how the team that won the

European Cup in 1971, 1972, and 1973 worked it to their advantage: "We discussed space the whole time. Johan Cruyff always talked about where people should run and where they should stand, and when they should not move" (BBC.co.uk, 2008)

The constant switching of positions that became known as total football came about only because of this spatial awareness. "It was all about making space, coming into space, and organizing space-like architecture on the football pitch," said Hulshoff. The system developed collaboratively: It was not down to coach Rinus Michels, his successor Stefan Kovacs, or Cruyff alone. In fact, Johan Cruyff summed up his (total football) philosophy by saying that "Simple football is the most beautiful. But playing simple football is the hardest thing."

The 1972 European Cup final proved to be total football's finest hour. After Ajax's 2–0 victory over Internazionale de Milan, newspapers around Europe reported the this new style was the end of the boring and ultra-defensive style of the Italian catenaccio. The Dutch newspaper *Algemeen Dagblad* noted: "The Inter system has been undermined. Defensive football is destroyed" (Britishcouncil.org, 2008).

Michels was appointed for the 1974 FIFA World Cup campaign by the Royal Netherlands Football Association (KNVB), and as noted earlier, most of the 1974 team were made up of players from Ajax and Feyenoord. However, Rob Rensenbrink, an outsider who played for clubs in neighboring Belgium, was unfamiliar with total football. Nonetheless, he was selected to the national team and adapted quite well. During the tournament, the Netherlands coasted through their first and second round matches, defeating Argentina (4–0), East Germany (2–0) and Brazil (2–0) to setup a meeting with hosts West Germany (FIFA, 2009).

In the 1974 final, Cruyff kicked off and the ball was passed around thirteen times before returning to Cruyff, who then went on a rush that eluded Berti Vogts and ended when he was fouled by Uli Hoeneb. The referee awarded the penalty, and teammate Johan Neeskens scored from the spot kick to give the Netherlands a 1–0 lead only 80 seconds of play into the game. The Germans had not touched the ball yet. Cruyff's playmaking influence was stifled in the second half of the match by the effective marking of Berti Vogts, while Franz Beckenbauer, Uli Hoeneb, and Wolfgang Overath dominated midfield, enabling West Germany to win the final game 2–1 (dw-world.de, 2008).

The ill-fated Austrian *Wunderteam* of the 1930s is also credited in some historical records as being the first national team to play total football. It is no coincidence that Ernst Happel, a talented Austrian player in the 1940s and 1950s, was coach in the Netherlands in the late 1960s and early 1970s. He introduced a tougher style of play at Feyenoord. Happel managed the Netherlands national team in the 1978 World Cup, where they again finished as runners-up to Argentina. Hungary also had a big role in laying down the tactical fundaments of total football in the 1950s, dominating international football with the remarkable "Magic Magyars" which included the legendary captain Ferenc Puskás.

With the Dutch a new phrase, "total football," entered football's ever-expanding vocabulary in an attempt to explain what the Dutch were up to. According to Gardner (1976), total football was seen as the ultimate marriage of the three B's of football: brawn, brain, and ball skills. The chemistry among the members of the Dutch team enabled them to attack and defend en masse with great precision while constantly rotating their positions, as can be seen in figure 17. This new breed of players was fit enough and skilled enough to play any position on the field, and intelligent enough to know exactly when to switch roles (Miller, 1979).

The Dutch team seemed always able to defend, and to attack in hordes, to flood midfield whenever they wished, all their players in constant motion, even their goalkeeper ever ready to leave his area to clear the ball (Gardner, 1976). The Germans, who won the World Cup in 1974, demonstrated a similar approach to the game, but exercised caution by not committing all 10 field players to the attack; their defense instead was tightly organized, and only about 80percent freedom of movement was used (Chyzowych, 1982).

The speed used by the Dutch to surround the ball with as many as five, six, or even ten players on both offense and defense was remarkable. The sudden charge of the whole team on offense left many forwards stranded yards off the play. Off-the-ball movement by the players was constant and done on purpose. Rinus Michels would say: "It is not difficult to get players to move about, but to get them to do it intelligently and with purpose, that is the problem."

Total movement of all 10 field players is feasible only when the players are thoroughly trained at all positions. The Dutch were able to use positionless football because they had a number of great players who could control the ball under extreme pressure and thus allow other players to push into the attack with confidence.

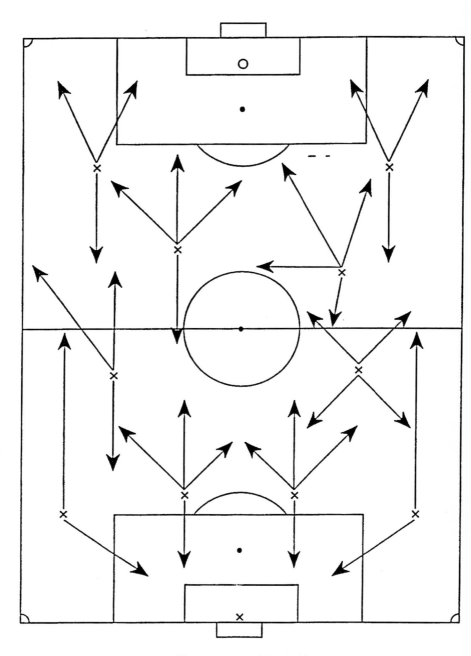

Figure 17. Total football.

Remarkably, the essence of the Dutch style had been foreseen nearly 20 years earlier by journalist Willy Meisl in 1955, who said,

> The future of football belongs to The Whirl. It must rotate on individuality rooted in *all-around* capacity.... A fullback seeing an opening in front must seize his chance without hesitation. A wing-half or winger will fall back, if necessary, and being an all-rounder, will not feel uncomfortable or out of place. The consciousness that he also is a capable forward will give the back's thrust weight and impetus. The knowledge that whoever has taken over from him (behind his back) will make a good job of it should the occasion arise, will enable him to carry on with his action (raid) without undo hurry or nervousness. He must and will be perfectly sure that he has left no expose flank behind himself (p.79).

Thus Meisl's "whirl" described exactly what the Dutch looked like to their opponents, a menacing whirl of orange shirts, with the great Johan Cruyff always at the center of things (Gardner, 1976; Rote Jr., 1978).

The Dutch whirl is too fluid to be given any meaningful expression in diagrams or numerical formations as those previously described. Their formation was 4-3-3, 4-2-4, 2-3-5, 4-4-2 and all other variations rolled into one; it was all of them, but it also was none of them.

As described by Gardner (1976), Rote (1978), and Chyzowych (1982), total football, with its elastic, positionless play and all 10 field players trying to score while at the same time trying to stop opponents from scoring, will be the style of the future. However, players will have to be in perfect physical shape for total football—probably fitter than any other sporting athlete, for they must spend most of their time running, either with the ball or in support.

Other Formations

The following formations are used in modern football. The formations are flexible according to the needs of a team, as well as to the players available. Variations of any given formation include changes in positioning of players, as well as replacement of a traditional defender by a sweeper.

4-4-2 Diamond or 4-1-2-1-2

The 4-4-2 diamond (also described as 4-1-2-1-2) staggers the midfield. The width in the team has to come from the fullbacks pushing forward. The defensive midfielder is sometimes used as a deep-lying playmaker. Its most famous example was Carlo Ancelotti's Milan, which won the 2003 UEFA Champions League Final and made Milan runners-up in 2005. Milan was obliged to adopt this formation so as to field talented central midfielder Andrea Pirlo, in a period when the position of offensive midfielder was occupied by Rui Costa and later Kaká (BBC News, 2005). This tactic was gradually abandoned by Milan after Andriy Shevchenko's departure in 2006. Milan then progressively adopted a "Christmas Tree" formation.

4-4-1-1

A variation of 4-4-2 with one of the strikers playing "in the hole," or as a "second striker," slightly behind a partner. The second striker is generally a more creative player, the playmaker, who can drop into midfield to pick up the ball before running with it or passing to teammates (BBC News, 2005).

4-3-2-1 "Christmas Tree" Formation

The 4-3-2-1, commonly described as the "Christmas Tree" formation, has another forward brought on for a midfielder to play "in the hole," leaving two forwards slightly behind the most forward striker. Terry Venables first brought in this system throughout England's UEFA Euro 1996 campaign.

Glenn Hoddle then used this formation during his time in charge of the England national football team. Since then the formation has lost its popularity in England It is, however, most known for being the formation Carlo Ancelotti utilized on and off during his time as a coach of Milan. In this approach, the middle of the three central midfielders acts as a playmaker while one of the attacking midfielders plays in a free role.

The "Christmas Tree" formation is considered a relatively narrow formation and depends on fullbacks to provide presence in wide areas. The formation is also relatively fluid. During open play, one of the side central midfielders may drift to the flank to add additional presence.

5-3-2

This formation has three central defenders with one of the three possibly acting as a sweeper. This system is heavily reliant on the wing-backs to provide width for the team. The two wide fullbacks act as wing-backs. It is their job to work their flank along the full length of the pitch, supporting both the defense and the attack (BBC News, 2005).

5-3-2 with Sweeper or 1-4-3-2

A variant of the above, this involves a more withdrawn sweeper, who may join the midfield, and more advanced fullbacks.

3-4-3

In a 3-4-3, the midfielders are expected to split their time between attacking and defending. Having only three dedicated defenders means that if the opposing team breaks through the midfield, they will have a greater chance to score than with a more conventional defensive configuration, such as 4-5-1 or 4-4-2. However, the three forwards allow for a greater concentration on attack. This formation is used by more offensive-minded teams.

3-5-2

This formation is similar to 5-3-2 except that the two wingmen are oriented more towards the attack. Because of this, the central midfielder tends to remain further back in order to help prevent counterattacks. It differs from the classical 3-5-2 of the WW by having a nonstaggered midfield. It was used for the first time at the international level by the Argentinean coach Carlos Salvador Bilardo (*The Guardian*, 2008). Many teams also use a central attacking midfielder and two defensive midfielders, so the midfielders form a W formation.

3-6-1

This uncommon but modern formation obviously focuses on ball possession in the midfield. In fact, it is very rare to see it as an initial formation, as it is better used to maintain a lead. Its more common variants are 3-4-2-1 or 3-4-3 diamond, which use two wingbacks. The lone forward must be tactically gifted, because he is focused not only in scoring, but to play back to the goal to assist with back passes to his teammates. Once the team is leading the game, the tactic focuses even more on ball control, short passes, and time wasting. On the other hand, when the team is losing, at least one of the playmakers will play more often in the edge of the area to add depth to the attack. Guus Hiddink is one of the few coaches who has used this formation, as when he coached Australia in the 2006 FIFA World Cup.

4-5-1

The 4-5-1 is a defensive formation; however, if the two midfield wingers play a more attacking role, it can be likened to 4-3-3. The formation can be used to grind out 0–0 draws or preserve a lead, as the packing of the center midfield makes it difficult for the opposition to build up play. Because of the "closeness" of the midfield, the opposing team's forwards will often be starved of possession. Due to the lone striker, however, the center of the midfield does have the responsibility of pushing forward as well. The defensive midfielder will often control the pace of the game (BBC News, 2005).

4-2-3-1

This formation is widely used by Spanish and French teams. It is a defensive formation which is quite flexible, as both the side midfielders and the fullbacks may join the attack, usually on the counter. In defense, this formation is similar to the 4-5-1. It is used to maintain possession of the ball and stop opponent attacks by controlling the midfield area. The lone striker may be very tall and strong to hold up the ball as his midfielders and fullbacks join him in attack. The striker could also be very fast. In these cases, the opponent's defense will be forced to fall back early, thereby leaving space for the offensive central midfielder. This formation is used especially when a playmaker is to be highlighted.

On the international level, this formation is used by the Dutch team, often with strikers as wide midfielders. The formation is also currently used by Brazil as an alternative to the 4-2-4 formation of the late 1950s to 1970. Implemented similarly to how the original 4-2-4 was used back then, use of this formation in this manner is very offensive, creating a six-man attack and a six-man defense tactical layout. The front four attackers are composed as wide forwards and playmaker forward in support of a target striker in front (*The Guardian*, 2008).

4-6-0

A highly unconventional formation, the 4-6-0 is an evolution of the 4-2-3-1 in which the center forward is exchanged for a player who normally plays as a *trequartista*[18] (that is, "in the hole"). Suggested as a possible formation for the future of football (*The Guardian*, 2008), the 4-6-0 sacrifices an out-and-out striker for the tactical advantage of a mobile front four attacking from a position that the opposition defenders cannot mark without being pulled out of position (The World, 2008). Owing to the intelligence and pace required by the front four attackers to create and attack any space left by the opposition defenders, however, the formation requires a very skillful and well-drilled front four. Due to these high requirements from the attackers, and the novelty of playing without a proper goal scorer, the formation has been adopted by very few teams, and rarely consistently. As with the development of many formations, the origins and originators are uncertain, but arguably the first reference to a professional team adopting a similar formation is Anghel Iordănescu's Romania in the 1994 World Cup round 16, when Romania won 3-2 against Argentina (*The Guardian*, 2010). The first team to adopt the formation systematically was Luciano Spalletti's Roma side during the 2005-2006 Serie A season, mostly out of necessity as his "strikerless" formation (Moore, 2008), and then notably by Alex Ferguson's Manchester United side in the 2007-2008 Premier League season in which they won both the Premier League and Champions League in the same year.

5-4-1

This is a particularly defensive formation, with an isolated forward and a packed defense. Again, however, a couple of attacking fullbacks can make this formation resemble something like a 3-4-3.

1-6-3

The 1-6-3 formation was first utilized by Japan at the behest of General Yoshijiro Umezu in 1936. Famously, Japan defeated the heavily favored Swedish team 3–2 at the 1936 Olympics with the unorthodox 1-6-3 formation, before going down 8-0 to Italy. The formation was dubbed the "kamikaze" formation sometime in the 1960s when former U.S. national team player Walter Bahr used it for a limited number of games as coach of the Philadelphia Spartans to garner greater media and fan attention for the struggling franchise (Robson, 2007).

4-2-2-2

Often referred to as the "Magic Rectangle," this formation was used most infamously by Wanderley Luxemburgo during his failed stint at Real Madrid in the latter part of the 2004–05 season and throughout the 2005–06 season. Although this formation was branded "deeply flawed" (Mirror Football, 2008), and "suicidal" (Simpson, 2010). Luxemburgo is considered the pioneer of this formation, although Brazil used it in the early 1980s (Wilson, 2009), and it was used by former Real Madrid manager Manuel Pellegrini to much appreciation and positive feedback (Goal, 2008).

Pellegrini had also used this formation while at Villarreal. The formation is closely related to the 4-2-4 and 4-4-2 diamond. It consists of the standard defensive four (right back, two center backs, and left back), with two center midfielders, two support strikers, and two out and out strikers (Football Line-ups, 2010). Similar to the 4-6-0, the formation requires a particularly alert and mobile front four to work successfully. The formation has also been used on occasion by the Brazilian national team (Deak, 2010) notably in the 1998 FIFA World Cup final (FIFA World Cup Finals — France 1998, 2010).

3-3-1-3

The 3-3-1-3 was formed of a modification to the Dutch 4-3-3 system Ajax had developed. Coaches like Louis van Gaal and Johan Cruyff brought it to even further attacking extremes and the system eventually found its way to FC Barcelona, where players such as Andrés Iniesta and Xavi learned the 3-3-1-3 philosophy. It demands intense pressing high up the pitch especially from the forwards, and also an extremely high defensive line, basically playing the whole game inside the opponents' half.

It requires incredible technical precision and rapid ball circulation since one slip or dispossession can result in a vulnerable counterattack situation. Cruyff's variant relied on a flatter and wider midfield, but Louis van Gaal used an offensive midfielder and midfield diamond to link up with the front three more effectively. Marcelo Bielsa has used the system with some success with Argentina's and Chile's national teams and is currently one of the only high-profile managers to use the system in competition today. Diego Simeone also tried it occasionally with River Plate.

4-2-1-3

The somewhat unconventional 4-2-1-3 formation has been developed by José Mourinho during his time at Inter Milan, including in the 2010 UEFA Champions League Final. By using captain Javier Zanetti and Esteban Cambiasso in holding midfield positions, he is able to push more players to attack. Wesley Sneijder filled the trequartista role and the front three operated as three strikers, rather than having a striker and one player on each wing. Using this formation, Mourinho won the Treble with Inter Milan in only his second season in charge of the club.

Choosing a Formation

The choice of formation is should always be related to the type of players available to the coach.

Teams with a surfeit of central midfielders, or teams that attack best through the center, may choose to adopt narrow formations such as the 4-1-2-1-2 or the 4-3-2-1, which allow teams to field up to four or five central midfielders in the team. Narrow formations, however, depend on the fullbacks to provide width and to advance upfield as frequently as possible to supplement the attack in wide areas.

Teams with a surfeit of forwards and wingers may choose to adopt wide formations such as 4-4-2, 3-5-2 and 4-3-3, which commit forwards and wingers high up the pitch. Wide formations allow the attacking team to stretch play and cause the defending team to cover more ground.

Teams may also choose to change formations during a game to aid their cause: When chasing a game for a desirable result, teams will change to an attacking formation and will have to sacrifice a defensive player or a midfield player for a forward in order to chase a result. An example of such a formation would be to change from 4-5-1 to a 4-4-2.

When a team is in the lead, or wishes to protect the score of a close game, the coach may choose to revert to a more defensive formation, moving a forward to a more defensive role. The extra player in defense or midfield adds solidity by giving the team more legs to chase opponents and recover possession.

Formations can be deceptive in analyzing a particular team's style of play. For instance, a team that plays a nominally attacking 4-3-3 formation can quickly revert to a 4-5-1 if a coach instructs two of the three forwards to track back in midfield.

No matter what tactical formation a team uses, without outstanding players it will never be great. Despite all the changes since the founding of the English FA in 1963, football is still a team game played by individuals. It is not a sport in which a coach can program athletes to carry out specific instructions. Every player must be able to make instant decisions during every game, and these decisions must be carried out with a combination of skill, agility, and a bit of luck. Football will always belong to the individual athlete and not the coaches, as in most American sports — particularly American football — and that is what makes football the best of all team sports, and thus "the people's game."

DEFENSIVE AND ATTACKING TACTICS

In order to win, a team must score more goals than the opposition. This is accomplished by coordinating the play of all 11 players into one collective effort through attacking and defensive tactics based on accepted principles of football. However, a player's skill limitations must be taken into consideration in a team's general tactical plan, and all the players must be aware of and adhere to the tactical plan regardless of their skill.

General Requirements

How long is a player in possession of the ball during a match? According to most statistics, the average player is in possession of the ball between two and three minutes per game (Csanadi, 1965). What a player does with the ball is of paramount importance for any and all tactics, be they on defense or offense. Many players are only "in" the game when the ball is near or when they are in possession of it. It is a player's duty to adjust his position continuously, according to the run of the ball and to the best advantage of his team. Positional play off the ball is a quality that distinguishes a great player from an ordinary one.

Positioning and passing are tactical tools by which teamwork is fashioned. Positioning is extremely important, and most bad passes are due not to the passer, but to his teammates. After all, it is not difficult for a top player to pass the ball accurately, but the ball will not reach a teammate who is not in a position to receive it.

Before a pass is made, the other players need to move into areas within comfortable reach of the player with the ball. They must find the open space by losing the opponent and create a clear path for the ball to travel without being intercepted.

Good positioning is more important to a defender than a strong tackle because it may prevent an opponent from obtaining the ball. A good rule of thumb is "It is always better to stop the ball from reaching an opponent than to try to dispossess him." Thus, a defender must be constantly adjusting his place on the pitch so that he is always within striking distance of his opponent and from cutting off a pass made into his area as well.

Proper positioning in defense entails two responsibilities — that of keeping on the goal side of the immediate opponent and being within striking distance. While preparing to make a tackle, a defender must guide his opponent away from danger and into an area packed with teammates. If the defender knows his attacker well enough, he should try to make the player switch the ball to his weaker foot.

With good forwards continually moving and trying to find open spaces and the defenders trying to block them, every player should be in continuous motion the entire game. The player who stands around "ball watching" is not helping his team or its tactical plan. A good player should always be adjusting his position on the pitch in relation to where the ball is.

Speed of delivery is needed for accurate passing. The longer a player holds to the ball the harder it is to find an open teammate. A general rule is three touches on the ball — one to receive the ball, one to adjust, and the third one to pass.

Talking and Tactics

In the beginning, talking during a match was limited to calling for a pass. It is clear however, that great benefits accrue to teams which talk well, and in a game between two teams that use good tactical talking, the team that communicates better may have a better chance to win the game.

It should be clear that talking is not prohibited, and will not be penalized by good referees. Sadly, many players are adversely affected by ill-informed coaches who prohibit talking during practices in the interest of discipline. Thus many young players grow up with the idea that talking goes against the laws of the game. This belief is reinforced at the junior level by inexperienced coaches and referees who penalize players that call advice to teammates and who do not indicate who the advice is for by mentioning the name of the player. Coaches and referees who do this are doing a great disservice to the game and to players, for talking is an integral part of the game and of tactics.[19]

Foul and abusive language does not need much explanation, but a word calling to mislead an opponent will not be out of place. For example: If a player calls "my ball" as he attempts to gain control of the ball, he may or may not be guilty of an offense. This, of course, will depend on the proximity of opponents and their chances of winning the ball had the advice not been given.

The majority of players who call "my ball" are not deliberately misleading an opponent, but seeking to advise a teammate. Players who intentionally mislead an opponent usually do it quietly with a soft "leave it" almost whispered as they move to control the ball.

Giving advice to a teammate is a definite advantage, and for this reason talking should be part of training and of tactical decisions. Players making passes are instructed to give advice regarding the situation on the back of the player receiving the ball, but it does not necessarily follow that only players who make passes should give advice. Giving advice along with the ball when a player makes a pass will enable the receiver to concentrate entirely on the ball — provided the advice given is good and not erroneous. Some basic calls which should be used by players when they give advice are:

1. Man-on
2. Turn-time-clear
3. Carry or Go with it
4. Square
5. Trail

The meaning of "man-on" is quite clear. The advice in this situation is a man is on the player's back and/or near, and thus it would be dangerous to turn and it should be played or passed away first-time. As long as the player receiving the ball moves to receive the ball and acts on the advice given, even the most tightly marking opponent is likely to be rendered impotent.

Similarly, the meaning of any of the three words turn-time-clear is quite simply that the player has time and space in which to control the ball and turn before being challenged by an opponent.

Carry or Go with it may seem more complicated, but is actually very simple. This type of advice should be given to a player who has no opponent near and, who relative to the speed at which the ball is travelling, would be wasting time and space if he were to stop the ball and then turn with it. To stop the ball and then push it forward to build speed again is a waste of precious time as well as space. Oftentimes, it is better for the player to let the ball pass him by without touching it, then turn and sprint after the ball and still be in possession before he is challenged.

"Square" and "trail" are information given to the player with the ball to let him know where to pass the ball to an open teammate. Square simply means a teammate is to either side and trail means a teammate is behind.

In a team with good talkers, it would be very difficult for a player with the ball to challenge from his blind side. The opposition may try to dispossess players in this way, but on a team with talkers there should be six or seven voices warning their teammate of any danger.

The most important voice in any team is that of the goalkeeper, for a keeper who does not give advice to his teammates regarding his intentions will surely put everyone in a great deal of trouble. In addition to constantly watching the ball and anticipating where an attack may develop, a good keeper should also note the danger of an opponent sneaking into a dangerous area unopposed. Therefore the goalkeeper should be constantly monitoring his penalty area. From his position, the keeper has everyone in front of him, and for this reason he is unique. No other player is so well placed to command the defense, and should an opposing player try to sneak into a danger area, he should decide which teammate is best positioned to cover the unexpected attacker and issue the appropriate instructions. These are just the beginning of the keeper's responsibilities. Whenever the keeper decides to intervene he should make his intentions very clear to all his teammates. If the keeper decides that he cannot reach a cross in time, it is his responsibility to make this known, and to call for a teammate who can and should deal with it. Oftentimes, two or more defenders may be trying to head the ball away from a cornerkick, and they can impede each other in such a way that neither is able to time the jump or head the ball away. If the keeper sees the situation and calls "Bobby's ball" a potentially dangerous situation may be avoided.

If the keeper decides to intercept the ball, he should yell "keeper's ball." This is a call that cannot be misunderstood by his teammates, the opposition, or the referee. Upon hearing the keeper's call, defenders should make sure not to obstruct their keeper, and immediately drop back behind him to cover the goal in case the keeper should fail to reach the ball.

Passing the ball back to the keeper can be dangerous, particularly if a defender passes the ball without verifying the position of the keeper, as this could multiply the danger. Quite often a player passes back to his keeper in situations where he had time to turn and move upfield — only to later discover that he had a "silent" teammate standing behind him or to his side. Another situation which often causes trouble is one in which a defender is covering the ball as it travels toward his goal with the keeper coming out. The goalkeeper in this situation must make his intentions quite clear and let his teammate know if he wants the ball or whether his colleague should play the ball back to him. All these situations can be avoided if the keeper and other teammates are alert, aware, and advising promptly as to what to do.

The keeper must continually make his decisions known loudly and clearly in order to avoid any embarrassing situations and prevent any potentially adverse plays from taking place.

Ball Possession

Scoring is generally accomplished by having possession of the ball, although on rare occasions a team may accidentally score on itself. Nonetheless, as a general rule a team cannot score goals if they do not have the ball, and at the same time, the opposition cannot score if they don't have the ball either. Thus, an important tactical decision is to maintain possession of the ball as much as possible.

Generally we talk and write about football in terms of attack and defense. Thus we need to think of the field of play as a pitch divided into three equal sections that are divided crosswise. The section nearest a team's own goal is known as the area of defense or defensive third, the central area is the area for midfield preparation (also called the mid-third), and the third section is the attack area or offensive third.

According to Csanadi (1965), Beim (1977), Rosenthal (1981), and Jones & Tranter (1999), in the defensive third of the pitch, a team should take no chances that may result in losing possession of the ball. Losing the ball in this area of the pitch could result in an immediate shot on goal by an opponent. In the mid-third, a player could take some chances in order to penetrate the opposition's defense, or to gain an advantage in preparation for an attack. However, losing the ball in this area could still be dangerous, because the opposition could create a quick counterattack. In the attacking third, a team may gamble if the result would create a goal or a shot on goal.

General Consideration in the Attacking Third

The attack begins at the moment that any player on a team gains possession of the ball — including the keeper. When in possession, the first pass made is as important as the last, and players must be prepared and anticipate a possible pass. The attack begins with the first pass, followed by the last pass, which should result on a shot on goal.

A successful attack generally follows the following pattern.

1. Running into open space
2. Playing without the ball
3. Depth — Width — Penetration
4. Dribbling — Improvisation
5. Shoot on goal

Running into Open Space

There are dead spaces and open spaces on the field of play. In order to maintain possession of the ball, all field players must run out of the dead space and into the open space. No one is faster than the ball, thus "use the ball" is the best advice for every attack. Each player must improve his peripheral vision, and think in advance so he can find the open space and be prepared for any situation (Jones & Tranter, 1999).

Playing Without the Ball

Running free into open space is the same as playing without the ball, and generally a player making this type of run should not expect to receive a pass. A good team is able to employ many tricks to mislead an opponent and open the space for a teammate.

Depth — Width — Penetration

Running without the ball is the preparation for the beginning of these three elements. The organization of the opposition's defense determines the style of attack. If the opposition is prepared to stop the attack, the midfield must be used in order to maintain possession until the open space is found. If the opposition is less organized, a good and fast counterattack should be employed.

Dribbling

Dribbling and other kinds of improvisation are important to any team. When these actions are missing, the match may become dull and predictable. Dribbling is the action of advancing the ball and beating an opposing player. To dribble and feint successfully, both speed and ball control must be augmented with the ability to elude or deceive an opponent.

Shot on Goal

Simply stated, there are no substitutes for goals. The aim of all the previous actions is to take a shot on goal and score. All these actions are meaningless if a shot on goal is not accomplished.

General Considerations in the Mid-Third

The link between defense and attack has always been vital and never more so than in the modern game. A major consideration here must the adequacy of the number of players with midfield responsibilities, regardless of the formation being used. Although the fullbacks can now take an integral part in developing and pressing attacks, it is the midfield players who have to accept the greater part of the physical burden involved (Winterbottom, 1960).

Screening their defensive teammates when possession of the ball is lost, sprinting out in support of their attacking teammates when the defense gains possession, and exploiting space within the opposition's defense will make too great a demand on one or two midfield players. It must also be taken into consideration that when one midfielder sprints forward, it will leave only one player in midfield for support. With three or more midfielders, the physical burden and responsibilities are shared over a broader base, and when one midfield player sprints forward to exploit space, he leaves behind other teammates behind as support should it become necessary.

Finally, a very important consideration is that a player with a very strong shot will probably find more opportunities to exploit his talent by coming from behind than he would if he were positioned up front. As a front player the potential scorer is likely to attract the attention of a defender, but coming from midfield he will be much less easier to mark. Except for very special circumstances the advantages of fielding three or more midfield players far outweigh having only one or two, as in the 4-2-4 formation.

General Considerations in the Defensive Third

When in defense, the first point to consider is that each of the opposition's front players must be marked by a defender. However, the term "man-to-man marking" is relative. Loose man-to-man cover can be just as effective as the tightest of markings, which seeks to deny an opponent even one touch on the ball. To what extent the defenders can devote themselves to their individual opponents depends entirely on the tactical formation adopted.

If the responsibility for covering in defense is shared equally, then the marking of individual opponents is relatively loose. Only with the introduction of a free back such as the libero can defenders be left to fight private battles with their individual opponents. It should be noted that even the most reliable libero is not invincible (Jones & Welton, 1973).

Probably the major covering problem in defense is the delegation of responsibility in the central area, and the easiest solution is to place two center fullbacks. This is the basis for the defensive aspects of the 4-2-4 and 4-3-3 formations. The key here is the understanding that must be developed by the two center backs, for when one is drawn into a duel for the ball, it is vital that his partner drops back to cover the empty space. Against an opponent that fields two center forwards this chemistry between the two defenders will be severely tested if each of the forwards is intelligent and moves around in order to create space by drawing his marker away from the central area.

In a 4-2-4 or 4-3-3 defense playing against a team with a lone center forward, this may not be a problem. One of the center backs is simply given the responsibility of marking the center forward while his partner covers the space. This will not be a problem either for a team with four defenders in the back line if the opposition fields two center forwards but only one winger as in a 4-3-3 or a 1-3-3-3 formation, or any other similar combination (Hughes, 1975).

If the covering of the center backs is considered to be inefficient, then an extra back may be used to (a) provide cover by positioning himself free behind the defensive line, or (b) to mark one of the opposition's center forwards. In this last situation, cover would then be provided by one of the center backs.

There is one alternative to the defensive systems such as the Swiss Bolt and the Italian catenaccio. In possession of the ball, the attacking team will be wasting a player if he is left free behind his offensive teammates. Once possession is gained, the free back should relieve one of the center backs, who will then be able to play at the very least a supporting role in midfield. When the attacking team loses possession, then the center back should sprint back to pick his personal opponent and thus relive the free back (Cramer, 1977).

It should be made clear that two center backs should be able to develop a chemical understanding which will enable them to do an adequate job. Except under very special circumstances the introduction of a free back should not be necessary in the modern game.

Space

The importance of space is vital to understand for both offense and defense in football. In attack, players must make use of space between and behind the defensive players, or they must create space by forcing defenders to move and spread out. The job of the defense is to deny and close space to the opposition.

Also, space is important in order to maintain ball possession. The more space a player has to play with, the more time he has to control a ball passed to him, to analyze the situation, and to make better passes to his teammates. Additionally, with more space, a player will generally make fewer errors that may result in losing the ball. Space and time are interdependent—the more a player has of one, the more he has of the other.

As attackers get closer to their opponent's goal the available space decreases. This, more than any other single factor, creates the need for the principles of attacking play (Greaves, 1966).

Mobility

It is easier for players to defend than it is to attack. Defenders are primarily concerned with preventing the opponents from scoring by breaking down their attack in any way they can, while the attacking players must be imaginative and creative in order to produce scoring opportunities. It is easier to destroy something than to create or build something, and in football it takes far less accuracy to simply kick a ball away than to work it through a defense and create a shot on goal.

Even forwards who seem to have possession of the ball rarely have it for longer than about 4 to 5 minutes per game. This fact emphasizes the great importance of each team player when he is not in possession of the ball, which is most of the match. Attacking players not in possession of the ball must concentrate on making the defender's job as difficult as possible, and must try to provide the man with ball the best penetrating and scoring opportunities (Csanadi, 1965). All these objectives require the application of the principle of "mobility." Movement of players without the ball is essential for a successful attacking game.

Mobility is essential for success in attack, but is also very demanding both physically and mentally. Players must constantly analyze the play to decide when a run will be helpful. They must watch the movement of the opponents as well as that of their teammates, and concentrate on the game constantly if they expect to be an asset to their team even when the ball is not at their feet. Such concentration can be very tiring. Thus, good support is essential for any tactic to succeed, and players must be in position to receive the ball as soon as their team wins position. This requires a great deal of running and is very physically strenuous. On average a good player will make several runs although he may not receive the ball. Although this can be frustrating and obviously tiring, it must be done. Unless a player is prepared both mentally and physically for all this running, he may stop this required running, and then will not be able to help his team effectively. Mobility is essential for good tactical football, but the total mental concentration and physical stress require a high degree of physical fitness.

Improvisation

Football is a game of constant motion, and although teams may have a general tactical formation and plan of attack, for the most part football does not lend itself to very organized set plays. The only time that set plays can be used effectively is during dead-ball/restart situations. A too-organized attack will be too predictable and less effective.

Players must be able to adapt to all situations as they take place during every match, which means that they should be able to improvise and anticipate every play. Football is a game of percentages, and players should do whatever will bring success by doing the unexpected, and gambling on even the low-percentage chances they may have in the attacking third of the pitch (Wade, 1967).

Good players have the ability to rise to any given occasion and act on the spur of the moment. Any football player should be adept at three ingredients in order to perform well in football: (a) fitness; (b) understanding of the game; and (c) good skills (Greaves, 1966). Any player with these ingredients should be able to deal with all situations that may arise during a match, and be better prepared to improvise.

The plan of attack has to be limitless. This is not possible without a great deal of improvisation, and for that reason, modern football requires "complete" players capable of playing any position on the pitch, and who can understand modern tactics. A very high work rate is also desirable.

The ultimate improvisation tactical style in modern football is "total football." Teams like Ajax of Amsterdam and the Dutch national team of the 1970s are excellent examples of this style. Both teams seem to have played with "total" disregard for allocated positions, as the players moved about with such fluidity and appeared to improvise constantly according to how each situation developed during a match. Their playmaking was very spontaneous and natural; and while this type of attack was effective, it was also great fun to watch.

Finishing and Shooting

Oftentimes teams control the ball quite a lot during a match, but they fail to win because they do not take chances and thus do not score goals. For the most part this type of teams works well in their defensive third and mid third, but breaks down in the attacking third when they don't take shots on goal. Scoring goals is what football is all about, and all the preparation in the midfield is totally useless if a team cannot finish and score goals.

Finishing is the culmination of the attack into shots on goal, and goal scoring, of course. Without good finishing and without shots on goal, a team will not win games. For the most part a team will get an opportunity to take a shot in two situations: (a) the defenders of the opposition make a mistake, or (b) the attacking players create their own opportunities. Thus players need to be aware of defensive errors that can result in good shooting chances (Jones & Welton, 1973).

Shooting is the culmination of good finishing. While the shooting range from which goals can be scored varies from player to player, usually good attacking players can score from as far as 30 yards away. If a player gets into shooting range, he can opt to do one of three things: (a) take a shot on goal, (b) dribble past a defender to get a closer or better shot, or (c) he can pass to a teammate in a better position to take a shot. A player will make his choice based on each specific situation dictated to him by the flow of the game. As a general rule, a player should take a shot anytime he has the opportunity. It is not a wise decision to try to get closer to the goal in order to take a shot, as the penalty area may be too crowded, diminishing the opportunity to score a goal. It is better to get a shot from 20 yards out than not to shoot at all.

Shots from outside the penalty area can be very effective, as they can surprise an unprepared keeper. Or they may be blocked by a defender. The ball could easily hit one of the players in the penalty area and be deflected to the goal. Additionally, if enough shots are taken from a long range, it may force the defenders to come out of their goal, thus opening space in the penalty area that attackers can then exploit for their advantage.

It is important to remember that the only way to score goals is to finish the attack by taking shots. Csanadi (1965) noted that it takes an average of nine to ten shots to score a goal, so it is logical to take as many shots as possible in order to increase the probabilities of scoring. No shots ... no goals!

9

GENERAL TACTICS

Football is a team game and the efforts of the team should be concentrated on a single purpose: to win. In order to achieve the best result, a team must play according to a specific plan that is agreed upon and implemented by the manager.

The common goal cannot be achieved if individual players do not adhere to the specified plan. Being able to work together as one is what makes eleven players a successful team.

Individual effort, however, plays an important role in teamwork. Often during the course of a game, success may well depend on the actions of a particular player. For example, a goalkeeper may be called upon to make a spectacular save to keep his team from losing. Or a forward may have to utilize his dribbling skills to take on a defender in order to create a scoring opportunity.

For that matter, tactics can be classified as individual and group tactics.. Tactics can also be classified as attacking tactics and defensive tactics. It should be understood that individual and group tactics as well as attacking and defensive tactics are influenced by many other factors, and some of these factors can have an influence through the entire game, or at particular times during a game.

Ball technique can exist independently of a game. A ball can be controlled, kicked, or headed without any particular purpose. People may kick or head the ball just for the pleasure of it.

Tactics, on the other hand, are entirely different. But even the simplest tactics cannot be adopted without the help of technique (Clues, 1980).

In modern football, tactics and technique must be in complete harmony. In making a tactical plan of play, the coach must above all reckon with the technical experience of his team. According to Miller (1975), the cardinal principle of coordinating tactics and technique is that the plan of play should fit the technical standards of the players and not the other way around. Tactics can be modified relatively quickly; but a long spell of training is always needed to improve technique.

Tactics can be adjusted to meet actual conditions in the manner best suited to achieve maximum results. Tactical sense is a matter of individual talent; and it can be developed by coaching, practice, and other activities related to football in general. Football is a team game, and the entire efforts of the team must be concentrated on a single purpose — to win. However, that cannot be achieved if the individual players fail to cooperate or if one or more players do not have the skills or knowledge necessary for teamwork. Working as one is what makes tactics and formations successful.

Individual effort can also play a decisive role in teamwork, although at times during the course of a game success may depend on the actions of a single player. For example, the goalkeeper who makes an incredible save to prevent a loss or maintain a tie, or a good dribbler, who is capable of creating scoring opportunities and/or converting those opportunities into goals.

On the basis of all that has been written, tactics include two stages: Individual tactics and team tactics. A team is not a machine and the players are not robots. A good football team requires good individual players, not uninformed teammates without self-confidence. At the moment when any player is contesting for the ball, he must think of his value to the team. If he wins his challenge, he has won the ball for his team, and his team is now able to go on attack, attempt to score, and win the game. Individual tactics include everything we require in order to maintain possession or to regain position. If a team loses over 60 percent of individual duels, then it will likely lose the game as well.

During a game, there is always one team on the attack while the other is on defense. Thus tactics while on attack are different from those employed while defending, and the manager should be able to adjust according to the needs of the game.

Defensive Tactics

A game cannot be won just by attacking. All teams and players are expected to defend during a game, not just the fullbacks and the goalkeeper.

In modern football, individual play, be that on attack or on defense, is starting to lose significance as most plays are harnessed to the interest of the whole team. Of course, each defender must be familiar with and capable of individual defensive play in order to be part of a successful team effort. The chief distinction in defensive tactics is between individual and team responsibility, reflected in the rise and fluctuating popularity of zonal defense and man-to-man marking.

Zonal Defense

Zonal defense is basically self-explanatory. To cover for a team or player's lack of pace or technique, every defender and midfielder is responsible for a particular zone on the pitch when the opposition has the ball. This is particularly important during set pieces, but does rely heavily on every player fulfilling his duties and keeping his concentration.

Ideally, the opposition will be facing two lines of four players covering the entirety of one half of the pitch. The defensive line is particularly important as, with proper communication and synchronized movement, it can exploit the offside rule and prevent all long-balls and through-balls succeeding. Generally speaking, zonal defense is fundamentally simple but allows sides to deal with all types of attackers on the opponent's team. However, it can be fraught with danger if any individual fails to cover his area of the pitch.

Man-to-Man Marking

The term is often associated with continental and in particular with Italian football and, once again, is extremely simple at its core. Whereas the defenders and midfielders are responsible for zones in zonal defense, man-to-man marking means certain individuals are responsible for guarding a particular opponent. Man-to-man marking is particularly effective alongside a sweeper who has a free role, enabling him/her to support anyone having problems with his opponent and reducing the potency of through-balls and balls played over the top of the defense for forward players to run onto.

However, man-to-man marking requires incredible discipline on the part of the marker, and good decision making on the part of the manager. If a slower defender is matched up with a fast and speedy striker, the results could prove disastrous!

Forwards on Defense

In modern football, forwards are required not only to attack but to help in defense as well. One of the defensive roles of a forward is to attempt to stop the opposition as they prepare to start an attack, or at the very least slow it down in order to allow his teammates to regroup so they can defend as a team.

As soon as the attacker loses control of the ball to a defender, he should immediately try to regain possession. The forward must not remain idle; he must chase after the defender and challenge him as long as he is still in possession of the ball, or at least until he reaches his teammates on defense. The forward must also challenge the keeper when appropriate so as to prevent him in his attempt to initiate an attack with a rapid pass.

Unfortunately, many forwards forget their defensive duties, and oftentimes do not switch to a defensive role after losing the ball, instead simply relaxing after the attack has ended.

The Goalkeeper Directing the Defense

The keeper must be able to direct the defense, as he is in the position to keep constant watch over the entire pitch during play. The defenders should be able to carry out the keeper's instructions, and those instructions should be definite, intelligible, and loud. A firm and definite tone can have a strong psychological effect, not only on the defenders, but on the opposition as well. If the defense is well disciplined and has complete understanding, one or two words may be sufficient to warn of danger and indicate how it should be countered. If the keeper regularly uses the same word or words for instruction, then his teammates become familiar with the word and will begin to respond to the instructions automatically.

A simple command such as "keeper's ball" may be enough when he needs the defenders to leave the ball alone and immediately move back to cover for him. "Clear" or "time" could be used to indicate to a teammate that he has ball possession and is in no danger of an immediate challenge. Other simple phrases and words to use are: "man on," "cover him," and "wall," among others. Of course, these instructions should be used only when necessary. If a defender is already in control of the situation, then unnecessary commands from the keeper could unsettle his teammate. At the same time, if a keeper gives instructions, they should be carried out without delay, particularly when defenders are facing their own goal.

Basic Attacking Team Tactics

The objective of the game is to score goals, but certain variables such as the score line can influence a particular team's desperation to ruffle the net. The following team styles represent some of the methods used to control the game and instigate attacks.

Possession Football

For years, the golden rule for managers everywhere has been pass and move, and this principle is still enshrined in possession football. In simple terms, teams attempt to hold onto the ball for as long as possible, at all times choosing the easiest possible pass. This is the reason we see defenders passing the ball along the defensive line.

There is logic behind this seemingly predictable style, though. Keeping control of the ball is likely to frustrate the opponent and draw out certain players from their starting positions, which in turn will create spaces for through-balls that would otherwise be impossible. Moreover keeping possession forces the opponents to chase all over the pitch, draining their stamina and further allowing the team in possession to control the pace of the match.

Counter-Attacking Football

With eleven players to get past, scoring a goal can be a difficult task even under the best of circumstances. However, the beauty of counterattacking football is to use the other team's desperation to score to your own advantage.

By withdrawing into one's own half, but keeping a man or two further up the pitch, the goal is to regain possession of the ball while the opposition has players committed to the attack and thus out of position. Once the team gains possession of the ball in their own half, they have more space to deliver a through-ball for the forwards, who should be lurking around the halfway line and with fewer players to deal with.

This tactic, while it can be considered extremely risky and dependent on solid defending, can generate impressive results and is often used by teams who are defending a lead and are utilizing a possible 4-5-1 formation. With this formation the lone striker can get isolated in front of four defenders, assuming that both sides are set up accordingly.

The Long Ball

This term is often used to describe boring teams. However, the long-ball style of play can be a genuine tactic in certain situations. Rather than spending time on the ball picking the pass, exploiting small gaps in the opposition's defense, or utilizing the flanks, the long ball can be employed as an opportunistic method of attack. By kicking the ball up the field from defense or midfield, the hope is that the strikers will either manage to control the hopeful pass or exploit any mistakes by the defenders.

Because the long ball is dealt with in the air most of the time, it may be wise for any team using this particular tactic to have a strong and tall target man. Additionally, the long ball can be effective on a waterlogged pitch, as keeping the ball on the ground could prove to be rather difficult.

Using the Flanks

Since the days of Sir Stanley Matthews, the wingers have always been a key part of attacking football. Spreading the ball wide provides a different angle of attack and offers a number of opportunities for the winger to take on a fullback and possibly drag central defenders out of position, cut inside and move forward at an angle, or kick-in a cross from deep for other strikers to attack.

A further development in wing play has been to alternate wingers on the left and right flanks. If a winger is losing the battle with his fullback, switching wings can provide a breakthrough for the team. This was effectively employed by Portugal on their way to the final of the 2004 European championships, with Luis Figo and Cristiano Ronaldo frequently exchanging wing positions.

Set-Plays

This is a common method for technically deficient teams. Using the set-plays means exploiting all types of free kicks, throw-ins, and corner-kicks. In the absence of quick, skilful players, such sides will use the break in play provided by set pieces to pack the box and attack the ball when it is delivered.

Tactics and Technique

In order to play with a defined plan, and/or to achieve a particular style, we must employ certain tactics, and therefore be able to deal with any situation. Everything that may influence the outcome of the game must be taken into consideration in order to decide the tactical system of play and the choice of the tactics, style, and formations will depend on several factors. Among these are:

- The technique being used by the opposition
- The physical fitness and abilities of both teams
- The player's knowledge of the rules

Of course, there are several other factors that must be taken into consideration before developing a tactical plan. For example, the coach must be aware of the theoretical knowledge of his players with regard to the game of football, and the tactics his opposition is expected to utilize.

Tactics and Condition

Even a superb tactical plan can fail if the physical condition of the players is left out of consideration. A most promising scheme on paper may fail miserably if the players have not enough strength to put it into practice. MacDonald (1972) indicates that several factors relating to the condition of the team should be taken into account when drawing out a tactical plan.

First, no particular task should be given to an individual, a part, or the whole of the team if players are not physically capable of carrying it out. In addition to taking one's own team into consideration, even greater attention should be given to the condition of the opposition. Many teams as a consequence of insufficient condition are unable to maintain the same standard of play in the second half. According to MacDonald (1972), many teams employ the tactic of not going all out for the first half, so as to hold strength and resources for the second half.

Because of inadequate preparation or insufficient stamina, some players are unable to keep pace with the game. Both the coach and the players should bear these factors in mind before and during the game (Thompson, 1977).

There is considerable tactical wisdom in exploiting superior condition. Forwards can tire out the opposing defense by forcing the defenders to keep constantly on the move. Sooner or later the opponents are bound to come to the end of their resources (Cramer, 1977).

If one or other of the opponents' defenders is known to dislike running, he must be forced to run. Play should be directed as often as possible to his side of the field. Long passes and four or five dashes in rapid succession are often enough to gain a decisive advantage over such a player (Thompson, 1977).

The coach must always seriously consider the strength and condition of his team, and the tactics adopted should be linked with training designed to bring the players to a state of physical preparation that will allow them to meet the demands of such tactics.

Tactics and External Factors

During a game, conditions are constantly changing. This applies to other sports, too, but it is doubtful if they vary to such an extent as in football.

Pitch Size

One of the external factors exercising an influence on tactics is the size of the pitch. Most teams have their own pitch to play, and not only do they train there, at least half of their games are played on home ground. The players are accustomed to the dimensions, the surface, and the feel of their own ground, and home game tactics are shaped accordingly (*Soccer*, 1967). That is one aspect of what we call the advantage of home ground.

In away games, the tactics which are successful at home may fail under unusual circumstances. The measurements of the pitch and other conditions are all factors to be reckoned with when giving tactical instructions to the players before the game (Maher, 1983).

According to Csanadi (1963), many pitches are 110 to 120 yards long by 80 to 85 yards wide. These grounds are too wide as compared to their length. When playing in such a pitch, he indicates that the forwards should draw the defenders to where they are spread out across the full width of the pitch. If short passes are used at first, the defenders will be caught on the wrong foot if the forwards then switch to long cross passes. Csanadi (1963) also mentions that on a wide pitch, the forwards can run into open spaces, and that this possibility should be exploited, while at the same time the defenders should not go too close to the touch-line, as this will leave a large gap in the middle.

Some pitches are too long (120 to 130 yards) in comparison to their width (60 to 65 yards). This type of ground is favorable for fast defenders (Winterbottom, 1959). Attackers and defenders are crowded in a relatively small area in front of the goal. The fact that the defense is on top of the attack gives it a distinct advantage (Csanadi, 1963). A fast breakaway is of particular significance on a large pitch. A well-controlled long pass ahead or a diagonal pass enables a team to start a fast surprise attack from a defensive position because it catches the defenders standing relatively wide apart on or near the halfway line (Woosman, 1972). This type of move, as described by Csanadi (1963), gives fast forwards space to work in and a chance to utilize their superiority in speed.

Tactics should be adjusted to the dimension of the pitch. A good-sized pitch is particularly suitable for building up fast attacks with long passes. It also favors a team in good physical condition. On a small pitch, passes have to be made in a relatively confined space, with opponents much closer and ready to challenge for the ball, and because there is so little room to work in, passes must be extra accurate. Maher (1983) mentions that dribbling, feinting, and shooting at goal are all made more difficult when there is less space to work in, and long passes from behind are seldom successful on a long pitch. Thus, short and accurate passes should be used.

Ground Quality

Csanadi (1963) explains that the quality of ground is another factor exerting an influence on tactics. A smooth ground is particularly suitable for a cultured, lowpassing game. But if the ground is uneven, it is unwise to keep the ball low since the direction is unsure, and the players are also hampered in performing the technical movements correctly. Csanadi indicates that it is advisable under this circumstance to keep the ball in the air as much as possible. On such grounds, players who have mastered volley-passing have a considerable advantage over their opponents.

Hard, loose, or grassy grounds have different effects on the ball. The ball bounces high on a hard surface. According to Hughes (1966), players should concentrate on taking possession of the ball or making a pass before or right at the moment the ball touches the ground. A moderately loose ground helps the player in working with the ball by absorbing its pace. A completely loose, in most cases sandy, ground always creates difficulties. Csanadi (1963) explains that on this type of ground the ball deceives the players, and the players tire quickly, since they use their strength in running over loose ground. He also indicates that unnecessary running and dribbling should be avoided on such pitches. In such situations, the ball should be allowed to do the work, and dribbling must be avoided if a pass will do.

On very grassy grounds, the angle at which the ball rebounds from the ground is not always identical with what a player might expect. Woosman (1972), says that a ball approaching at a steep angle generally bounces up at a similar angle, but a low ball often deceives a player who lacks experience because the ball is likely to bounce in a different direction.

The Weather

An exclusively outdoor game, Association Football is influenced immensely by the weather. Rain can make a fundamental transformation in the condition of the ground in a relatively short time. The condition of the pitch will vary according to the quantity of rain, and tactics should be adjusted accordingly. When the ground is only slightly wet, the team can work with short passes since a slippery pitch has no effect on the direction of the ball (Csanadi, 1963). Most errors, according to Csanadi, are made when players use cross passes. If the ball is sent in front of a running teammate in the same manner as when passing on hard ground, it is likely the ball will go too far ahead because of the treacherous conditions. On a wet pitch, the ball must be sent directly to the foot of a teammate.

A wet or slippery pitch is favorable for short and technically experienced players who run with short strides. Tall players are usually slow moving and experience great difficulties if the pitch is slippery (Kobyashi, 1978).

Csanadi (1963) advises against running at full speed in wet conditions, because it is extremely difficult to come to a sudden stop or change directions; thus, defenders should be advised to move more slowly, and tall or heavily built players should bend the trunk to place the center of gravity as low as possible to the ground when running. As for the attackers, Csanadi advises moving rapidly because the defenders are greatly hampered in reacting to their movements.

When the ground is soaking wet or muddy, special tactics are required. It is incorrect to work with low passes on such a pitch, not only because the ball is bound to stick in the mud, but also because this method of passing needs too much energy and tires players out (Kobyashi, 1978). In muddy or snow-covered pitches, the foot must go well under the ball like a scoop, and lobs as well as long passes should be used.

Csanadi (1963) accurately mentions that special care is required if the ball is in the goal area and the ground is muddy and wet. The ball is liable to stick in a pool, and both the attackers and defenders should anticipate this possibility. Since the ball becomes greasy on a muddy or slippery ground, the goalkeeper is bound to have difficulties in clutching and holding the ball, so the goalkeeper should be advised to catch the ball only if this can be done with safety. If he cannot, then is better to use the fists to punch it clear.

Sunny and Hot Weather

Sunny weather is another factor that influences tactics. The sun shining directly into the eyes of the players can greatly hamper the defenders, especially when the ball is in the air. Csanadi (1963) recommends that if the attack has a forward or forwards that are good in the air, particularly in heading, it will be a good tactic to lob the ball into the goal area as often as possible. Additionally, after winning the toss, the position of the sun should be considered. On a hot sunny day, light-colored jerseys should be worn if possible. (Dark jerseys, or long-sleeved jerseys, should be worn when it is cold.) In a hot climate area such as Africa or South America, the short-passing game is more appropriate. Running is minimized and players will not tire quickly. This is why the short-pass style game is common in warm climates.

Windy Weather

The effects of the wind can greatly influence the game; thus, tactics which take this factor into account can be decisive. Playing against the wind places greater demands on the strength of the players. Passing requires a greater amount of strength, and it is more tiring to run against the wind than with it (Kobyashi, 1978). Against the wind it is logical to operate with short, low passes, avoiding unnecessary running.

Altitude

Games played at high altitude, as in Bolivia, Mexico, and Ecuador, can affect not only the fitness of a player but the movement of the ball, as the lighter air can change the flight path of the ball once it has been kicked.

Equipment

The playing kit can be adapted to meet changes in ground conditions and weather. Boots with longer studs should be worn when playing on slippery or grassy pitches in order to help the players with their movements. On hard or frozen ground, boots with very short studs should be worn.

The boots worn by Tony Singleton during the 1954 FA Cup (won by Preston North End).

It is advisable to smear the boots, especially the soles, with grease when the ground is muddy. This prevents mud from sticking between the studs (Csanadi, 1963).

Tactics and the Laws of the Game[20]

According to Csanadi (1963), Rosenthal (1980), and Vogelsinger (1982), a profound knowledge of the laws of the game is of immense value in extending the range of tactics that can be employed. Several sections of the laws are valuable from a tactical point of view. Many referees, for example, do not give a separate signal to the kicker to take a free kick. The placed ball can be kicked at once. If the kick is taken quickly, the offensive team will not have the time to position themselves to form up in defense. The same applies to the throw-in. Tactically inexperienced players are inclined to go after the ball at a slow pace, giving the opposition time to regroup themselves in defense (it is only wise to go after the ball at a slow pace when trying to waste time).

The offside law, as explained by Csanadi (1963), offers a wide variety of tactical possibilities to defenders and attackers. By adopting what is described as "the offside trap," the defenders can use the law to nullify attacks. From the point of view of attack, it is important to remember that a player is not offside if he receives the ball directly from a goal kick, from a throw-in, a corner kick, and when the ball is dropped by the referee (FIFA, 1994).

The "advantage rule" can also be exploited tactically. When an opponent commits an infringement while a player is taking possession of the ball, even if the opponent is almost bound to be penalized because the foul was so obvious, the player in possession should carry on until the referee's whistle is blown (Csanadi, 1963). Many scoring opportunities are never converted into goals because players come to a stop after an infringement by an opponent, expecting the referee to blow the whistle, when the referee has decided to give the advantage rule and not deny a possible scoring opportunity.

The newest change in the laws of the game indicates that the goalkeeper is not allowed to touch the ball with his hands if he receives a pass from a teammate, unless it is a header (FIFA, 2009). This change has increased the possibilities of the forwards to charge the goalkeeper, and thus create a scoring opportunity. With the new rule the goalkeeper is now forced to play the ball with his feet while under a lot of pressure. Forwards should take advantage of this new law and pressure the goalkeeper at all times.

A player with insufficient knowledge of the laws of the game will almost certainly commit an offense at the worst possible time, or lose the opportunity to score, thus giving the tactical advantage to the opposing side.

"Waste Time Tactics"

Late in a game a player may choose to walk to retrieve the ball, rather that jogging or running, thus wasting precious seconds and therefore minimizing the opposition's chance to gain possession of the ball. During a throw-in, a coach may instruct the player to throw the ball downfield but not onto the pitch, thus the throw-in must be retaken and again waste additional seconds (as the author did on many occasion during his coaching stints). A keeper may choose to hold onto the ball for a little longer after a save, instead of releasing it too soon. Players could make long passes to a teammate on an offside position, which would require stoppage of the game, again wasting precious seconds.

Counter Tactics

When making the tactical plan, the manager must bear in mind that the other team too will adopt certain tactics, or more precisely counter-tactics designed to take the opposition by surprise. The value of a tactical plan depends on how much of it can actually be put into practice or to what extent it can be realized in the face of active opposition (Csanadi, 1963).

The tactics the opponents use may in some cases be difficult to define, and so the other team must be prepared to adopt alternative tactics or counter-tactics. The timing of counter-tactics is all-important since a delayed antidote is of no avail.

In the game of football, only three substitutions are allowed per game. The use of substitutions in a tactical sense should be well thought out by the manager. If the other team substitutes for an offensive-minded player, the other team should in certain occasions reply with a substitution of a defensive player. The time of the substitution is another factor that should be taken into consideration when making a change. Sometimes a team is reduced in numbers because of injury or the fact that a player is ordered off. On such occasions, it is a fundamental principle that if the defense has suffered the loss, then the missing player must be replaced with a player who can function as a defender. While a forward line can be incomplete, the defense should never be a man short (Csanadi, 1963).

If the opponents have lost a player, they are now outnumbered, and this involves a tactical counter-tactic of great importance: What role should be given to the man who is now without an opposite number? If the other team is superior in play, the free player should help in defense. If there is a balance in power, he should assist in building up the attacks. Hughes (1966) called it unwise to put the extra player into the forward line, since this results in making the opponents' goal area more crowded, operating to the advantage of the defenders.

Tactics as well as counter-tactics sometimes fail to live up to expectations, and during the game it is impossible to give new tactical information to the team, except at halftime. The ideal situation is one in which all the players have highly tactical experience, where they as a whole team can be inspired into executing the tactical instructions given by the manager and be capable of adapting as the situations of the game demand.

10

SUMMARY AND CONCLUSIONS

The purpose of this book is to describe team tactics in football, from 1863 to the present. In addition to the description of tactics, an attempt has been made to identify coaches and players who have been instrumental in developing and implementing the various tactics. Prominent teams which have had any significance in regards to team tactics were also described. I attempted to accomplish several goals through this descriptive history:

1. To provide a descriptive history of football, from 1863 to the present.
2. To trace the evolution and development of tactics.
3. To describe the significant tactics, formations, and trends that have been beneficial to the development of football.
4. To identify the most influential people and leaders in the development of football.
5. To identify the major reasons or influences that affected tactical changes.
6. To assist the coach, the player, and the fan to understand and appreciate the different aspects of team tactics in football.
7. To consolidate and to preserve a history of team tactics in football.

Summary

The following summarizes the main areas in the development of tactics in football.

1. During the early days of football, the game was unorganized and there were an unlimited number of players with no real organized formations. Dribbling and crowding were the main characteristics of the game.

2. The introduction of the pass changed the game considerably. By 1873, formations began to develop, and this in turn gave an opportunity for better offensive and defensive team tactics.

3. As the offense began to find weaknesses in the opposing defenses, defenders began to change their tactics, and coaches started to play more defenders.

4. In 1970, a trend towards a more attack-minded game began to appear, and with it came hope that football tactics would become more exciting and entertaining.

Conclusions

This historical description has established the following aspects of current team tactics in football.

A picture showing the similarities between the game of *kemari* and modern football.

General Position of Players on the Pitch

It is generally accepted that is difficult for a team to function properly with fewer than four defenders, two midfielders, and at least two forwards. This makeup allows for other players to be maneuvered in order to create a desired formation. If a coach can motivate the players to adhere effectively to the principles of attack and defense, it is possible for the coach to place the remaining two players in more appropriate tactical positions anywhere on the pitch.

Importance of Players, Coaches, and Environmental factors

It is the players on a team who make tactics work. The tactics used are simply based on a particular team and a coach who designates the roles of the players. In doing so, the coach should always remember to fit the tactics according to the players, their strengths, and their weaknesses. The weather and conditions of the pitch, including size and quality, should also be taken into consideration.

Strengths and Weaknesses of Rigid Formations

Not very knowledgeable coaches often impose a particular formation upon a weak team. When that happens, play becomes codified and players cannot think or read the game well, or even if they can, they are usually not allowed to do what they think is best at the moment. In times like this, good teams can exploit the weaknesses of rigid formations. Superior teams that have players who are quick, versatile, and capable of intelligent thinking are more effective and successful in rigid formations and team tactics.

Effect of Rules on Tactics

Football, like all other sports, is played under certain rules. Depending on the nature of the change, football tactics may or may not be affected by a rule change or rule modification. A rule change which made the penalty spot 10 yards from the goal instead of 12 would make very little difference to the game. On the other hand, if an offensive player were allowed to handle the ball in the other team's penalty box, a great impact on the game, particularly in scoring, would result. If a kick-in was to be used instead of a throw-in from the sidelines, it would certainly bring about new changes in tactics and formations.

Effect of Substitutions

The allowance of substitutes during a game seems to be a simple rule with no consequences to the game at all. However, substituting can have tactical repercussions. A deep defensive midfielder may be substituted for a fast forward to try to preserve a win or a tie. An extra forward could be substituted to try to win a game or to tie it. Allowing a fourth substitution exclusively for a goalkeeper after the allowed three have taken place can have a big impact on the outcome of a game.

Allowing three additional substitutions during extra time can mean a significant change, particularly during a championship game. The addition of new, fresh players after ninety minutes of regulation could be the difference between winning and losing, and possibly avoid the dreaded penalty shootout.

Effect of Physical Fitness

Increased fitness has come from the application of scientific research. More emphasis is being placed on the development of players' physical assets of speed, power, skill, endurance, and versatility. In the future, the player must be all-around and complete. He must be able to defend and attack effectively according to the circumstances of the game. The training of a player's peripheral vision may prove a significant aspect of a player's overall fitness, particularly for a goalkeeper.

The Future of Team Tactics

As has been mentioned, playing systems are relatively rigid in form and do not change rapidly from one game to another. At the same time, systems do develop and change in the long run. This can be seen clearly from the manner in which the present systems have evolved from the chaotic style of early days, through the defensive center-half game, to the 4-2-4, the 3-3-4, and other formations.

While certain radical alterations to the rules of the game and progress in technical standards have played a part in these changes, it is the constantly changing tactical methods that have been a major influence in the development of playing systems and team formations.

Improved tactics have led to the formation of the many systems in use today. Positional switching and sudden counterattacks have led to the increase in the number of defenders. To sum up, this struggle between offense and defense has given rise to new and improved tactics. In time these changes begin to form a pattern, and a new system begins to emerge.

It will be difficult to forecast the shape of future tactics in football. The experience of the players and the standard of play, rather than the team formations, should ensure the supremacy of football. Players capable of playing the game with skill and versatility, and filling out with initiative to give it life, are all-important in regard to the future of tactics in the people's game.

According to David Barber (2006), archivist at the English FA in Soho Square, London, many other changes in tactics and formations will take place due to improved fitness of the players, and since teams need to win and make money as well, formations will have to be modified as the game changes. He adds that because of changes in the environment, pitches may have to be altered and artificial turf could become the standard, which would in turn modify tactics and formations.

Alum Evans of the Welsh FA (2006) noted that tactics and formations evolved from the laws of the game as they were written back in 1863. For example, as lines were being marked on the pitch, tactics had to be changed as well. He believes that the biggest impact on tactics and formations is that resulting from changes in the laws of the game, as happened when the offside rule was changed.

As Mr. Barber noted above, teams need to make money, and in order to make money they have to win games. Thus, it is likely that the days of the opportunistic goal scorer — players such as Gary Lineker (England), Gerd Muller (Germany), and Ronaldo (Brazil), among others — may give way to the rebirth of the libero and/or the traditional stopper in the next few years.

Considering the way football has evolved since 1863, it is likely that major revolutions in tactics are over, and the future development of tactics will more than likely be in small increments, rather than radically, as in the early years.

All the great tactics of the past such as the 2-3-5, the W-M, catenaccio, and total football came about mostly due to rule changes, as Mr. Evans pointed out, or they simply evolved because the players of the day did not really know how to play the game, had little or no experience, and were therefore less rigid about how the game should be played. In other words, they were more willing to experiment and try new things.

Whether there is a revolution or not, evolution will continue. The move has been apparent in club football for some time; in fact, it may be that 4-2-3-1 is beginning to be supplanted by variants of 4-3-3 at club level, but international football these days lags behind the club game, and the recent 2010 FIFA World Cup confirmed the trend that began to emerge at Euro 2008. Formations, though, are one thing; their employment is completely something else, and this was quite noticeable during the recent World Cup in South Africa by the vast range use of 4-2-3-1s. Spain, when they finally adopted it against Germany and stopped trying to squeeze Fernando Torres and David Villa into the same side, fiddled with the line of three, pulling Xavi back and pushing Andrés Iniesta and Pedro forward so their formation was almost 4-2-1-3, which seems to be the route club football is taking. It has had very attacking fullbacks and has pressed high up the pitch, essentially using the Barcelona formula.

Germany, too, played with a 4-2-3-1 in South Africa, and although Philipp Lahm broke forward occasionally, the German formation was essentially a defensive set-up. Here again goals are the great betrayers; it was bewildering how much praise was heaped on their supposedly fresh, open approach just because they scored four goals in three games. This Germany was superb on the counterattack, and the interaction of the front four — Miroslav Klose, Thomas Müller, Lukas Podolski, and Mesut Ozil — was at times breathtaking. But this was reactive football. In fact, in the South Africa World Cup, reactive football was a major feature, which is one of the reasons the proactive style of Spain was rather welcome in some circles. It's probably too early to highlight it as a definite trend, for the world seemed headed in a similar direction back in 2004 when José Mourinho's Porto won the Champions League and Greece won the European Championship, only for attacking football to return the next season, but after Mourinho's success with Inter, it may be that the great creative boom of the past decade is drawing to a close.

Even the mighty Brazilians had a small element of reactivity, often sitting deep, pressing only when the opponent had crossed the midfield, and then hitting the space behind them. They played an angled 4-2-3-1 that had the advantage of getting Robinho into an area other 4-2-3-1s found difficult to counteract. Although they capitulated miserably in the second half against Holland, and although they have an utter disregard for the samba stereotype of yesteryear, they still are one of the strongest sides in the world. Over the past few years, they have won the Copa América, the Confederations Cup, and finishing at the top of Conmebol qualifying. What a joy it would be if Brazil and Spain could meet in a game carrying so much at stake.

The rise of 4-2-3-1 has had knock-on effects. Attacking fullbacks have become rarer, and the difference in attitude of the respective pairs of fullbacks is more than likely the major difference between the two 4-2-3-1s (Spain vs. Netherlands) that met in the final. It had seemed that the advance of lone-central-striker systems would definitely mean the end of three at the back. As it turns out, nowadays teams are simply intent on surviving, playing for goalless draws, and that is what Uruguay did against France, North Korea against Brazil, and New Zealand on a regular basis. Again, that suggests a preparedness to absorb pressure that it's hard to believe wasn't in some way, if not inspired then at least encouraged, by José Mourinho's success with Inter Milan. There was evidence that a technically inferior side could, through discipline and industry, endure a prolonged assault. It was that battle between proactivity and reactivity that we witnessed in the 2010 final, and it was sadly the Dutch who found themselves cast as the destructive force.

The 2010 World Cup will not be remembered for tactical innovation. What was obvious is that the prevailing 4-2-3-1 will continue to be improved. According to recent reports, 40percent of teams deployed a clear 4-2-3-1 formation at some time or another during the competition. This type of formation has managed to spread to all areas of the football world. Additionally, a higher percentage of teams played a variation of a one-man striker system, further illustrating the paradigm shift in world football.

In the 2006 World Cup, the most popular system was still the regimented 4-4-2 with eight teams using it as their primary system. In fact, only two teams, Portugal and Ivory Coast, used the 4-2-3-1 as their preferred formation throughout their World Cup campaign. Seemingly, within four years a coup d'état has taken place, removing the once popular 4-4-2 with a violent surge to the reactive 4-2-3-1.

So why is the 4-2-3-1 popular now? Well, it offers the opportunity for teams to dominate the midfield area, getting extra numbers in midfield and subsequently being able to control possession. The importance of keeping possession is becoming more and more of a mainstream belief in management, and by playing one-striker up front; it allows a team to do this.

Whether there is a revolution or not, evolution will continue. Over the past few years in the English Premier League there has been a turn back towards 4-4-2 (or 4-4-1-1), but single-striker systems remain common, and in Spain 4-2-3-1 has been the default system for some time. Either way, the situation has emerged whereby a striker's primary function is no longer to score goals, but to create the space for others to do so. Obviously it's advantageous if he can take chances, or even conjure up goals out of nothing, which is what makes Drogba and Fernando Torres so special, but increasingly goals alone are an inadequate measure by which to judge a forward. If the opportunistic goal scorer is not dead yet, it is possible that may be the case in the next ten years or so.

It has become quite obvious that the player with most space is no longer the fullback, but the center-back, which as pointed out earlier, may lead to the return of the libero, something that can already be seen in the performances of Gerard Piqué of Spain. With the liberalization in the off-side law stretching the game so it tends to be played in four bands and not three, it seems likely that in the next few years we will see some elision of the roles of attacking center-back and holding midfielder, and thus to teams effectively playing with three and a half players at the back. A return to the past!

APPENDIX A.
LAWS OF THE GAME

These are the 2009-2010 rules of football as authorized by the International Football Association Board (IFAB) and published by the Fédération Internationale de Football Association (FIFA) — all rights are reserved by FIFA. Their official title is Laws of the Game, and they are the basis for playing football all over the world. The Laws of the Game are reprinted here with the kind permission of FIFA.

FÉDÉRATION INTERNATIONALE DE FOOTBALL ASSOCIATION

President: Joseph S. Blatter
Secretary General: Jérôme Valcke
Address: FIFA-Strasse 20
P.O. Box 8044
Zurich, Switzerland
Telephone: +41 (0)43 222 7777
Telefax: +41 (0)43 222 7878
Internet: www.FIFA.com

INTERNATIONAL FOOTBALL ASSOCIATION BOARD (IFAB)

Members: The Football Association
The Scottish Football Association
The Football Association of Wales
Irish Football Association (1 vote each)
Fédération Internationale de Football Association (FIFA)
(4 votes)

Notes on the Laws of the Game

Modifications

Subject to the agreement of the member association concerned and provided the principles of these Laws are maintained, the Laws may be modified in their application for matches for players of under 16 years of age, for women footballers, for veteran footballers (over 35 years of age) and for players with disabilities.

Any or all of the following modifications are permissible:

- size of the field of play
- size, weight and material of the ball
- width between the goalposts and height of the crossbar from the ground
- duration of the periods of play
- substitutions

Further modifications are only allowed with the consent of the International Football Association Board.

Male and Female

References to the male gender in the Laws of the Game in respect of referees, assistant referees, players and officials are for simplification and apply to both men and women.

Key

A single line in the left-hand margin indicates new Law changes.

Laws

1 — The field of play
2 — The ball
3 — The number of players
4 — The players' equipment
5 — The referee
6 — The assistant referees
7 — The duration of the match
8 — The start and restart of play
9 — The ball in and out of play
10— The method of scoring

11 — Offside
12 — Fouls and misconduct
13 — Free kicks
14 — The penalty kick
15 — The throw-in
16 — The goal kick
17 — The corner kick

Law 1—The Field of Play

Field Surface

Matches may be played on natural or artificial surfaces, according to the rules of the competition.

The color of artificial surfaces must be green.

Where artificial surfaces are used in either competition matches between representative teams of member associations affiliated to FIFA or international club competition matches, the surface must meet the requirements of the FIFA Quality Concept for Football Turf or the International Artificial Turf Standard, unless special dispensation is given by FIFA.

Field Markings

The field of play must be rectangular and marked with lines. These lines belong to the areas of which they are boundaries.

The two longer boundary lines are called touch lines. The two shorter lines are called goal lines.

The field of play is divided into two halves by a halfway line, which joins the midpoints of the two touch lines.

The center mark is indicated at the midpoint of the halfway line. A circle with a radius of 9.15 m (10 yds) is marked around it.

Marks may be made off the field of play, 9.15 m (10 yds) from the corner arc and at right angles to the goal lines and the touch lines, to ensure that defending players retreat this distance when a corner kick is being taken.

Dimensions

The length of the touch line must be greater than the length of the goal line.

Length (touchline):	minimum	90 m	(100 yds)
	maximum	120 m	(130 yds)
Width (goal line):	minimum	45 m	(50 yds)
	maximum	90 m	(100 yds)

All lines must be of the same width, which must be not more than 12 cm (5 ins).

International Matches

Length:	minimum	100 m	(110 yds)
	maximum	110m	(120 yds)
Width:	minimum	65 m	(70 yds)
	maximum	75 m	(80 yds)

The Goal Area

Two lines are drawn at right angles to the goal line, 5.5 m (6 yds) from the inside of each goalpost. These lines extend into the field of play for a distance of 5.5 m (6 yds) and are joined by a line drawn parallel with the goal line. The area bounded by these lines and the goal line is the goal area.

Law 1—The Field of Play

The Penalty Area

Two lines are drawn at right angles to the goal line, 16.5 m (18 yds) from the inside of each goalpost. These lines extend into the field of play for a distance of 16.5 m (18 yds) and are joined by a line drawn parallel with the goal line. The area bounded by these lines and the goal line is the penalty area.

Within each penalty area, a penalty mark is made 11 m (12 yds) from the midpoint between the goalposts and equidistant to them.

An arc of a circle with a radius of 9.15 m (10 yds) from the center of each penalty mark is drawn outside the penalty area.

Flagposts

A flagpost, not less than 1.5 m (5 ft) high, with a non-pointed top and a flag must be placed at each corner.

Flagposts may also be placed at each end of the halfway line, not less than 1 m (1 yd) outside the touch line.

The Corner Arc

A quarter circle with a radius of 1 m (1 yd) from each corner flagpost is drawn inside the field of play.

Goals

A goal must be placed on the center of each goal line.

A goal consists of two upright posts equidistant from the corner flagposts and joined at the top by a horizontal crossbar. The goalposts and crossbar must be made of wood, metal or other approved material. They may be square, rectangular, round or elliptical in shape and must not be dangerous to players. The distance between the posts is 7.32 m (8 yds) and the distance from the lower edge of the crossbar to the ground is 2.44 m (8 ft).

Both goalposts and the crossbar have the same width and depth, which do not exceed 12 cm (5 ins). The goal lines must be of the same width as the goalposts and the crossbar. Nets may be attached to the goals and the ground behind the goal, provided that they are properly supported and do not interfere with the goalkeeper.

The goalposts and crossbars must be white.

Safety

Goals must be anchored securely to the ground. Portable goals may only be used if they satisfy this requirement.

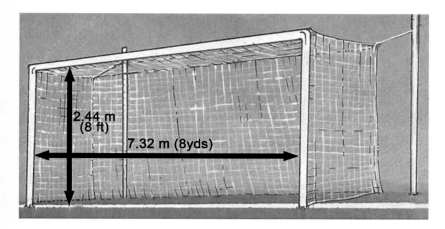

The Field of Play

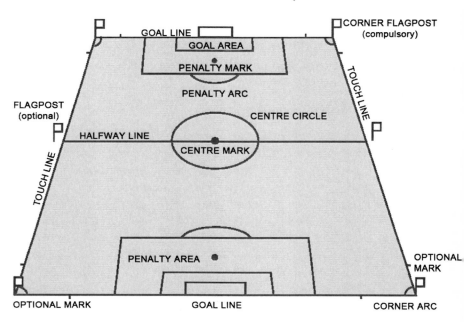

Corner Flagpost

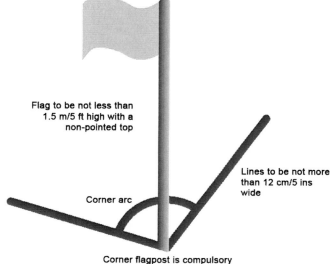

Metric Measurements

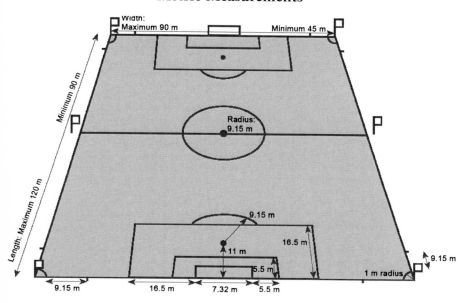

Imperial Measurements

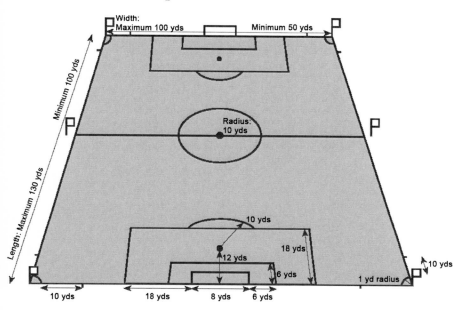

Decisions of the International FA Board

DECISION 1

Where a technical area exists, it must meet the requirements approved by the International FA Board, which are contained in the section of this publication entitled The Technical Area.

Law 2—The Ball

Qualities and Measurements

The ball is:

- spherical
- made of leather or other suitable material
- of a circumference of not more than 70 cm (28 ins) and not less than 68 cm (27 ins)
- not more than 450 g (16 oz) and not less than 410 g (14 oz) in weight at the start of the match
- of a pressure equal to 0.6–1.1 atmosphere (600–1,100 g/cm³) at sea level (8.5 lbs/sq in–15.6 lbs/sq in)

Replacement of a Defective Ball

If the ball bursts or becomes defective during the course of a match:

- the match is stopped
- the match is restarted by dropping the replacement ball at the place where the original ball became defective, unless play was stopped inside the goal area, in which case the referee drops the replacement ball on the goal area line parallel to the goal line at the point nearest to where the original ball was located when play was stopped.

If the ball bursts or becomes defective whilst not in play at a kick-off, goal kick, corner kick, free kick, penalty kick or throw-in:

- the match is restarted accordingly

The ball may not be changed during the match without the authority of the referee.

Decisions of the International FA Board

DECISION 1

In addition to the requirements of Law 2, acceptance of a ball for use in matches played in an official competition organized under the auspices of FIFA or the confederations is conditional upon the ball bearing one of the following: the official FIFA APPROVED logo, the official FIFA INSPECTED logo, the INTERNATIONAL MATCHBALL STANDARD logo. Such a logo on a ball indicates that it has been tested officially and found to be in compliance with specific technical requirements, different for each logo and additional to the minimum specifications stipulated in Law 2. The list of the additional requirements specific to each of the respective logos must be approved by the International FA Board. The institutes conducting the tests are subject to the approval of FIFA.

Member association competitions may also require the use of balls bearing any one of these three logos.

DECISION 2

In matches played in an official competition organized under the auspices of FIFA, the confederations or the member associations, no form of commercial advertising on the ball is permitted, except for the emblem of the competition, the competition organizer and the authorized trademark of the manufacturer. The competition regulations may restrict the size and number of such markings.

Law 3—The Number of Players

Players

A match is played by two teams, each consisting of not more than eleven players, one of whom is the goalkeeper. A match may not start if either team consists of fewer than seven players.

Official Competitions

Up to a maximum of three substitutes may be used in any match played in an official competition organized under the auspices of FIFA, the confederations or the member associations.

The rules of the competition must state how many substitutes may be nominated, from three up to a maximum of seven.

Other Matches

In national A team matches, up to a maximum of six substitutes may be used.

In all other matches, a greater number of substitutes may be used provided that:

- the teams concerned reach agreement on a maximum number
- the referee is informed before the match

If the referee is not informed, or if no agreement is reached before the match, no more than six substitutes are allowed.

All Matches

In all matches, the names of the substitutes must be given to the referee prior to the start of the match. Any substitute whose name is not given to the referee at this time may not take part in the match.

Substitution Procedure

To replace a player with a substitute, the following conditions must be observed:

- the referee must be informed before any proposed substitution is made
- the substitute only enters the field of play after the player being replaced has left and after receiving a signal from the referee
- the substitute only enters the field of play at the halfway line and during a stoppage in the match
- the substitution is completed when a substitute enters the field of play
- from that moment, the substitute becomes a player and the player he has replaced becomes a substituted player
- the substituted player takes no further part in the match
- all substitutes are subject to the authority and jurisdiction of the referee, whether called upon to play or not

Changing the Goalkeeper

Any of the other players may change places with the goalkeeper, provided that:

- the referee is informed before the change is made
- the change is made during a stoppage in the match

Infringements and Sanctions

If a substitute or substituted player enters the field of play without the referee's permission:

- the referee stops play (although not immediately if the substitute or substituted player does not interfere with play)
- the referee cautions him for unsporting behavior and orders him to leave the field of play
- if the referee has stopped play, it is restarted with an indirect free kick for the opposing team from the position of the ball at the time of the stoppage (see Law 13 — Position of Free Kick)

If a player changes places with the goalkeeper without the referee's permission before the change is made:

- the referee allows play to continue
- the referee cautions the players concerned when the ball is next out of play

In the event of any other infringements of this Law:

- the players concerned are cautioned
- the match is restarted with an indirect free kick, to be taken by a player of the opposing team from the position of the ball at the time of the stoppage (see Law 13 — Position of Free Kick)

Players and Substitutes Sent Off

A player who has been sent off before the kick-off may be replaced only by one of the named substitutes.

A named substitute who has been sent off, either before the kick-off or after play has started, may not be replaced.

Law 4—The Players' Equipment

Safety

A player must not use equipment or wear anything that is dangerous to himself or another player (including any kind of jewelry).

Basic Equipment

The basic compulsory equipment of a player comprises the following separate items:

- a jersey or shirt with sleeves — if undergarments are worn, the color of the sleeve must be the same main color as the sleeve of the jersey or shirt.
- shorts — if undershorts are worn, they must be of the same main color as the shorts
- stockings
- shinguards
- footwear

Shinguards

- are covered entirely by the stockings
- are made of rubber, plastic or a similar suitable material
- provide a reasonable degree of protection

Colors

- The two teams must wear colors that distinguish them from each other and also the referee and the assistant referees
- Each goalkeeper must wear colors that distinguish him from the other players, the referee and the assistant referees

Infringements and Sanctions

In the event of any infringement of this Law:

- play need not be stopped
- the player at fault is instructed by the referee to leave the field of play to correct his equipment
- the player leaves the field of play when the ball next ceases to be in play, unless he has already corrected his equipment
- any player required to leave the field of play to correct his equipment must not re-enter without the referee's permission
- the referee checks that the player's equipment is correct before allowing him to re-enter the field of play
- the player is only allowed to re-enter the field of play when the ball is out of play

A player who has been required to leave the field of play because of an infringement of this Law and who re-enters the field of play without the referee's permission must be cautioned.

Restart of Play

If play is stopped by the referee to administer a caution:

- the match is restarted by an indirect free kick taken by a player of the opposing team, from the place where the ball was located when the referee stopped the match (see Law 13 — Position of Free Kick)

Decision of the International FA Board

DECISION 1

Players must not reveal undergarments showing slogans or advertising. The basic compulsory equipment must not have any political, religious or personal statements. A player removing his jersey or shirt to reveal slogans or advertising will be sanctioned by the competition organizer. The team of a player whose basic compulsory equipment has political, religious or personal slogans or statements will be sanctioned by the competition organizer or by FIFA.

Law 5—The Referee

The Authority of the Referee

Each match is controlled by a referee who has full authority to enforce the Laws of the Game in connection with the match to which he has been appointed.

Powers and Duties

The Referee:

- enforces the Laws of the Game
- controls the match in cooperation with the assistant referees and, where applicable, with the fourth official
- ensures that any ball used meets the requirements of Law 2
- ensures that the players' equipment meets the requirements of Law 4
- acts as timekeeper and keeps a record of the match
- stops, suspends or abandons the match, at his discretion, for any infringements of the Laws
- stops, suspends or abandons the match because of outside interference of any kind

- stops the match if, in his opinion, a player is seriously injured and ensures that he is removed from the field of play. An injured player may only return to the field of play after the match has restarted
- allows play to continue until the ball is out of play if a player is, in his opinion, only slightly injured
- ensures that any player bleeding from a wound leaves the field of play. The player may only return on receiving a signal from the referee, who must be satisfied that the bleeding has stopped
- allows play to continue when the team against which an offense has been committed will benefit from such an advantage and penalizes the original offense if the anticipated advantage does not ensue at that time
- punishes the more serious offense when a player commits more than one offense at the same time
- takes disciplinary action against players guilty of cautionable and sending-off offenses. He is not obliged to take this action immediately but must do so when the ball next goes out of play
- takes action against team officials who fail to conduct themselves in a responsible manner and may, at his discretion, expel them from the field of play and its immediate surrounds
- acts on the advice of the assistant referees regarding incidents that he has not seen
- ensures that no unauthorized persons enter the field of play
- indicates the restart of the match after it has been stopped
- provides the appropriate authorities with a match report, which includes information on any disciplinary action taken against players and/or team officials and any other incidents that occurred before, during or after the match

Decisions of the Referee

The decisions of the referee regarding facts connected with play, including whether or not a goal is scored and the result of the match, are final.

The referee may only change a decision on realizing that it is incorrect or, at his discretion, on the advice of an assistant referee or the fourth official, provided that he has not restarted play or terminated the match.

Decisions of the International FA Board
DECISION 1

A referee (or where applicable, an assistant referee or fourth official) is not held liable for:

any kind of injury suffered by a player, official or spectator

any damage to property of any kind

any other loss suffered by any individual, club, company, association or other body, which is due or which may be due to any decision that he may take under the terms of the Laws of the Game or in respect of the normal procedures required to hold, play and control a match.

Such decisions may include:

- *a decision that the condition of the field of play or its surrounds or that the weather conditions are such as to allow or not to allow a match to take place*
- *a decision to abandon a match for whatever reason*
- *a decision as to the suitability of the field equipment and ball used during a match*
- *a decision to stop or not to stop a match due to spectator interference or any problem in spectator areas*
- *a decision to stop or not to stop play to allow an injured player to be removed from the field of play for treatment*
- *a decision to require an injured player to be removed from the field of play for treatment*
- *a decision to allow or not to allow a player to wear certain apparel or equipment*
- *a decision (where he has the authority) to allow or not to allow any persons (including team or stadium officials, security officers, photographers or other media representatives) to be present in the vicinity of the field of play*
- *any other decision that he may take in accordance with the Laws of the Game or in conformity with his duties under the terms of FIFA, confederation, member association or league rules or regulations under which the match is played*

DECISION 2

In tournaments or competitions where a fourth official is appointed, his role and duties must be in accordance with the guidelines approved by the International FA Board, which are contained in this publication.

Law 6—The Assistant Referees

Duties

Two assistant referees may be appointed whose duties, subject to the decision of the referee, are to indicate:

- when the whole of the ball leaves the field of play
- which team is entitled to a corner kick, goal kick or throw-in
- when a player may be penalized for being in an offside position
- when a substitution is requested
- when misconduct or any other incident occurs out of the view of the referee
- when offenses have been committed whenever the assistant referees have a better view than the referee (this includes, in certain circumstances, offenses committed in the penalty area)
- whether, at penalty kicks, the goalkeeper moves off the goal line before the ball is kicked and if the ball crosses the line

Assistance

The assistant referees also assist the referee to control the match in accordance with the Laws of the Game. In particular, they may enter the field of play to help control the 9.15 m (10 yds) distance.

In the event of undue interference or improper conduct, the referee will relieve an assistant referee of his duties and make a report to the appropriate authorities.

Law 7—The Duration of the Match

Periods of Play

The match lasts two equal periods of 45 minutes, unless otherwise mutually agreed between the referee and the two teams. Any agreement to alter the duration of the periods of play (for example, to reduce each half to 40 minutes because of insufficient light) must be made before the start of play and must comply with competition rules.

Half-time Interval

Players are entitled to an interval at half-time.
The half-time interval must not exceed 15 minutes.

Competition rules must state the duration of the half-time interval. The duration of the half-time interval may be altered only with the consent of the referee.

Allowance for Time Lost

Allowance is made in either period for all time lost through:

- substitutions
- assessment of injury to players
- removal of injured players from the field of play for treatment
- wasting time
- any other cause

The allowance for time lost is at the discretion of the referee.

Penalty Kick

If a penalty kick has to be taken or retaken, the duration of either half is extended until the penalty kick is completed.

Abandoned Match

An abandoned match is replayed unless the competition rules provide otherwise.

Law 8—The Start and Restart of Play

Preliminaries

A coin is tossed and the team that wins the toss decides which goal it will attack in the first half of the match.

The other team takes the kick-off to start the match.

The team that wins the toss takes the kick-off to start the second half of the match.

In the second half of the match, the teams change ends and attack the opposite goals.

Kick-off

A kick-off is a way of starting or restarting play:

- at the start of the match
- after a goal has been scored
- at the start of the second half of the match

- at the start of each period of extra time, where applicable A goal may be scored directly from the kick-off.

Procedure

- all players must be in their own half of the field of play
- the opponents of the team taking the kick-off are at least 9.15 m (10 yds) from the ball until it is in play
- the ball must be stationary on the center mark
- the referee gives a signal
- the ball is in play when it is kicked and moves forward
- the kicker must not touch the ball again until it has touched another player

After a team scores a goal, the kick-off is taken by the other team.

Infringements and Sanctions

If the player taking the kick-off touches the ball again before it has touched another player:

- an indirect free kick is awarded to the opposing team to be taken from the position of the ball when the infringement occurred (see Law 13 — Position of Free Kick)

In the event of any other infringement of the kick-off procedure:

- the kick-off is retaken

Dropped Ball

If, while the ball is still in play, the referee is required to stop play temporarily for any reason not mentioned elsewhere in the Laws of the Game, the match is restarted with a dropped ball.

Procedure

The referee drops the ball at the place where it was located when play was stopped, unless play was stopped inside the goal area, in which case the referee drops the ball on the goal area line parallel to the goal line at the point nearest to where the ball was located when play was stopped.

Play restarts when the ball touches the ground.

Infringements and Sanctions

The ball is dropped again:

- if it is touched by a player before it makes contact with the ground
- if the ball leaves the field of play after it makes contact with the ground, without a player touching it

Law 9—The Ball In and Out of Play

Ball Out of Play

The ball is out of play when:

- it has wholly crossed the goal line or touch line whether on the ground or in the air
- play has been stopped by the referee

Ball In Play

The ball is in play at all other times, including when:

- it rebounds off a goalpost, crossbar or corner flagpost and remains in the field of play
- it rebounds off either the referee or an assistant referee when they are on the field of play

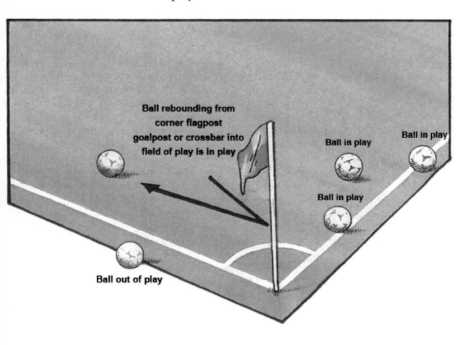

Law 10—The Method of Scoring

Goal Scored

A goal is scored when the whole of the ball passes over the goal line, between the goalposts and under the crossbar, provided that no infringement of the Laws of the Game has been committed previously by the team scoring the goal.

Winning Team

The team scoring the greater number of goals during a match is the winner. If both teams score an equal number of goals, or if no goals are scored, the match is drawn.

Competition Rules

When competition rules require there to be a winning team after a match or home-and-away tie, the only permitted procedures for determining the winning team are those approved by the International FA Board, namely:

- away goals rule
- extra time
- kicks from the penalty mark

Law 11— Offside

Offside Position

It is not an offense in itself to be in an offside position. A player is in an offside position if:

- he is nearer to his opponents' goal line than both the ball and the second-last opponent

A player is not in an offside position if:

- he is in his own half of the field of play or
- he is level with the second-last opponent or
- he is level with the last two opponents

Offence

A player in an offside position is only penalized if, at the moment the ball touches or is played by one of his team, he is, in the opinion of the referee, involved in active play by:

- interfering with play or
- interfering with an opponent or
- gaining an advantage by being in that position

No Offence

There is no offside offense if a player receives the ball directly from:

- a goal kick
- a throw-in
- a corner kick

Infringements and Sanctions

In the event of an offside offense, the referee awards an indirect free kick to the opposing team to be taken from the place where the infringement occurred (see Law 13 — Position of Free Kick).

Law 12 — Fouls and Misconduct

Fouls and misconduct are penalized as follows.

Direct Free Kick

A direct free kick is awarded to the opposing team if a player commits any of the following seven offenses in a manner considered by the referee to be careless, reckless or using excessive force:

- kicks or attempts to kick an opponent
- trips or attempts to trip an opponent
- jumps at an opponent
- charges an opponent
- strikes or attempts to strike an opponent
- pushes an opponent
- tackles an opponent

A direct free kick is also awarded to the opposing team if a player commits any of the following three offenses:

- holds an opponent
- spits at an opponent
- handles the ball deliberately (except for the goalkeeper within his own penalty area)

A direct free kick is taken from the place where the offense occurred (see Law 13 — Position of Free Kick).

Penalty Kick

A penalty kick is awarded if any of the above ten offenses is committed by a player inside his own penalty area, irrespective of the position of the ball, provided it is in play.

Indirect Free Kick

An indirect free kick is awarded to the opposing team if a goalkeeper, inside his own penalty area, commits any of the following four offenses:

- controls the ball with his hands for more than six seconds before releasing it from his possession
- touches the ball again with his hands after he has released it from his possession and before it has touched another player
- touches the ball with his hands after it has been deliberately kicked to him by a teammate

- touches the ball with his hands after he has received it directly from a throw-in taken by a teammate

An indirect free kick is also awarded to the opposing team if, in the opinion of the referee, a player:

- plays in a dangerous manner
- impedes the progress of an opponent
- prevents the goalkeeper from releasing the ball from his hands
- commits any other offense, not previously mentioned in Law 12, for which play is stopped to caution or send off a player

The indirect free kick is taken from the place where the offense occurred (see Law 13 — Position of Free Kick).

Disciplinary Sanctions

The yellow card is used to communicate that a player, substitute or substituted player has been cautioned.

The red card is used to communicate that a player, substitute or substituted player has been sent off.

Only a player, substitute or substituted player may be shown the red or yellow card.

The referee has the authority to take disciplinary sanctions from the moment he enters the field of play until he leaves the field of play after the final whistle.

A player who commits a cautionable or sending-off offense, either on or off the field of play, whether directed towards an opponent, a teammate, the referee, an assistant referee or any other person, is disciplined according to the nature of the offense committed.

Cautionable Offences

A player is cautioned and shown the yellow card if he commits any of the following seven offenses:

- unsporting behavior
- dissent by word or action
- persistent infringement of the Laws of the Game
- delaying the restart of play
- failure to respect the required distance when play is restarted with a corner kick, free kick or throw-in

- entering or re-entering the field of play without the referee's permission
- deliberately leaving the field of play without the referee's permission

A substitute or substituted player is cautioned if he commits any of the following three offenses:

- unsporting behavior
- dissent by word or action
- delaying the restart of play

Sending-off Offences

A player, substitute or substituted player is sent off if he commits any of the following seven offenses:

- serious foul play
- violent conduct
- spitting at an opponent or any other person
- denying the opposing team a goal or an obvious goal-scoring opportunity by deliberately handling the ball (this does not apply to a goalkeeper within his own penalty area)
- denying an obvious goal-scoring opportunity to an opponent moving towards the player's goal by an offense punishable by a free kick or a penalty kick
- using offensive, insulting or abusive language and/or gestures
- receiving a second caution in the same match

A player, substitute or substituted player who has been sent off must leave the vicinity of the field of play and the technical area.

Law 13 — Free Kicks

Types of Free Kick

Free kicks are either direct or indirect.

The Direct Free Kick

BALL ENTERS THE GOAL

- if a direct free kick is kicked directly into the opponents' goal, a goal is awarded

- if a direct free kick is kicked directly into the team's own goal, a corner kick is awarded to the opposing team

The Indirect Free Kick

SIGNAL

The referee indicates an indirect free kick by raising his arm above his head. He maintains his arm in that position until the kick has been taken and the ball has touched another player or goes out of play.

BALL ENTERS THE GOAL

A goal can be scored only if the ball subsequently touches another player before it enters the goal:

- if an indirect free kick is kicked directly into the opponents' goal, a goal kick is awarded
- if an indirect free kick is kicked directly into the team's own goal, a corner kick is awarded to the opposing team

Procedure

For both direct and indirect free kicks, the ball must be stationary when the kick is taken and the kicker must not touch the ball again until it has touched another player.

Position of Free Kick

FREE KICK INSIDE THE PENALTY AREA

Direct or indirect free kick to the defending team:
- all opponents must be at least 9.15 m (10 yds) from the ball
- all opponents must remain outside the penalty area until the ball is in play
- the ball is in play when it is kicked directly out of the penalty area
- a free kick awarded in the goal area may be taken from any point inside that area

Indirect free kick to the attacking team:
- all opponents must be at least 9.15 m (10 yds) from the ball until it is in play, unless they are on their own goal line between the goalposts
- the ball is in play when it is kicked and moves

- an indirect free kick awarded inside the goal area must be taken on the goal area line parallel to the goal line at the point nearest to where the infringement occurred

FREE KICK OUTSIDE THE PENALTY AREA

- all opponents must be at least 9.15 m (10 yds) from the ball until it is in play
- the ball is in play when it is kicked and moves
- the free kick is taken from the place where the infringement occurred or from the position of the ball when the infringement occurred (according to the infringement)

Infringements and Sanctions

If, when a free kick is taken, an opponent is closer to the ball than the required distance:

- the kick is retaken

If, when a free kick is taken by the defending team from inside its own penalty area, the ball is not kicked directly out of the penalty area:

- the kick is retaken

FREE KICK TAKEN BY A PLAYER OTHER THAN THE GOALKEEPER

If, after the ball is in play, the kicker touches the ball again (except with his hands) before it has touched another player:

- an indirect free kick is awarded to the opposing team, the kick to be taken from the place where the infringement occurred (see Law 13 — Position of Free Kick)

If, after the ball is in play, the kicker deliberately handles the ball before it has touched another player:

- a direct free kick is awarded to the opposing team, the kick to be taken from the place where the infringement occurred (see Law 13 — Position of Free Kick)
- a penalty kick is awarded if the infringement occurred inside the kicker's penalty area

FREE KICK TAKEN BY THE GOALKEEPER

If, after the ball is in play, the goalkeeper touches the ball again (except with his hands), before it has touched another player:

- an indirect free kick is awarded to the opposing team, the kick to be taken from the place where the infringement occurred (see Law 13 — Position of Free Kick)

If, after the ball is in play, the goalkeeper deliberately handles the ball before it has touched another player:

- a direct free kick is awarded to the opposing team if the infringement occurred outside the goalkeeper's penalty area, the kick to be taken from the place where the infringement occurred (see Law 13 — Position of Free Kick)
- an indirect free kick is awarded to the opposing team if the infringement occurred inside the goalkeeper's penalty area, the kick to be taken from the place where the infringement occurred (see Law 13 — Position of Free Kick)

Law 14 — The Penalty Kick

A penalty kick is awarded against a team that commits one of the ten offenses for which a direct free kick is awarded, inside its own penalty area and while the ball is in play.

A goal may be scored directly from a penalty kick.

Additional time is allowed for a penalty kick to be taken at the end of each half or at the end of periods of extra time.

Position of the Ball and the Players

The ball:

- must be placed on the penalty mark

The player taking the penalty kick:

- must be properly identified

The defending goalkeeper:

- must remain on his goal line, facing the kicker, between the goalposts until the ball has been kicked

The players other than the kicker must be located:

- inside the field of play
- outside the penalty area

- behind the penalty mark
- at least 9.15 m (10 yds) from the penalty mark

Procedure

- After the players have taken positions in accordance with this Law, the referee signals for the penalty kick to be taken
- The player taking the penalty kick must kick the ball forward
- He must not play the ball again until it has touched another player
- The ball is in play when it is kicked and moves forward

When a penalty kick is taken during the normal course of play, or time has been extended at half-time or full time to allow a penalty kick to be taken or retaken, a goal is awarded if, before passing between the goalposts and under the crossbar:

- the ball touches either or both of the goalposts and/or the crossbar and/or the goalkeeper

The referee decides when a penalty kick has been completed.

Infringements and Sanctions

IF THE REFEREE GIVES THE SIGNAL FOR A PENALTY KICK TO BE TAKEN AND, BEFORE THE BALL IS IN PLAY, ONE OF THE FOLLOWING OCCURS:

the player taking the penalty kick infringes the Laws of the Game:

- the referee allows the kick to be taken
- if the ball enters the goal, the kick is retaken
- if the ball does not enter the goal, the referee stops play and the match is restarted with an indirect free kick to the defending team, from the place where the infringement occurred

the goalkeeper infringes the Laws of the Game:

- the referee allows the kick to be taken
- if the ball enters the goal, a goal is awarded
- if the ball does not enter the goal, the kick is retaken

a teammate of the player taking the kick infringes the Laws of the Game:

- the referee allows the kick to be taken
- if the ball enters the goal, the kick is retaken
- if the ball does not enter the goal, the referee stops play and the

match is restarted with an indirect free kick to the defending team, from the place where the infringement occurred

a teammate of the goalkeeper infringes the Laws of the Game:

- the referee allows the kick to be taken
- if the ball enters the goal, a goal is awarded
- if the ball does not enter the goal, the kick is retaken

a player of both the defending team and the attacking team infringe the Laws of the Game:

- the kick is retaken

IF, AFTER THE PENALTY KICK HAS BEEN TAKEN:

the kicker touches the ball again (except with his hands) before it has touched another player:

- an indirect free kick is awarded to the opposing team, the kick to be taken from the place where the infringement occurred (see Law 13 — Position of Free Kick)

the kicker deliberately handles the ball before it has touched another player:

- a direct free kick is awarded to the opposing team, the kick to be taken from the place where the infringement occurred (see Law 13 — Position of Free Kick)

the ball is touched by an outside agent as it moves forward:

- the kick is retaken

the ball rebounds into the field of play from the goalkeeper, the crossbar or the goalposts, and is then touched by an outside agent:

- the referee stops play
- play is restarted with a dropped ball at the place where it touched the outside agent, unless it touched the outside agent inside the goal area, in which case the referee drops the ball on the goal area line parallel to the goal line at the point nearest to where the ball was located when play was stopped

Law 15—The Throw-In

A throw-in is a method of restarting play.

A throw-in is awarded to the opponents of the player who last touched the ball when the whole of the ball crosses the touch line, either on the ground or in the air.

A goal cannot be scored directly from a throw-in.

Procedure

At the moment of delivering the ball, the thrower:

- faces the field of play
- has part of each foot either on the touch line or on the ground outside the touch line
- holds the ball with both hands
- delivers the ball from behind and over his head
- delivers the ball from the point where it left the field of play

All opponents must stand no less than 2 m (2 yds) from the point at which the throw-in is taken.

The ball is in play when it enters the field of play.

After delivering the ball, the thrower must not touch the ball again until it has touched another player.

Infringements and Sanctions

THROW-IN TAKEN BY A PLAYER OTHER THAN THE GOALKEEPER

If, after the ball is in play, the thrower touches the ball again (except with his hands) before it has touched another player:

- an indirect free kick is awarded to the opposing team, the kick to be taken from the place where the infringement occurred (see Law 13 — Position of Free Kick)

If, after the ball is in play, the thrower deliberately handles the ball before it has touched another player:

- a direct free kick is awarded to the opposing team, the kick to be taken from the place where the infringement occurred (see Law 13 — Position of Free Kick)
- a penalty kick is awarded if the infringement occurred inside the thrower's penalty area

THROW-IN TAKEN BY THE GOALKEEPER

If, after the ball is in play, the goalkeeper touches the ball again (except with his hands), before it has touched another player:

- an indirect free kick is awarded to the opposing team, the kick to be taken from the place where the infringement occurred (see Law 13 — Position of Free Kick)

If, after the ball is in play, the goalkeeper deliberately handles the ball before it has touched another player:

- a direct free kick is awarded to the opposing team if the infringement occurred outside the goalkeeper's penalty area, the kick to be taken from the place where the infringement occurred (see Law 13 — Position of Free Kick)
- an indirect free kick is awarded to the opposing team if the infringement occurred inside the goalkeeper's penalty area, the kick to be taken from the place where the infringement occurred (see Law 13 — Position of Free Kick)

If an opponent unfairly distracts or impedes the thrower:

- he is cautioned for unsporting behavior

For any other infringement of this Law:

- the throw-in is taken by a player of the opposing team

Law 16—The Goal Kick

A goal kick is a method of restarting play.

A goal kick is awarded when the whole of the ball passes over the goal line, either on the ground or in the air, having last touched a player of the attacking team, and a goal is not scored in accordance with Law 10.

A goal may be scored directly from a goal kick, but only against the opposing team.

Procedure

- The ball is kicked from any point within the goal area by a player of the defending team
- Opponents remain outside the penalty area until the ball is in play
- The kicker must not play the ball again until it has touched another player
- The ball is in play when it is kicked directly out of the penalty area

Infringements and Sanctions

If the ball is not kicked directly out of the penalty area from a goal kick:

- the kick is retaken

GOAL KICK TAKEN BY A PLAYER OTHER THAN THE GOALKEEPER

If, after the ball is in play, the kicker touches the ball again (except with his hands) before it has touched another player:

- an indirect free kick is awarded to the opposing team, the kick to be taken from the place where the infringement occurred (see Law 13 — Position of Free Kick)

If, after the ball is in play, the kicker deliberately handles the ball before it has touched another player:

- a direct free kick is awarded to the opposing team, the kick to be taken from the place where the infringement occurred (see Law 13 — Position of Free Kick)
- a penalty kick is awarded if the infringement occurred inside the kicker's penalty area

GOAL KICK TAKEN BY THE GOALKEEPER

If, after the ball is in play, the goalkeeper touches the ball again (except with his hands) before it has touched another player:

- an indirect free kick is awarded to the opposing team, the kick to be taken from the place where the infringement occurred (see Law 13 — Position of Free Kick)

If, after the ball is in play, the goalkeeper deliberately handles the ball before it has touched another player:

- a direct free kick is awarded to the opposing team if the infringement occurred outside the goalkeeper's penalty area, the kick to be taken from the place where the infringement occurred (see Law 13 — Position of Free Kick)
- an indirect free kick is awarded to the opposing team if the infringement occurred inside the goalkeeper's penalty area, the kick to be taken from the place where the infringement occurred (see Law 13 — Position of Free Kick)

In the event of any other infringement of this Law:

• the kick is retaken

Law 17—The Corner Kick

A corner kick is a method of restarting play.

A corner kick is awarded when the whole of the ball passes over the goal line, either on the ground or in the air, having last touched a player of the defending team, and a goal is not scored in accordance with Law 10.

A goal may be scored directly from a corner kick, but only against the opposing team.

Procedure

• The ball must be placed inside the corner arc nearest to the point where the ball crossed the goal line
• The corner flagpost must not be moved
• Opponents must remain at least 9.15 m (10 yds) from the corner arc until the ball is in play
• The ball must be kicked by a player of the attacking team
• The ball is in play when it is kicked and moves
• The kicker must not play the ball again until it has touched another player

Infringements and Sanctions

CORNER KICK TAKEN BY A PLAYER OTHER THAN THE GOALKEEPER

If, after the ball is in play, the kicker touches the ball again (except with his hands) before it has touched another player:

• an indirect free kick is awarded to the opposing team, the kick to be taken from the place where the infringement occurred (see Law 13 — Position of Free Kick)

If, after the ball is in play, the kicker deliberately handles the ball before it has touched another player:

• a direct free kick is awarded to the opposing team, the kick to be taken from the place where the infringement occurred (see Law 13 — Position of Free Kick)

- a penalty kick is awarded if the infringement occurred inside the kicker's penalty area

CORNER KICK TAKEN BY THE GOALKEEPER

If, after the ball is in play, the goalkeeper touches the ball again (except with his hands) before it has touched another player:

- an indirect free kick is awarded to the opposing team, the kick to be taken from the place where the infringement occurred (see Law 13 — Position of Free Kick)

If, after the ball is in play, the goalkeeper deliberately handles the ball before it has touched another player:

- a direct free kick is awarded to the opposing team if the infringement occurred outside the goalkeeper's penalty area, the kick to be taken from the place where the infringement occurred (see Law 13 — Position of Free Kick)
- an indirect free kick is awarded to the opposing team if the infringement occurred inside the goalkeeper's penalty area, the kick to be taken from the place where the infringement occurred (see Law 13 — Position of Free Kick)

In the event of any other infringement:

- the kick is retaken

Procedures to Determine the Winner of a Match or Home-and-Away

Away goals, extra time and kicks from the penalty mark are the three methods approved for determining the winning team where competition rules require there to be a winning team after a match has been drawn.

Away Goals

Competition rules may provide that where teams play each other home and away, if the aggregate score is equal after the second match, any goals scored at the ground of the opposing team will count double.

Extra Time

Competition rules may provide for two further equal periods, not exceeding 15 minutes each, to be played. The conditions of Law 8 will apply.

Kicks from the Penalty Mark

PROCEDURE

- The referee chooses the goal at which the kicks will be taken
- The referee tosses a coin and the team whose captain wins the toss decides whether to take the first or the second kick
- The referee keeps a record of the kicks being taken
- Subject to the conditions explained below, both teams take five kicks
- The kicks are taken alternately by the teams
- If, before both teams have taken five kicks, one has scored more goals than the other could score, even if it were to complete its five kicks, no more kicks are taken
- If, after both teams have taken five kicks, both have scored the same number of goals, or have not scored any goals, kicks continue to be taken in the same order until one team has scored a goal more than the other from the same number of kicks
- A goalkeeper who is injured while kicks are being taken from the penalty mark and is unable to continue as goalkeeper may be replaced by a named substitute provided his team has not used the maximum number of substitutes permitted under the competition rules
- With the exception of the foregoing case, only players who are on the field of play at the end of the match, which includes extra time where appropriate, are eligible to take kicks from the penalty mark
- Each kick is taken by a different player and all eligible players must take a kick before any player can take a second kick
- An eligible player may change places with the goalkeeper at any time when kicks from the penalty mark are being taken
- Only the eligible players and match officials are permitted to remain on the field of play when kicks from the penalty mark are being taken
- All players, except the player taking the kick and the two goalkeepers, must remain within the center circle
- The goalkeeper who is the teammate of the kicker must remain on the field of play, outside the penalty area in which the kicks are being taken, on the goal line where it meets the penalty area boundary line

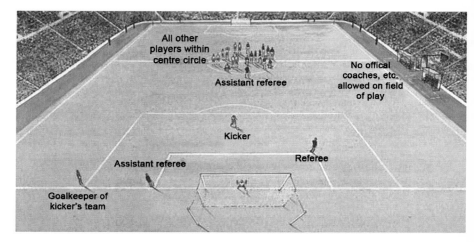

- Unless otherwise stated, the relevant Laws of the Game and International FA Board Decisions apply when kicks from the penalty mark are being taken
- If at the end of the match and before the kicks start to be taken from the penalty mark, one team has a greater number of players than its opponents, it must reduce its numbers to equate with that of its opponents and the team captain must inform the referee of the name and number of each player excluded. Any player thus excluded may not participate in kicks from the penalty mark
- Before the start of kicks from the penalty mark, the referee must ensure that an equal number of players from each team remains within the center circle and they shall take the kicks

The Technical Area

The technical area relates to matches played in stadiums with a designated seated area for technical staff and substitutes as described below.

While the size and position of technical areas may differ between stadiums, the following notes are issued for general guidance:

- the technical area extends 1 m (1 yd) on either side of the designated seated area and extends forward up to a distance of 1 m (1 yd) from the touch line
- it is recommended that markings are used to define this area

- the number of persons permitted to occupy the technical area is defined by the competition rules
- the occupants of the technical area are identified before the beginning of the match in accordance with the competition rules
- only one person at a time is authorized to convey tactical instructions from the technical area
- the coach and other officials must remain within its confines except in special circumstances, for example, a physiotherapist or doctor entering the field of play, with the referee's permission, to assess an injured player
- the coach and other occupants of the technical area must behave in a responsible manner

The Fourth Official and the Reserve Assistant Referee

- A fourth official may be appointed under the competition rules and officiates if any of the three match officials is unable to continue, unless a reserve assistant referee is appointed. He assists the referee at all times
- Prior to the start of the competition, the organizer states clearly whether, if the referee is unable to continue, the fourth official takes over as the referee or whether the senior assistant referee takes over as referee with the fourth official becoming an assistant referee
- The fourth official assists with any administrative duties before, during and after the match, as required by the referee
- He is responsible for assisting with substitution procedures during the match
- He has the authority to check the equipment of substitutes before they enter the field of play. If their equipment does not comply with the Laws of the Game, he informs the referee
- He supervises the replacement balls, where required. If the match ball has to be replaced during a match, he provides another ball, on the instruction of the referee, thus keeping the delay to a minimum
- He must indicate to the referee when the wrong player is cautioned because of mistaken identity or when a player is not sent off having been seen to be given a second caution or when violent conduct

occurs out of the view of the referee and assistant referees. The referee, however, retains the authority to decide on all points connected with play

- After the match, the fourth official must submit a report to the appropriate authorities on any misconduct or other incident that occurred out of the view of the referee and the assistant referees. The fourth official must advise the referee and his assistants of any report being made
- He has the authority to inform the referee of irresponsible behavior by any occupant of the technical area
- A reserve assistant referee may also be appointed under competition rules. His only duty shall be to replace an assistant referee who is unable to continue or to replace the fourth official, as required

APPENDIX B.
GLOSSARY

Football, like any other sport, has its own language. In fact, it has many languages, as the terms and words come from Spanish, Portuguese, German, French, Italian, and of course British English. Which creates a problem for many Americans, since many of the words can be confused with similar or identical words that have different meanings in traditional American sports.

"Tackle" in American football means a player grabbing another player to bring him crashing to the ground. In football that action is prohibited, and to tackle means to use the feet to take away the ball from an opponent's feet.

Most people around the world accept the British definitions for fundamental words and terms. Below is a list of selected words that are commonly used to interpret and understand the people's game.

Advantage rule — The referee does not have to blow the whistle every time he determines there is an infraction. For example, a player may grab another player's jersey in order to stop or slow his forward movement, but fails in his attempt. If the referee stops play he would be penalizing the attacking player, and possibly deny him of a scoring opportunity. Thus, if he chooses not to blow the whistle, the referee would be applying the "advantage rule."

Aggregate score — Many competitions worldwide (except for the Olympics and the World Cup), are played on a knock-out basis. For example, in the Champions Cup two teams play each other twice, home and away. The winner is decided by adding together the scores from the two games. If the aggregate score is tied, then the team that scored more goals in the opponent's stadium (referred as the "away goals" rule) is declared the winner. If the score is still tied under the away goals rule, the an additional 30 minutes of extra time are played, followed by a penalty shoot-out if the score remains tied after extra time.

Ball in and out of play— For the ball to be in or out of play ALL of it must be outside ALL of the sideline or goal line (lines are up to five inches wide). Therefore, if a ball is on the line, then it is still in play, even if the ball is on the ground just outside the field of play. A goal is not scored until all the ball has crossed/passed over the goal line. The player controlling or dribbling the ball does not matter, as he can be standing with both feet outside the field of play, but as long as the ball is in play the game will continue.

Boots— Soccer shoes.

Box— This refers to the penalty area, often called the 18-yard box (16.5 meters) to distinguish it from the 6-yard box (5.5 meters), or keeper's box.

Clear— To kick or head the ball away from the goalmouth, in order to eliminate any possible threat to the goal.

CONCACAF— Confederation of North, Central American and Caribbean Association Football. Regional confederation to which the United States is a member. FIFA has divided the world into six continental confederations: Europe, Asia, Africa, Oceania, South America, and North/Central America and the Caribbean (*USSF Administrative Handbook*, 2009).

Dead ball— When play is stopped and the ball is not moving it is called a dead ball. All free kicks, penalty kicks, and corner kicks are taken from a dead ball, and substitutions are only allowed in dead ball situations.

Defenders/Fullbacks— Position whose primary role is to prevent the opposition from scoring and to delay their attack.

Direct free kick— A goal may be scored directly from a free kick (FIFA, 2009).

FIFA— Fédération Internationale de Football Association, founded in 1904. The world governing body of football associations. All national and international competitions are played under the rules and laws established by FIFA, and any changes in rules must be approved by the organization. (FIFA, 2009).

FIFA World Cup — Quadrennial world championship for all members of FIFA. Played every four years since 1930, excluding 1942 and 1946 due to World War II.

Forwards — Players responsible for scoring the majority of goals.

Free kick — Free kicks can be classified as direct or indirect. They are awarded when a player commits a foul or misconduct as stated by FIFA in the Laws of the Game (2009).

Goalkeeper — Also called "keeper," a player whose priority is to prevent the ball from going into the goal. The keeper is the only player allowed to use the hands, but only within the penalty area.

Halfbacks — Players whose main responsibilities are to organize the attacks and assist in defense.

Indirect free kick — A goal cannot be scored unless the ball has been played or touched by a player other than the kicker (FIFA, 2009).

International Football Association Board (IFAB) — Governing body which reviews, revises, and implements new rules/changes to football worldwide.

Libero — Italian word for "free man." A player whose main job is to mark unguarded attackers behind the last line of defense. Another defensive position.

Manager — The coach and technical advisor of a football team.

Marking — When a player attempts to dispossess an opposing player of the ball, or simply guards him to prevent him from becoming an offensive threat.

Midfielder — Also called halfback. A player who acts as a link between the defense and the offense and usually coordinates and initiates the attacks.

Net/Goalnet — Net placed behind and around the goal to ensure that a goal has been scored.

Offside — "A player is offside when he is nearer the opponents' goal line than the ball at the moment the ball is played, unless he is in his own half of the field; There are at least two opponents nearer to their goal line than he is; The ball was last touched by an opponent or was last played by him. There is no offside following a goalkick, a cornerkick, a throw-in or a dropped ball by the referee" (FIFA, 2009).

Own goal— When a player accidentally kicks, heads, or deflects the ball into his own goal, is called an own goal and is counted as a goal in favor of the opposition. The player is then listed as the scorer with the letters o.g. (for own goal) after his name.

Pitch— The field of play.

Promotion/Relegation— Football leagues around the world have a number of divisions. The weaker clubs are in the lower divisions, and the big clubs are part of the top tier of their respective leagues. The top clubs at the end of a season (generally the first two or three) are promoted to the division above, and those in the bottom including the top tier are relegated to replace them. That is, if the New York Yankees were to finish dead last at the end of their MLB season, they would be demoted to Triple A, and the Triple A team that finishes at the top would be promoted to MLB. For all practical purposes, during a football season across all tiers around the world, there are two competitions: one to decide the champion, and another to decide who gets relegated.

Referee— The only one with a whistle and whose authority is final. He is assisted by two assistant referees (linesmen), but their function is strictly advisory, and the referee can overrule a call made by the assistant referees.

Scoreline— It is the accepted convention worldwide to name the home team first. Thus Arsenal vs. Manchester United means that Arsenal is the home team. A scoreline of Arsenal 2–Man U 1 indicates that Arsenal won the game, but if the scoreline shows Arsenal 1–Man U 2, then it means an away win for Man U. This is vital and important during international competitions when the "aggregate score" is used to determine a winner.

Shoulder Charge — Using the shoulder to knock an opponent off the ball or to unbalance him. The only legal charge in football.

Soccer— The term used in the United States to refer to the game of football.

Stopper— Player whose main job is to guard and defend tightly the opposing striker or most dangerous player, usually the top scorer. Stoppers also are the first to avert an attack by the opposition.

Striker— A forward player in a central position. The top scorer on a team.

Sweeper— The last defensive hope before the goalkeeper. This player's main role is to provide coverage against unguarded attackers and to sweep the defensive line.

Tackle—To use the feet to attempt to take the ball from an opponent's feet. A tackle can be accompanied by a shoulder charge, but not holding, pushing, tripping, or hitting.

Time-out—Only the referee has the authority to stop the clock, and coaches are not permitted to call time-outs.

Transfer fee—Around the world a footballer's contract still belongs to his club even after the contract has expired. When a player is transferred to another club, the new team has to "purchase" the contract, often paying large amounts of money in order to acquire his services. This is known as the transfer fee.

USSF—United States Soccer Federation. The internationally recognized national federation governing body for football in the United States (*USSF Administrative Handbook*, 2009).

Winger—A forward player, whose main responsibility is to spread out the opposing defenders and to make crosses from the sides to teammates in position to score.

APPENDIX C.
IMPORTANT DATES IN THE
EVOLUTION OF FOOTBALL

1860s Football is played with eleven men on the pitch, but there are no tactical formations and passing is still absent. It is generally played with one defender and nine forwards.

1863 The English Football Association is founded in London, England

1870 Forwards are reduced to five or six, but dribbling predominates.

1872 First International: Scotland 0–0 England (Partick, Scotland, attendance: 4,000)

1872 The size of the ball is determined, and touchlines are marked. Crossbars replace goal tapes.

1874 Shin guards are introduced, and a wooden crossbar is added to the goalpost. Teams change sides at halftime, rather than after every goal.

1879 The passing game is introduced by the Scots.

1881 Referees replace umpires.

1882 The one-handed throw-in is replaced by the two-handed throw.

1883 Forwards are reduced to four or five.

1886 First meeting of the International Football Association Board (IFAB).

1891 Goal nets are introduced.

1902 Markings on the pitch are marked as they are in force today.

1904 FIFA is founded.

1908 England beats France in the first Olympic football game.

1913 FIFA joins the IFAB.

1913 The USFA, later known as the USSF, is founded in the USA.

1914 The Brazilian FA is founded.

1923 The first Cup Final is played at Wembley. Bolton Wanderers 2-West Ham 0.

1925 The offside rule is changed to its current format.

1930 Uruguay wins the first World Cup match and the USA finishes third.

1931 First jersey swap takes place after France defeats England for the first time. However, it would be Bobby Moore and Pele's exchange in the 1970 World Cup that popularized this show of respect.

1933 Herbert Chapman develops the WM system.

1950 The USA beats England 1–0 during the World Cup in Brazil.

1958 The Brazilians win the World Cup with a 4-2-4 formation, and become the first nation to win the World Cup outside its continent.

1966 England wins the World Cup on home soil with a 4-4-2 formation.

1970 Brazil beats Italy 4–1 to win the World Cup for a third time.

1974 Franz Beckenbauer and Gerd Muller lead West Germany 2–1 over the Dutch team and "total football" in the World Cup final.

1975 Pele signs an unprecedented $4.5 million contract with the New York Cosmos of the NASL.

1978 Argentina defeats the Dutch team and "total football" 3–1 for the World Cup.

1994 The USA hosts the World Cup.

1996 Professional football reappears in the USA as MLS begins play.

1998 France hosts and wins the World Cup for the first time.

2002 The first ever co-hosted World Cup (Korea/Japan). Brazil wins an unprecedented fifth World Cup and becomes the only nation to win the World Cup outside its continent twice.

2010 South Africa hosts the first ever World Cup on the African continent.

APPENDIX D.
WORLD CUP HISTORY

The FIFA World Cup is open to all eligible national teams from all member nations of FIFA. It takes place every four years, between the Olympic Games cycle, in a pre-determined host nation.

Thirty-two teams take part in the final tournament. A series of regional elimination games are played within each confederation, starting about two years before the finals in order to reduce the number of entries. When the elimination rounds are over, 30 nations join the host nation and the defending champion to make up the final 32.

At the World Cup draw, which is held about six months before the final tournament begins, the 32 nations are divided into eight groups of four. Within each group, each team plays the other three once. First and second place in each group advance to the knock-out stage; the pairings have been decided in advance.

The six regional FIFA Confederations are:

- **AFC** Asian Football Confederation, with 46 members, and six qualify for the final 32.
- **CAF** Confédération Africaine de Football, with 53 members, and six qualify for the final 32.
- **CONCACAF** Confederation of North, Central American and Caribbean Federation with 35 members, and three qualify for the final 32.
- **CONMEBOL** Confederación Sudamericana de Fútbol, with 10 members, and five qualify for the final 32.

- **OFC** Oceania Football Confederation, with 11 members, and two qualify for the final 32.
- **UEFA** Union des Associations Européennes de Football, with 53 members, and 13 qualify for the final 32.

South Africa 2010

European title-holders Spain overcame an opening loss to Switzerland to win their remaining six matches, the last four by a 1–0 scoreline. Champions of Europe and now champions of the world, Spain captured football's Holy Grail for the first time with a 1–0 victory over the Netherlands thanks to Andrés Iniesta's 116th-minute strike at Soccer City. Defeat was especially harsh on the Dutch, who must face up to their third loss in a FIFA World Cup Final, the 1974 and 1978 showpieces also having passed the Oranje by.

- Winner: Spain
- Runners-Up: Netherlands
- Third: Germany
- Fourth: Uruguay

Germany 2006

Italy won its fourth world crown in Germany, beating France on penalties in Berlin. Sadly, Zinedine Zidane's red card was the final's image that resonated around the world. Italy's triumph would be remembered as a team effort with ten different Azzurri players finding the net. It was also a special month for Germany, the goals of Miroslav Klose helping secure third place in a tournament memorable for the festival mood across the host country.

- Winner: Italy
- Runners-Up: France
- Third: Germany
- Fourth: Portugal

Korea/Japan 2002

Brazil became champion for the fifth time with Ronaldo scoring both goals in the final against Germany. This was Asia's first FIFA World Cup and both host nations made history by reaching the knockout rounds. Korea reached the last four. It was indeed a tournament of surprises, as the competition began with France losing to Senegal and closed with Turkey third in the world.

- Winner: Brazil
- Runners-Up: Germany
- Third: Turkey
- Fourth: Republic of Korea

USA v. Czech Republic lined up before their kick-off during the 2006 World Cup.

USA 1994

The United States hosted a very successful FIFA World Cup that became the best attended in history, and ended with Brazil celebrating its first world title since 1970, and fourth overall. Forwards Romario and Bebeto were the Brazilians' star performers while Roberto Baggio was the star for Italy despite his penalty miss during the final. It was the first final to be decided by penalty kicks.

- Winner: Brazil
- Runners-Up: Italy
- Third: Sweden
- Fourth: Bulgaria

Italy 1990

When Lothar Matthaus lifted the FIFA World Cup for Germany, it was Franz Beckenbauer's triumph as well, as he became only the second winner of the trophy as both player and coach. Italy 1990 was low on goals but high on drama — from the feats of Italy's top scorer Toto Schillaci, to the tears of England's Paul Gascoigne, to the historic run of Roger Milla's Cameroon to the quarter-finals.

- Winner: Germany FR
- Runners-Up: Argentina
- Third: Italy
- Fourth: England

Mexico 1986

The FIFA World Cup returned to Mexico for the second time. It was a tournament marked by the mastery of Diego Maradona, as Argentina overcame West Germany in an exciting final. However, the defining match was a quarter-final against England featuring two of history's most famous goals: the "Hand of God" followed by the dribble of the genius of Maradona.

- Winner: Argentina
- Runners-Up: Germany FR
- Third: France
- Fourth: Belgium

Spain 1982

Paolo Rossi was the hero in Spain. His six goals led Italy to a third world crown. The Azzurri defeated a German team that had survived the competition's first penalty shoot-out in a dramatic semifinal against France. Brazil took a small share of the glory for some exciting football before succumbing to Rossi's hat trick in the best game of the tournament.

- Winner: Italy
- Runners-Up: Germany FR
- Third: Poland
- Fourth: France

Argentina 1978

Hosts Argentina captured their first world title as the Netherlands suffered heartache for the second tournament in a row. Mario Kempes sealed Argentina's triumph, scoring twice against the Dutch in the confetti-covered Estadio Monumental and earning the top score. Brazil, denied a place in the final by Argentina's 6–0 win over Peru, took third place from an enterprising Italy side.

- Winner: Argentina
- Runners-Up: Netherlands
- Third: Brazil
- Fourth: Italy

Germany 1974

West Germany was champion on home soil, and just as in 1954 their victory came at the expense of a team widely considered the world's finest. Johan Cruyff's Netherlands "total football" team were favorites before the final, but the hosts, beaten earlier in their competition by their East German neighbors, recovered from a first-minute Dutch goal to win.

- Winner: Germany FR
- Runners-Up: Netherlands
- Third: Poland
- Fourth: Brazil

Mexico 1970

For the first time the FIFA World Cup was broadcast in color, and Brazil's yellow shirts were everywhere. With a healthy Pele and Jairzinho scoring in every game, Mario Zagallo's men were unstoppable. They defeated Italy rather easily in the final and, with this their third triumph, Brazil retained the Jules Rimet Cup.

- Winner: Brazil
- Runners-Up: Italy
- Third: Germany FR
- Fourth: Uruguay

England 1966

England, the country that invented modern football, finally found success on the world's stage. Sir Alf Ramsey's "Wingless Wonders" overcame final opponents West Germany thanks to Geoff Hurst's historic hat trick, though the debate over whether his middle strike crossed the line continues to this day.

- Winner: England
- Runners-Up: Germany FR
- Third: Portugal
- Fourth: Soviet Union

Chile 1962

1966 World Cup ball used for final game, England v. West Germany.

Brazil was a worthy winner and retained the World Cup by defeating Czechoslovakia in the final that showcased the sublime skills of Garrincha. With Pele injured, Garrincha made sure that his teammate's absence was not felt, and he inspired the Seleção to victory and finished as top scorer as well.

- Winner: Brazil
- Runners-Up: Czechoslovakia
- Third: Chile
- Fourth: Yugoslavia

Sweden 1958

Brazil's string of success in the FIFA World Cup began in earnest as they won the world title for the first time. A 17-year-old player, Edson Arantes Do Nascimento, nicknamed "Pele," introduced his prodigious skills to the world in Sweden, epitomizing the Brazilians' attacking flair and scoring six goals, two of them in the final against the hosts.

- Winner: Brazil
- Runners-Up: Sweden
- Third: France
- Fourth: Germany FR

Switzerland 1954

West Germany was surprise winner of the 1954 FIFA World Cup, as they came from two goals down to defeat Hungary in a final forever remembered as the "Miracle of Berne." The Hungarians were unbeaten in 31 matches and scored 25 goals en route to the final — eight of them against the Germans in the first round. Yet it was Fritz Walter, not Ferenc Puskas, who picked up the Jules Rimet Cup.

- Winner: Germany FR
- Runners-Up: Hungary
- Third: Austria
- Fourth: Uruguay

Brazil 1950

Brazil was determined to put on a show, and they built the world's biggest football stadium, the Maracana, for the 1950 FIFA World Cup. Unfortunately, their dream of becoming the world's best died in that huge bowl, as Uruguay captured their second crown by defeating the hosts in front of some 200,000 stunned spectators. It was not the only shock of a tournament where debutants England were humbled by the part-timers from United States by a 1–0 score.

- Winner: Uruguay
- Runners-Up: Brazil

- Third: Sweden
- Fourth: Spain

France 1938

Italy captured a second successive title with a rebuilt team. With Silvio Piola's goals and Giuseppe Meazza's leadership, Italy defeated Hungary in the final, having overcome in the semifinal a Brazil side missing top scorer Leonidas. Three of his strikes came in a 6–5 victory over Poland.

- Winner: Italy
- Runners-Up: Hungary

- Third: Brazil
- Fourth: Sweden

Italy 1934

Italy delighted its fans by coming from behind to beat Czechoslovakia in the first FIFA World Cup Final played on European soil. Angelo Schiavio scored the winning goal for the Azzurri, who had overcome the highly-rated Austrian Wunderteam in the semifinals. It was a tournament missing holders Uruguay, whose refusal to take part made them the first and only champions not to defend their crown.

- Winner: Italy
- Runners-Up: Czechoslovakia

- Third: Germany
- Fourth: Austria

Uruguay 1930

FIFA president Jules Rimet's dream of a world tournament was realized when Uruguay hosted the inaugural FIFA World Cup in its centenary year of its independence. Only four European teams made the long sea journey, and the final was an all–South American affair, with Uruguay defeating neighbors Argentina just as they had done in the 1928 Olympic final. Trailing at half-time, the hosts triumphed 4–2 in the newly built Estadio Centenario to become football's first world champions.

- Winner: Uruguay
- Runners-Up: Argentina

- Third: USA
- Fourth: Yugoslavia

APPENDIX E.
FAMOUS PLAYERS

Virtually every country throughout the history of football has produced great players. These players are the men who have delighted the fans not only with their achievements on and off the pitch but with their personalities as well. They certainly drew spectators who may not have had any previous attachment to the clubs they represented, but who were simply attracted by the beauty of their talents and skills.

These are just some of the players who have been part of systems and formations we have witnessed since the founding of the English FA at Freemasons Tavern back in 1863.

The Players

Luigi Allemandi: A left back and one of the outstanding personalities of the Italian Calcio during the great years of Inter Milan. He played 25 times for his country and would have made more appearances but for a match-fixing scandal. He was accused of having accepted a bribe from a director of Torino FC to fix a match while playing for Juventos in 1927. Despite being one of the best players of his time, he was found guilty of match fixing, and was suspended for life. By the time of his suspension he was playing for Inter Milan, who challenged and won a reprieve of the ban. In 1929 he again played for the Italian team against Czechoslovakia, and went on to win a World Cup Medal in 1934.

Amasildo (Amarildo Tavares de Silveira): He was an attacking inside-left whose slight appearance belied his a wiry frame. He burst onto the international scene at the 1962 World Cup after the great Pele was injured. Amarildo was not expecting to play when he was called to replace "The King" in a decisive match against Spain. Brazil recovered from a goal down to win 2–1 thanks to two late goals from Amarildo, and he scored another goal in the final against Czechoslovakia. A year later his contract was bought by Inter Milan, and he enjoyed a successful career in Italy with Milan and Fiorentina. He won the Italian championship with Fiorentina in 1969.

José Leandro Andrade: He was an old-fashioned winger of the 2-3-5 system, which was used by most of the football world for the first half of the 20th century. He was a stalwart of the great Uruguayan teams of the 1920s and 1930s, winning gold medals at the Olympic games in 1924 and 1928. He played 41 times for his native Uruguay, winning the World Cup in the inaugural 1930 tournament.

Osvaldo Ardiles: Ardiles combined legal and football studies in the mid 1970s when he earned his reputation as a midfield general of Argentina under manager César Luis Menotti. Soon after winning the 1978 World Cup he was the subject of a remarkable transfer to Tottenham Hotspurs of the English League for $500,000 transfer fee, which made him one of the greatest bargains of modern football. He completed his outstanding career, which included Tottenham's FA Cup, in 1984.

Roberto Baggio: He became the world's most expensive player when Juventos bought his contract from Fiorentina on the eve of the 1990 World Cup for $13 million. His transfer provoked three days of riots by angry fans in the streets of Florence, but he proved his value by scoring a glorious goal in the World Cup against Czechoslovakia. He then helped Juventus win the UEFA Cup and was voted player of the year in 1994, despite missing a penalty in the World Cup final shoot-out against Brazil. He won the league with Juventus in 1995 and with Milan in 1996 before moving to Bologna.

Gordon Banks: A product of Chesterfield goalkeeper academy, Banks went on to undying fame with the English national team. Against Brazil in the 1970 World Cup, he made what is considered to be the best World Cup save ever. He flew across his goal to palm away a close-range header from Pele. Banks set all kinds of goalkeeping records, including 73 caps, 23 consecutive international, and seven consecutive shut-outs, which ended with Eusébio's penalty kick in the 1966 World Cup semifinal. His late withdrawal from the 1970 quarter-final probably cost England the match after being 2–0 up; and he lost two FA Cup finals with Leicester.

Franceschino "Franco" Baresi: Perhaps the greatest in a long line of outstanding Italian sweepers. He began as an attacking midfielder with Milan in the late 1970s. In 1987 Baresi made his debut for the Italian side, providing the defensive foundation on which coach Arrigo Sacchi built Milan.

Bebeto (José Roberto Gama de Oliveira): He could have made an international impact earlier in his career, but his temperament seems always to have gotten the best of him. He was outstanding for Flamengo when they won the Rio championship in 1986, and was the club's top scorer four years in a row. He was transferred to Vasco da Gama in 1989 and won Brazil's fans by scoring six goals in the 1989 South American Championship. He then moved to Spain's La Coruna, and then scored three goals for Brazil in the 1994 World Cup and three more in the 1998 tournament.

Franz Beckenbauer: "The Kaise" can boast that he has lifted the World Cup for Germany both as captain in 1974 and as manager in 1990. However, his achievements are the measure of his true greatness. Beckenbauer's innovative strength was through the revolutionary role as an attacking sweeper, which with his majestic calm and precision, he introduced in the 1960s. He spent most of his career with Bayern Munich, and no other German player reached such incredible heights. He was the first German to reach 100 caps, before leaving Bayern Munich for spells with the New York Cosmos of the former NASL and finally with Hamburg, where he ended his career. His honors include: the World Cup in 1974, and runner-up in 1966; the European championship in 1972, and runner-up in 1976; the World Club Cup in 1976; the European Cup in 1974, 1975, and 1976; the European Cup Winners Cup in 1967 and the West German League and Cup. With the New York Cosmos he won the NASL Soccer Bowl in 1977, 1978, and 1979.

Dennis Bergkamp: A youth product of Ajax, Bergkamp starred for Holland at the 1992 European championship, and soon after Inter Milan nabbed him when they outbid Barcelona, Juventus, and AC Milan for $11 million. He never settled in Italy, and in 1995 was transferred to Arsenal for $10 million, inspiring the Gunners to their league and cup double in 1998. He was one of the stars of France '98, scoring a glorious goal against Argentina and guiding Holland to fourth place.

George Best: Possibly the most outstanding British player of all time, despite a career much shorter than it could and should have been. Genius is a word that cannot describe a player with such incredible skills built

into such a small frame: perfect balance, twinkling feet, a surprisingly
high leap, and a keen eye for scoring goals. Georgie Best won the league
with Manchester United, and also won both the European Cup and the
European Player of the Year in 1968. Sadly, fame, fortune, and the temp-
tations of the world beyond football combined to force a sad finale scattered
with retirements and comebacks.

Tomas Brolin: One of Sweden's most outstanding attackers, he was
called to represent his country at Italy '90, and his great displays alerted
Italian clubs. Parma soon bought his services. He starred for Sweden at
the 1992 European championships, scoring a marvelous goal against
England, and then helped Parma to success in the 1993 European Cup
Winners Cup. In 1994 he led Sweden to third place at the World Cup.

Emilio Butragueno: Nicknamed "the Vulture," he was once considered not good enough to play for Real Madrid, yet he became one of its
leaders throughout the 1980s. His close control and talent helped Madrid
win the UEFA Cup in 1985 and 1986, and in both years he also won the
Prix Bravo award as Europe's best young player. He made his scoring debut
for Spain in 1984, and in 1986 became a World Cup sensation when he
scored four times in a five-goal trashing of Denmark in the second round
of the tournament in Mexico.

Claudio Paul Caniggia: He was one of the most intriguing stars of
the 1994 World Cup, after having just completed a 13-month drug suspension in Italy. He scored on his international return in a 3–0 win over
Israel, but was injured when Argentina lost to Romania. Caniggia began
his career with River Plate, and eventually moved to Italy in 1988. His
play was one of Argentina's positive features at the 1990 World Cup, when
he scored the quarter-final winner against Brazil, and was an equalizer in
the semis against Italy. He missed the final due to suspension, and unfortunately Argentina had nothing to offer in attack without him.

Eric Cantona: Cantona had a career that mixed glorious success and
discipline issues. Born in Marseille, he was discovered by Auxerre and
moved to Marseille, his contract sold for $3 million, in 1998. Two months
later he scored in his international debut against West Germany. He was
later banned from the national team for a year for insulting manager Henri
Michel, and bounced around between Bordeaux, Montpellier, and Nimes
before quitting the game after a shouting match with a disciplinary panel.
He later re-launched his career in England, winning the championship in
1992 with Leeds and four more times with Manchester United. A fight

with a Crystal Palace fan cost him another seven-month ban from football. Upon his return he was voted Footballer of the Year and as captain, sealed Man U's double in 1996 by scoring the winning goal in the FA Cup Final against Liverpool. He retired abruptly a year later.

Antonio Carbajal: He set a record at the 1966 World Cup as the only player then to have appeared in five different World Cup tournaments. An agile goalkeeper, he played for Mexico in 1950, 1954, 1958, and in 1962. He retired after the 1966 tournament, having made his first appearance at the 1948 London Olympics. He was presented with FIFA's gold award for his service to the game.

Careca (Antonio de Oliveira Filho): He was one of the spearheads of the world game through the 1980s and 1990s. Born in Brazil, he helped the unrated Guarani team win the 1987-88 national championship. His contract was later sold to São Paulo. He missed the 1982 World Cup to injuries, but made amends with five goals in Mexico in 1986. He was named Brazil's sportsman of the year and eventually transferred to Italy where he partnered with Diego Maradona and won the 1989 UEFA Cup and Italian league title with Napoli.

Bobby Charlton: Charlton is probably the one English player who has ever thrilled a crowd. He won 106 caps, and his name is synonymous with some of the best moments of English football, as well as for his highest tradition of sportsmanship, modesty, and integrity. In 1966 he won the World Cup and the European Footballer of the Year award. In 1968 he scored two goals as Manchester United won the European Cup over Benfica. In 1994 he received his knighthood.

Luis Chilavert: A goalkeeper from Paraguay who is also known for his skills as a free kick specialist, and often took penalties. He scored 62 goals in his professional career, many of them crucial, including eight in international matches. Four of his international goals were scored during Paraguay's qualification for the 2002 FIFA World Cup. As goalkeeper he earned 74 caps for Paraguay, scoring eight goals in his international career. Chilavert was also known for his eccentricity and his at times fiery temper, which brought him his fair share of controversies.

Johan Cruyff: Not only the greatest Dutch player but certainly one of the greatest players of all time. He made his debut at 17 years of age, and his international goal-scoring debut at 19. He went on to inspire Ajax and Holland through the 1970s, during the era of "total football." His position as a center forward was as strange as his number 114 jersey he wore during his career. He always turned up at the "apex" of the attack, and was always meandering the midfield and out on the wings unhinging defenses from all angles and positions. He pulled apart Inter Milan in the 1972 European Cup final and scored both goals for Ajax in their win. In 1973 his contract was sold to Barcelona for a world record transfer fee of $1.5 million, and after his first season Barcelona was crowned champion. In 1974 he captained Holland and their unstoppable total football round after round. No one, it seemed, could handle the inspiring Cruyff until Holland was defeated in the final by West Germany. Holland reached the final again in 1978 when they lost to Argentina in overtime. He retired from the national team in 1978 and joined the Los Angeles Aztecs of the NASL and won the MVP award that same year. Next he moved to the Washington Diplomats. In late 1981, he returned to Holland where he won the Dutch title, first with Ajax and once more with their bitter rivals Feyenoord. In 1984 he returned to Ajax as technical director, and guided Ajax to victory in the European Cup Winners Cup before being appointed Barcelona's manager. In 1992 he managed Barcelona to victory in the European Cup final.

Teofilo Cubillas: A key figure in Peru's greatest international success at the 1970 and 1978 World Cup finals in which he scored a total of 10 goals. A powerful inside left, Cubillas also packed a powerful shot, scoring a memorable goal against Scotland in the 1978 World Cup. He scored 38 goals and won 88 caps for his native Peru.

Kenny Dalglish: The most decorated British footballer, he won 26 major trophies as a player and as a manager, in addition to a record 102 caps for Scotland, including 30 goals. He inspired Celtic to European Cup triumph in 1967 before joining Liverpool in 1977. After his retirement he managed Blackburn Rovers to the 1995 Premier League title and then replaced Kevin Keegan at Newcastle United, guiding them to the 1998 FA Cup final.

Didi (Waldyr Pereira): He was the key to Brazil's 4-2-4 success at the 1958 World Cup. Known as a midfield general, Didi had superb technique and skill. His teammates often commented that he could "make the ball talk" and could drop the ball on a coin from any distance. He was one of the first players to become a proficient goal scorer from set pieces (free kicks), scoring over a dozen of his 31 goals in his 85 appearances for Brazil. He won the World Cup 1958 and 1962.

Alfredo Di Stéfano: He was the most dominant European player of the 1950s and 1960s. His greatness is in, not only his achievement while leading Real Madrid to victory in the first five consecutive European Cup Finals, but in his uncanny individual ability to organize a team to play to his command. Born in the suburbs of Buenos Aires, he made his debut for River Plate in 1944, and in 1947 won the South American Championship with the national team. In 1949 he was lured away to play for Millonarios FC in Colombia, where he was spotted by Real Madrid. That team outbid their rivals Barcelona, who had originally sealed a deal with Di Stefano's old club River Plate. A Spanish court ruled that Di Stefano should play one season for Madrid and one for Barcelona. After a slow start for Real Madrid, Barcelona sold their share to Madrid, and four days later Di Stéfano scored a hat trick in a 5–0 trashing — against none other than Barcelona. He played one season for Espanyol before becoming a coach for Argentina and Spain.

Dunga (Carlos Bledorn Verri): Dunga is one of Brazil's most controversial and criticized players. He won the 1994 World Cup for Brazil as captain in their victory over Italy. Dunga was criticized because as a defensive midfielder player he was strong and a great tackler, but rather clumsy and slow on the ball when compared to the rest of his teammates. Nonetheless, he possessed a strong shot with either foot, and in 1994 coach Carlos Alberto Parreira considered Dunga's tactical discipline vital to Brazil's success. Dunga captained Brazil again in 1998 before losing to France in the final.

Eusébio Da Silva Ferreira: Known popularly simply as Eusebio, he is nicknamed the "black panther" and perhaps the greatest Portuguese player in history. He was actually born in Mozambique, then still one of Portugal's colonies. Fans around the world loved Eusébio not only for his ability and skills, but also for the sportsmanlike way he played the game. At Wembley in the 1968 European Cup final against Manchester United he was stopped in his attempt to score and win the cup for Benfica by Alex Stepney on Man U; Eusébio reacted by patting Stepney on the back and applauding such a worthy opponent. He won the European Cup in 1962 against Real Madrid, and in 1965 was voted European Footballer of the Year. He won the Portuguese championship with Benfica seven times before ending his career in Mexico and Canada. A statue in his honor was unveiled in 1992 at the entrance to Benfica's Estádio da Luz in Lisbon.

Just Fontaine: He secured his place in the annals of history when he scored 13 goals in the 1958 World Cup for France. Born in Morocco, he was a quick and skillful center forward who had only played twice for France before the 1958 World Cup. Sadly, he had to retire in 1961 due to two double fractures to a leg. He was twice top league scorer and totaled 27 goals for France in 20 appearances.

Garrincha (Manoel Francisco dos Santos): He ranked alongside Pele in the national side. A childhood illness left his legs badly twisted, and the surgeons who performed his corrective surgery noted that he would be lucky just to walk again. Yet he went on to become one of the most feared wingers of all time. He was part of Brazil's 1958 World Cup winning side in Sweden, and in 1962 was the dominant Brazilian football personality after an early injury to Pele. Sadly, his personal life was chaotic, and he died prematurely of alcohol poisoning.

Paul Gascoigne: His career was blighted by his own indiscipline and misfortune with injuries. Known as Gazza, he was a great midfielder with a great touch, he was England's star of the 1990 World Cup and was inconsolable when his second yellow card ruled him out of the third place match. Gascoigne left Newcastle for Tottenham and led them to the 1991 FA Cup final, where he suffered a bad knee injury. After missing a year he signed for Lazio, and due to injuries played only 42 games in three years. He moved to Rangers in 1995, and won two league titles, as well as the Scottish Footballer of the Year Award. In 1998 he joined Middlesbrough and soon helped them win promotion to the top tier of English Football. Gazza's English career was over when he was omitted from England's World Cup team in 1998.

Sergio Javier Goycochea: He earned his fame at the 1990 World Cup when he stepped into action during Argentina's match against the Soviet Union after Nery Pumpido broke his leg during the course of the game. He made heroic saves in penalty shootout victories over Yugoslavia and Italy and led Argentina to the final.

Ruud Gullit: He was one of Europe's most outstanding players in the late 1980s and early 1990s. He started his career as a sweeper for Dutch side PSV but soon began to play as a forward after his $10 million move to Milan in 1987. A year later he led Holland to victory in the European championship, and won the European Cup with Milan.

Gheorghe Hagi: He played for Romania's youth team at 15, and was a top league player by 17. He started his international career at 18. In 1985 he scored 20 goals and in 1986, 31. After the 1990 World Cup he played in Spain and Italy, and then returned to Spain's Barcelona after an inspiring performance at the 1994 World Cup in which he led Romania to third place. He played again at the 1998 World Cup.

Rene Higuita: Higuita played the majority of his goalkeeping career with Colombian side Atlético Nacional, where he helped the team win the Colombian League on numerous occasions as well as the Copa Libertadores and Copa Interamericana, both in 1989. He is known for scoring throughout his career from penalties and free-kicks, and scored eight goals from 68 international caps for the Colombian national team. Higuita is also famed for inventing the scorpion kick, a clearance in which the keeper jumps forward, arches his legs over his head, and in doing so kicks the ball away with his heels. This save earned him notoriety when he pulled it off in a friendly game against England in September 1995, blocking a shot by Jamie Redknapp. On the pitch, Higuita was known for his eccentric playing style, often taking unnecessary risks and actively trying to score goals. Because of his eccentricity he was also prone to blunders, and it was a blunder that knocked Colombia out of the 1990 World Cup, when he seemingly dithered with the ball at his feet near the halfway line enabling Cameroon's striker Roger Milla to dispossess him and score, putting Cameroon through to the quarter-finals. Because of such behavior, Higuita was nicknamed "El Loco" by media and fans alike.

Jairzinio (Jair) Ventura Filho: He signed with Brazil's Botafogo at 15 and played on the same 1966 World Cup team as his hero Garrincha. In 1970 he made history by scoring in every round of the World Cup on the way to victory. He won the South American Club Cup with Cruzeiro at the age of 32.

Pat Jennings: A keeper with character and charm equal to his size. He retired from football by earning his 119th cap on his 41st birthday. Jennings played over 1,000 senior matches in a 24-year career, won two FA Cups, and lost in two others. He also scored a goal with a punt in the 1967 Charity Shield game against Manchester United. He is to this date one of the finest British keepers of all time.

Kevin Keegan: He is the only British player to have won the European Footballer of the Year award twice. At Liverpool he was a success, first in his original position as an outside right, then as a free attacking forward. He won two league titles with Liverpool, and won a European Cup with Hamburg in 1977.

Mario Alberto Kempes: Kempes was an aggressive striker who had a first taste of World Cup football in 1974, and soon earned a transfer to

Spain from Argentina's River Plate to play for Valencia. In 1978 he was the only foreign based Argentinean to be called to play in the World Cup squad under Luis Cesar Menotti. He was the tournament top scorer with six goals, including two in the victory over Holland in the final.

Jurgen Klinsmann: He won Germany's Footballer of the Year on his first Bundesliga spell with VfB Stuttgart. He spent three years at Inter Milan before moving to France with Monaco, and subsequently to England to play for Tottenham before returning to Germany and Bayern Munich in 1995. In 1996 he won the UEFA Cup with Bayern, and eventually the World Cup with Germany in 1990, and the European Championship in 1996. He retired from international football after the 1998 World Cup.

Sandor Kocsis: At attacking inside right for Honved and Hungary in the 1950s, Kocsis along with inside forward Ferenc Puskas were part of the great Hungarian team known as the "Magic Magyars." He scored 75 goals in 68 internationals, and was three-time Hungarian league top scorer. He also scored 11 goals at the 1956 World Cup. In 1956, after the Hungarian revolution, he joined Barcelona and won the Fairs Cup in 1960.

Leonidas da Silva: He was Brazil's superstar of the 1930s and although he only earned 23 caps, it is believed that he is the inventor of the "bicycle kick," which he performed when he scored twice during his international debut against Uruguay in 1932. He was top scorer at the 1938 World Cup with eight goals.

Gary Lineker: His smiling sincerity and his incredible skill for scoring made him a popular figure. He scored 48 goals for England, ten of which were in the World Cup. He also won an FA Cup, but retired early after suffering injuries in Japan.

Josef "Sepp" Maier: He reached the pinnacle of his career in 1974 when he won the European Cup with Bayern Munich and a few weeks later the World Cup for West Germany on home soil. He was a talented goalkeeper and played 473 league matches, and made his international debut in the 1966 World Cup. Additionally, he won the European Cup three times with Bayern and the World Club in 1976.

Paolo Maldini: He began his career with Milan's youth squad, and played for the first team at age 17. He won the European Cup in 1989, 1990, and 1994, and was soon acclaimed as one of the finest all-around players in the world after helping Italy reach the final of the 1994 World Cup. He was voted 1994 World Player of the Year, and captained the Italian national team under the management of his father, Cesare Maldini, at the 1998 World Cup.

Diego Armando Maradona: He was not just the best player in the world during the 1980s and early 1990s, he was also one of the most controversial and enigmatic. He was unable to appear in public without arousing the most contrasting of emotions. His admirers in Argentina during his years with Boca Juniors considered him a god, and the *tifosi* (fans) in Italy where he triumphed with Napoli worshipped his shoelaces. All of Argentina idolized him after he led them to World Cup victory in 1986. English fans are still angry over his "hand of God" goal, but fans all over remember clearly his other goal in the same game when he controlled the ball inside his own half, and outwitted five English players and goalkeeper Peter Shilton, before gliding to the back of the net one of the greatest goals in World Cup history. After the 1990 World Cup, a drug test showed traces of cocaine, and he was banned for 15 months. He returned to Argentina and was arrested there for cocaine procession. He made a disappointing return to Sevilla in Spain, and his return to the 1994 World Cup ended with another failed drug test and a new 15-month ban. He won a league title with Napoli in 1987 and a UEFA Cup in 1988.

Lothar Matthaus: An outstanding leader for Germany's midfield and an excellent sweeper. He reached his zenith in 1990 when he captained the West German World Cup–winning team, and was voted Player of the Tournament by the world's media. He won the UEFA Cup with Bayern Munich in 1996 and the league title as well. He returned to the World Cup at age 37 in 1998.

Stanley Matthews: He was probably the first great player of the modern era. His nickname, the "wizard of dribble," stayed with him until the last days of his career when he returned to play for his original club, Stoke City. He retired at age 50, but insisted he could have played a few more years. Matthews was one of the players at the 1950 World Cup when the USA defeated the English side by a 1–0 score. An outside right, he was an inspiring personality for all youngsters to emulate. He started his professional career for Stoke City in 1932, and made his English debut in 1934 against Wales. In 1948 he was voted Footballer of the Year, and he won the FA Cup with Blackpool in 1953. In 1957 he played the last of his 84 caps in a World Cup qualifying victory over Denmark. In 1961 he returned to Stoke for a modest fee at 46 years of age, and was the leader in a successful campaign to get the team back to the first division. He retired in

1965 after a star-filled farewell match at Stoke's Victoria Ground featuring the likes of Di Stefano, Puskas, and Yashin. He was knighted in 1965.

Roger Milla: He delighted the crowds as a center forward at the 1990 World Cup with his celebratory dances around the corner flags. His goals, and in particular the one against Colombia, made him the first player to be named African Footballer of the Year twice. He played most of his football career in France, winning the league with Monaco in 1980 and in 1981 with Bastia. At age 42 he became the oldest player ever to appear in the World Cup, for his native Cameroon in 1994.

Bobby Moore: The inspirational ice-cool captain of England's victory at the 1966 World Cup. He led by example and won an FA Cup, a European Cup Winners Cup with West Ham, and of course the 1966 World Cup. Unfortunately he developed cancer and died in 1993.

Gerd Muller: A short and stocky center forward for Bayern Munich, he had a keen eye for scoring goals, and was a powerful header as well. His goals helped Bayern win the European Cup Winners Cup, and he went on to score over 600 goals in the Bundesliga, and an incredible 68 goals in 62 internationals. His most famous goal was his last at the 1974 World Cup which helped Germany defeat Holland in the final. He won the European Cup three times.

Johan Neeskens: An aggressive, intelligent midfielder who was perfect for the "total football" concept set by Ajax and Holland in the early 1970s. Neeskens was the structure that supported the more technical skills of teammates such as Cruyff. He scored 17 goals in 49 internationals. With Ajax, Neeskens won the European Cup, the Dutch League, and the Dutch Cup. In 1974 he moved to Barcelona where he won the Spanish Cup and the European Cup Winners Cup.

Daniel Passarella: One of the special kind of players who has captured the World Cup as a winning captain. His moment took place at River Plate stadium — his club team home ground — in 1978, when he guided the Argentinean team as a central defender. He powered the midfield to serve Ardiles and Kempes with his extraordinary free-kicks and at strength in the air during corner kicks, which added pressure on opposing defenses. He later guided Argentina in France 1998.

Pele (Edson Arantes do Nascimento): remains to this day a great example of inspiration, not just for football, but to sports the world over. He was a poor boy who at 17 broke onto the world stage and reached peaks of achievement, fame, and fortune. Yet he retained his innate sense of sportsmanship, a love and passion for his calling, and the love, respect, and admiration of teammates and opponents alike. Pele started his career at age 15 with his club Santos. Soon he earned national and then international recognition when at age 16 he debuted for Brazil in a match against Argentina. At age 17 he won the 1958 World Cup, scoring one of the unforgettable goals in the final against Sweden. Santos was quick to see his talents, and began touring the world for lucrative match fees. The income from these tours allowed Santos to buy a supporting cast, which helped them win the World Club Championship in 1962 and 1963. Pele missed the 1962 World Cup because of an injury in the first round. In 1966, he again led Brazil in England, but unfortunately, the referees were unprepared to give players of skill and creativity the necessary protection; he missed the rest of the tournament after a series of vicious tackles and had to be carried off the pitch. Four years later at Mexico 1970, Pele took revenge in a magnificent way. As long as the game of football is played, the 1970 finals will be revered as the glorification of a great player at his very best, and the final game against Italy as the best World Cup final ever. He remains the only player to have won the World Cup three times. In 1975 he ended an 18-month retirement to play for the New York Cosmos of the NASL for a record $4.5 million three-year contract. He retired after guiding the Cosmos to their third NASL Soccer Bowl title.

Michel Platini: He first appeared on the international stage at the 1976 Olympics in Montreal, and two years later he played in the 1978 World Cup in Argentina. In 1982, he inspired France to a dramatic semi-final defeat against West Germany. He joined Juventus after the World Cup, where he was three times the top scorer in the Italian league. In 1985 he scored the winning goal to win the European Cup for Juventus. He guided France as manager to the finals of the 1992 European Championship, and later became the lead organizer of the 1998 World Cup in France. He currently serves as president of UEFA.

Ferenc Puskas: One of the greatest players of all time, and a symbol of the legendary "Magic Magyars" of Hungary who dominated European football in the 1950s, and who remain as perhaps one of the two greatest teams never to have won the World Cup (Holland of the 1970s being the other). An inside left, Puskas was terrorizing goalkeepers by age 16 with his "magical" left foot and the power of his shot. It has been written that he rarely used his right foot — except to stand on — but his left was so powerful that he hardly ever needed it. By the age of 18 he was part of Hungary's national team where, along with Sandor Kocsis, he became part of the new tactical concept of two inside forwards to spearhead the attack. In 1952 he captained Hungary to a gold medal at the Olympics, and in 1953 he inspired Hungary to a historic 6–3 win over England at Wembley. The following year they trashed the English 7–1 in Budapest, and were the favorites to win the World Cup in 1954. However, they lost to West Germany 3–2 despite leading early by 2–0. In 1958 he signed to Real Madrid. He was part of Spain's World Cup team at the 1962 finals in Chile. He was top scorer in Spain for four years and his partnership with Alfredo Di Stefano at Real Madrid was one of the best of all time.

Frank Rijkaard: One of the most versatile players at both club and country. He turned professional under Johan Cruyff at Ajax in 1979 and debuted for Holland at age 19. During seven years at Ajax, he won the Dutch league and the Dutch Cup three times and the European Cup Winners Cup once. In 1988 he signed to Milan and for five seasons played alongside his countrymen Marco van Basten and Ruud Gullit. Rijkaard won the European Cup twice: in 1989 against Steaua Bucuresti and in 1990 against Benfica. He won the Serie A championship twice, and in 1990 in the European Cup final he scored the only goal, to win the cup for Milan. In 1993 he returned to Ajax where he won the first two of three consecutive Dutch Championships. Ajax was the unbeaten champion of the Netherlands in the 1994-95 season and carried that success into Europe. In his final game, Rijkaard won the European Cup (which had been renamed as the Champions League) with a 1–0 victory over his former team Milan in the 1995 final.

Roberto Rivelino: A deep left winger who was not particularly quick but who had a superb technique with his banana-bending free kicks and corners. He earned over 100 caps, and was part of the successful Brazilian campaign in the 1970 FIFA World Cup, scoring three goals, including a powerful free-kick against Czechoslovakia, which earned him the nickname "Patada Atómica" (Atomic Kick) from Mexican fans. Rivelino also played in the 1974 and 1978 FIFA World Cups, though with less success (fourth and third places, respectively).

Ronaldo (Ronaldo Luiz Nazario da Lima): He was one of the most talked about players in Europe, being one of the most prolific scorers in the world in the 1990s and the early 2000s. He won his first Ballon d'Or as the European Footballer of the Year in 1997, and again won the award in 2002. Additionally, he is one of only two men to have won the FIFA

Player of the Year award three times (Zinedine Zidane is the other). Ronaldo played for Brazil in 97 international matches, amassing 62 goals. He was part of the Brazilian squad that won the 1994 and 2002 World Cups. During the 2006 FIFA World Cup, Ronaldo became the highest goal scorer in the history of the World Cup with his fifteenth goal, sur-passing Gerd Muller's previous record of 14.

Paolo Rossi: He made his debut in professional Italian football with Como, to which Juventus had sent him to gain experience after three oper-ations on his knees. They tried to get him back but were outbid by Perugia, who paid a world record fee of $5.5 million. While at Perugia he was involved in a famous betting scandal (known as Totonero), and as a result of this Rossi was disqualified for three years, though this was later reduced to two years. He returned just in time to lead Italy to the 1982 World Cup triumph, where he led in goal scoring with six goals. Rossi scored a total of 20 goals in 48 caps for Italy. Undoubtedly, his most important goal was the winner against Brazil in the 1982 World Cup which completed a famous hat trick and enabled the Azzurri to advance at the expense of the South Americans. He retired at 29.

Hugo Sanchez: A Mexican player who was top league scorer in Spain for five seasons in a row in the late 1980s and early 1990s. Sanchez played twelve seasons in the Spanish league and is the second highest goal scorer in the history of that league. He also played for Mexico's national team for 17 years and participated in the World Cups of 1978, 1986, and 1994. He won two championships, as head coach of the club Pumas de la UNAM and with Club Necaxa, both teams in the Mexican Primera Division. He also had a sixteen-month stint with the Mexican national team which ended in 2008.

Djalma Santos: The cornerstone of the Brazilian side which won the 1958 and 1962 World Cup, and lost in 1966. He became the first Brazilian to earn 100 caps. Santos is considered to be one of the greatest right-backs of all time. While primarily known for his defensive skills, he often ven-tured up-field and displayed some impressive attacking skills.

Peter Schmeichel: Voted the best goalkeeper in 1992 and 1993, he is best remembered for his most successful years at English club Manchester United, whom he captained to the 1999 UEFA Champions League to com-plete the Treble. He was a key member of the Danish national team that won Euro 92. Schmeichel is also known for his trademark shouts at his defense. He would often berate the defenders for blunders and poor defending and would occasionally single out individual defensive players to make his feelings heard. Today, he is widely regarded as one of the greatest goalkeepers in the history of football.

Uwe Seeler: The central figure of West Germany's team in the 1960s and 1970s. Seeler followed in his father's footsteps as a player for Hamburg SV, making his first team debut in 1954 in a German Cup match, scoring four goals. He was a gifted striker who, among other things, was renowned for his overhead kick. He scored 137 times in 239 Bundesliga games, 43 times in 72 international games for the German national team, and 21 times in 29 European club tournament games.

Alan Shearer: He played as a striker in the top level of English league football for Southampton, Blackburn Rovers, Newcastle United, and for the England national team. Considered heir apparent to Gary Liniker, he is widely considered as one of the greatest strikers of all time, being both Newcastle's and the Premier League's record goal scorer. He earned 63 caps and scored 30 goal for the English team.

Peter Shilton: A former goalkeeper who holds the record for playing more games for England than any other player. His international career earned him 125 caps, making him England's most capped player. His last appearance for England came during the 1990 World Cup, and it was his 17th game in such competition. He conceded 80 goals in his international career, each one a blow to such a perfectionist. He was the English keeper when Maradona scored his famous "hand of God" goal. A famous photograph subsequently showed Maradona out-jumping Shilton and his fist making contact with the ball as Shilton was still midway through his own stretch, arm extended but, curiously, jumping only an inch or two. Shilton largely escaped criticism for the goal because the English media focused on Maradona's cheating.

Hristo Stoichkov: He was a member of the Bulgarian national team that finished fourth at the 1994 World Cup, and aside from his footballing skills, he was notable for his on-pitch temper. In 1996 he moved to Barcelona, where he was part of Johan Cruyff's "Dream Team." Stoichkov helped Barcelona to one of the most successful eras of the club, winning the Primera Division four years in a row between 1991 and 1994 and the European Cup after defeating Sampdoria in 1992. During his stay in Barcelona, he had become an idol to the club's fans, and was Barca's most popular player at the time, having earned a place in the supporters' hearts much like Johan Neeskens in the past. Stoichkov played as a left winger who was known for his explosive acceleration and speed dribbling, and for taking unpredictable shots on goal. He was also notable for taking free kicks and penalties as well as being among the best crossers in the world at his prime. He gained much popularity because of his aggressive temper on the pitch, and he could often be seen arguing with the referee or with his opponents. He was honored as European Footballer of the Year in 1994 and scored 37 goals in 83 appearances for Bulgaria.

Tostão (Eduardo Goncalves de Andrade): He was a small but nimble center forward known as the "white Pele" when he made his debut for Brazil at the 1966 World Cup. In the 1970 FIFA World Cup, Tostão scored two of his 32 goals for Brazil, as the national team won its third World Cup, while finding the net on 19 occasions. The previous year, after being hit in the face by a ball during a match against Corinthians, he suffered a detached retina from which he never fully recovered. A qualified doctor, he recognized that the longer he played, the greater the risk of permanent injury, and he retired at the tender age of 26 to become an eye specialist.

Carlos Valderrama: His mass of blond, frizzy hair made him one of Colombia's most recognizable footballers. He was voted South American Footballer of the year in 1987 after leading Colombia to a third place in the Copa America. He won the award again in 1994 after guiding Colombia to an impressive record, including a 5–0 victory over Argentina in Buenos Aires. He earned 111 caps and scored 11 goals in his international career. Valderrama was a pleasure to watch when he had the ball at his quick and light feet, giving the impression of gliding as opposed to running. Perhaps his most remarkable strengths were his positioning and passing accuracy. These were the reason he could play at walking pace: with one or two touches on the ball he would do enough damage to make himself felt. Another very distinctive quality was that Valderrama was completely two-footed when dribbling and passing the ball. This, combined with his quick-footed technique made it near impossible to intercept his passes; his two-footed ability was very apparent when he played his trademark one-two plays.

Marco Van Basten: He is regarded as one of the greatest forwards of all time and scored 277 goals in a high-profile career cut short by injury. Known for his strength on the ball, his tactical awareness, and his spec-tacular strikes and volleys, Van Basten was named European Footballer of the Year three times (1988, '89, and '92) and FIFA World Player of the Year in 1992. He earned 58 caps and scored 24 goals for the Dutch national team. During his tenure with Ajax he won the UEFA Cup Winners Cup, the Dutch league three times, and the Dutch Cup three times. In 1987 he signed with Milan, where he won the European Cup twice, the Intercontinental Cup twice, the European Supercup twice, the Italian league thrice, and the Supercoppa Italiana three times as well.

George Weah: Weah spent 14 years of his professional football career playing for clubs in France, Italy, and England, winning titles in these three countries. In 1995, he was named FIFA World Player of the Year, European Footballer of the Year, and African Footballer of the Year. Weah has since become a humanitarian and politician in Liberia, and ran unsuccessfully in the 2005 Liberian presidential election. For all his remarkable achievements, Weah is the only FIFA World Player of the Year who failed to qualify for FIFA World Cup with his national team.

Lev Yashin: A Soviet goalkeeper considered by many as probably the best keeper of all times. In Latin America he was called "Black Spider" and in Europe the "Black Panther." Portugal's Eusébio described him as "the peerless goalkeeper of the century." His fame spread around the world, not only for his ability to stop shots that no one else could reach, but also for his role as a great sportsman and ambassador of the game. He spent his entire professional football career with Dynamo Moscow, from 1949 to 1971, winning the USSR football championship five times and the USSR Cup three times. He also won the gold medal at the Melbourne Games in 1958, and the European Cup with the Soviet Union in 1960, earning 75 caps. In 1963 he was voted European Footballer of the Year.

Zinedine Zidane: He proved to be one of the world's finest midfielders when he scored twice in the 1998 World Cup for France, and became a national hero after he masterminded a 3–0 victory over Brazil, and lived to his reputation as the new Platini. At the club level he won the 2002 UEFA Champions League and a La Liga title with Real Madrid. Additionally, he won two Serie A league championships with Juventus. Zidane and Ronaldo are the only three-time FIFA World Player of the Year winners; Zidane also won the Ballon d'Or in 1998. For all his talents and glorious career he will always be remembered for head-butting Marco Materazzi in the chest in the 110th minute of the final game against Italy. He was sent off and was unable to participate in the penalty shoot-out, which Italy won 5–3. He earned an impressive 108 caps for France and scored 31 times.

APPENDIX F.
FOOTBALL FACTS

- On average, each player in a match has the ball for only three minutes, the time it takes to soft-boil an egg.
- In 1965, substitutes were allowed for the first time, but only when a player was injured. Substitutes featured in the World Cup for the first time in 1970.
- Luis Chilavert, goalkeeper for Paraguay, rushed out of his goal and scored for his team in a match against Argentina in 1998. The final score was 1–1.
- The first person to score from a penalty in a World Cup was Johan Neskens from Holland in 1974.
- In the 1994 World Cup, Russia failed to qualify for the second round even though they scored more goals in the first round of the competition than any other team.
- The referee for the 1930 World Cup final wore a shirt, tie, jacket, and knickerbockers.
- Johann Cruyff's mother was a cleaner for the club Ajax in Amsterdam, Holland. When she persuaded them to give her then 10-year old son a trial, they signed him as a youth player. He went on to become an international football star.
- The goal crossbar was introduced in 1875, and the goal net became mandatory in 1892.
- The first time that teams used numbered jerseys in an FA Cup final was in 1933. Everton wore numbers 1 to 11, and Manchester City wore 12 to 22.

- Eight of the players who won the World Cup for Brazil in 1958 were on the team that retained the World Cup in 1962.
- Only eight different countries have won the World Cup, although there have been 18 finals.
- The FA Cup is the oldest competition in football. The highest scoring FA Cup victory was on October 15, 1887, when Preston North End defeated Hyde United 26–0 in the first round of the competition. The score was 12–0 at half time and 25–0 at 90 minutes. The final goal was scored in the extra five minutes added by the referee.
- Pele scored 1,283 goals in his professional career.
- Half of the world's registered football players are from Asia. Hide Nakata was one of the first Japanese players to make a career outside his country.
- After Brazil defeated Italy 4–1 in the 1970 World Cup, reporters pursued Pele into the locker room and interviewed him while he was in the shower.
- Uruguay, the host nation of the first World Cup in 1930, offered to pay travel expenses for all the teams.
- The first international match played by a side with 12 players was in 1952, between France and Northern Ireland. One of the French players was injured and substituted, but after treatment he continued playing, and no one noticed until half-time.
- Two pairs of brothers, John and Mel Charles and Len and Ivor Allchurch, played on the Welsh national team that defeated Northern Ireland 3–2 in 1955. John Charles scored a hat trick.
- Brazil has won the World Cup a record five times — more than any other country.
- The oldest football club in the world is Sheffield FC, formed in 1857. The club has never played at the top echelon of English football.
- Lev Yashin of Russia is the only goalkeeper who has been chosen as European Footballer of the Year.
- In 1999, Manchester United became the first team to win the treble of the Premier League, the FA Cup, and the Champions League.
- Real Madrid has won the European Champions League eight times, more than any other team.
- In 1957, Sir Stanley Matthews became the oldest footballer to play for England when he won his 84th international cap at the age of 42. He continued playing until he was 50 years old.

- The first recorded use of floodlights was at Bramall Lane, Sheffield, in 1878. The lamps were placed on wooden gantries and were powered by dynamos.
- France became the first country to be knocked out of a World Cup in a penalty shoot-out. They lost to West Germany 5–4 in the semi-final of the 1982 World Cup.
- The first official women's match was played in 1895, when Netty Honeyball of the British Ladies Football Club organized the first game.
- The first Women's World Cup took place in China in 1991. The final was held in Guangzhou, where the USA beat Norway 2–1.
- The Copa America is the oldest major international competition, first held in 1910. It was originally played only by South American clubs, but in recent years Mexico and the USA have taken part.
- World Cup Willie was the first World Cup mascot. He was designed for the 1966 tournament in England.
- The Jules Rimet trophy was stolen before the 1966 World Cup in England, and was later found in a garbage pile by a dog named Pickles. Brazil was presented with permanent possession of the trophy after they won it three times. It was stolen again, and has not been seen or recovered since.
- The Maracana stadium in Rio de Janeiro, Brazil, was built for the 1950 World Cup, and with a capacity of nearly 200,000 spectators it is the largest stadium in the world.
- Roger Milla of Cameroon, twice African Player of the Year, was the oldest player to appear and score in a World Cup. He was 42 in the 1994 tournament.
- Shin pads were developed in 1874 by Nottingham Forest's Samuel Widdowson in response to the physical punishment that players suffered during games. The earliest shin pads were worn outside the socks and were extended to include ankle protectors, which rested on the top of the boot.
- The first studs for football boots were made entirely of leather. The studs had to be hammered into the soles.
- In the 1930s, the wearing of illegal boots was a sending-off offense, mostly for sharp edges or protruding nails from the studs.
- Balls in the mid–1800s were often made by stitching together eight segments of leather, the ends of which were secured by a central disc. The leather was unprotected and could absorb water on wet days, so

View of the National Football Museum.

the ball increased in weight. Heading the ball could be dangerous, even fatal, and therefore this technique was not often used in those days. The dribbling game was the popular style of the time.

- The first World Cup balls to have a color other than black were used in the final in France 1998.
- Until 1909, goalkeepers were distinguishable only by their cap, making it difficult for the referee to judge who, in the goalmouth scramble, was handling the ball.
- Until the 1970's keeper's gloves were worn only when it was wet, and they were made of thin cotton.
- Penalties were introduced in 1891 as a punishment for foul play.
- A referee was introduced in the 1880s to settle disputes, and in 1891, the referee was moved onto the pitch and linesmen were introduced. This is a system that has continued ever since.
- The first linesmen waved a handkerchief to alert the referee. Today the use of a flag is standard.

NOTES

1. For the purpose of this book, soccer is referred to as "football" throughout.

2. The author, a native of El Salvador, lived through that short war as a 13-year-old.

3. Four sets of laws made a significant contribution to today's game. They are the Cambridge Rules (1848), Sheffield (1857), Uppingham (1862), and the English FA (1863). At that time one set of rules did not supersede another; it was up to the clubs to decide which set of rules to play under. It was the merger of the Sheffield and English FA rules in 1878 that provided the platform for the growth of the game all over the world.

4. The original Freemasons Tavern burned down and was rebuilt in the early 20th century. It is now called the Freemasons Arms, and as of 2006 it is owned by John and Linda Annetts. On this very spot in 1863, the public house hosted several meetings between London clubs and schools before the laws of the game, the FA rules of 1863, were finally "etched in stone."

5. The author was fortunate to be there for the opening game of the 2006 World Cup

6. It was students' slang that we have to thank for the word "soccer." It seems it was the practice of the students at Oxford to abbreviate words by adding "er" or "ers" to the end (e.g., "brekkers" for breakfast). Thus were coined the two words "rugger" for rugby, and "soccer," based on the abbreviation "assoc," for the football association game.

7. Formations always start with the defense. The goalkeeper comes first, but as this is a position that has remained unchanged, the formations in football always begin with the fullbacks and progress up to the forwards (e.g., 2-3-5 means two fullbacks, three halfbacks, and five forwards).

8. In England, as in the rest of the world, to be "capped" means to be chosen for the national team. A player is said to be capped each time he represents his country in international games.

9. Preston North End was the first club for which David Beckham played. From there he moved to Manchester United.

10. The acronym FIFA comes from the official French title of the organization: Fédération Internationale de Football Association. In English, it is the International Federation of Association Football.

11. Unlike the Major League Baseball World Series, the World Cup is truly a world championship; it is open to teams from all over the world.

12. At the 1946 congress FIFA voted to call the World Cup the "Jules Rimet Cup" to honor its president, who had led the organization for the past 25 years. The first to win it three times would keep the cup for life.

13. The English soon pointed out that baseball was nothing but a form of rounders (an English game played generally by girls). Americans responded by claiming that Abner Doubleday had invented baseball in 1839. Such was the desire of Americans to Americanize their sports that this story was accepted as the gospel truth.

14. Under the "single-entity" agreement, the teams are owned and run by the league, although financially supported by wealthy investors.

15. Title IX is a law passed in 1972 that requires gender equity for boys and girls in every educational program that receives federal funding. Title IX of the Educational Amendments of 1972 is the landmark legislation that bans sex discrimination in schools, whether it is in academics or athletics.

16. This pyramid formation is the one generally used in the popular table game of foosball found in many game rooms across the world.

17. The words "system" and "formation" are used interchangeably throughout this book.

18. *Trequartista*, which means "three quarters" in Italian, is the position employed by the playmaker of the team, who generally sports the Number 10 jersey.

19. It should be made clear that there are situations in which talking contravenes the laws of the game: (1) Using foul or abusive language; (2) Seeking to gain an unfair advantage by calling to mislead an opponent.

20. As long as the laws of the game are not being broken, a manager and his players can use the rules to their advantage, thus it is imperative that they are well aware of any changes or modifications.

BIBLIOGRAPHY

Adam, P. (1907). *La Morale des Sports.* Paris: Librarie Mondiale.
Agnew, P. (2006). *Forza Italia: A Journey in Search of Italy and Its Football.* London: Ebury Press.
Alcock, C.W. (1895). *Association Football.* London: George Bell.
Allen, J. (1973). *Soccer for Americans.* New York: Grosset & Dunlap.
Allison, M. (1967). *Soccer for Thinkers.* London: Pelham Books.
Andrew, C. (1980). *Soccer.* Scarborough, Ontario: Prentice-Hall.
Annetts, J., and L. Annetts. (2006). Personal communication at Freemasons Tavern.
Arbena, J. (ed.). (1998). *Sport and Society in Latin America.* New York: Greenwood Press.
Armstrong, G., and R. Giulianotti (eds.). (1997). *Entering the Field: New Perspectives on World Football.* Oxford, UK: Berg.
Azikiwe, N. (1970). *My Odyssey.* London: C. Hurst.
Baker, W. (1982). *Sports in the Western World.* Totowa, NJ: Rowman & Littlefield.
Bale, J. (1982). *Sport and Place.* London: Hurst.
_____, and J. Maguire (eds.). (1994). *The Global Sports Arena.* London: Frank Cass.
Ball, D. (1975). *Sport and Social Order.* Boston: Addison-Wesley.
Ball, P. (2001). *The Story of Spanish Football.* London: WSC Books.
Barber, D. Personal communication, June 10, 2006.
Barclay, P. (2000). *The Fab Four: France Win the European Championship.* In C. Ruhn (ed.) *Le Foot: The Legends of French Football.* London: Abacus.
Batty, E. (1969). *Soccer Coaching the Modern Way.* London: Faber & Faber.
Bauer, G. (1975). *Football.* London: E.P. Sport.
BBC News. (2010). Formations guide. http://news.bbc.co.uk/sport1/low/football/rules_and_equipment/4197518.stm. Retrieved May 2, 2010.
Bebbington, J. (1976). *Football in Color.* London: Blanford.
Beck, P. (1999). *Scoring for Britain: International Football and International Politics.* London: Frank Cass.
Beckenbauer, F. (1978). *Soccer Power.* New York: Simon & Schuster.
Beim, G. (1977). *Principles of Modern Soccer.* Boston: Houghton Mifflin.
Bernard, J. (1956). *Soccer Tactics.* London: Phoenix House.
Bottemburg, M. (2001). *Global Games.* Urbana: University of Illinois Press.
Brasch, R. (1970). *How Did Sports Begin.* New York: McKay.
Brera, G. (1978). *Storia Critica del Calcio Italiana.* Italy: Limina.
Brown, A. (ed.) (1978). *Fanatics: Power, Identity and Fandom in Football.* London: Routledge.

Cantor, A. (1996). *Goooal! A Celebration of Soccer.* New York: Simon and Schuster.
Chandos, J. (1984). *Boys Together: English Public Schools.* New Haven: Yale University Press.
Chyzowych, W. (1982). *Official Soccer Book.* Chicago: Rand McNally.
Clues, J. (1980). *Soccer for Players and Coaches.* Englewood Cliffs, NJ: Prentice-Hall.
Corry, E. (1989). *Catch and Kick.* Dublin: Poolberg.
Cottrell, J. (1970). *A Century of Great Soccer Drama.* London: Hart-Davis.
Cramer, D. (1977). *Coaches Manual.* Chicago: U.S. Soccer Federation.
Csanadi, A. (1963). *Soccer.* New York: Sport Shell.
Douglas, P. (1974). *The Football Industry.* London: Howard House.
Eastman, G. (1966). *Soccer Science.* Chicago: Quadrangle Books.
European Cup History.com, 2010. http://www.europeancuphistory.com/eur072.html, 2010.
Evans, A. Personal communication, June 21, 2006.
Fabian, A., and G. Green. (1960). *Association Football.* London: Caxton.
FIFA. (2009). FIFA Laws of the Game. http://www.fifa.com/mm/document/affedera tion/federation/81/42/36/lawsofthegameen.pdf. Retrieved December 9, 2009.
_____. (2010). Classic football. http://www.fifa.com/classicfootball/history/index.html. Retrieved February 4, 2010.
_____. (2010). The history of FIFA: The Blatter years. http://www.fifa.com/classic football/history/fifa/historyfifa9.html. Retrieved June 4, 2009.
_____. (2010). The history of the laws of the game: The International FA Board. http://www.fifa.com/classicfootball/history/law/ifab.html. Retrieved June, 3, 2010.
FIFA World Cup Finals — France 1998. (2010). http://www.cartage.org.lb/en/themes/ sports/football/br-fr.html. Retrieved May 6, 2010.
Foer, F. (2004). *How Soccer Explains the World.* London: HarperCollins.
Foot, J. (2006). *Calcio: A History of Italian Football.* London: Fourth Estate.
Ford, G. (1937). *Basic Soccer.* Boston: Allyn & Bacon.
Fouls, S. (1979). *A History of the Game.* Los Angeles: Soccer for America.
Freddi, C (2006). *Complete Book of the World Cup.* London: Collins Willow.
Gardiner, E. (1930). *Athletics of the Ancient World.* New York: Oxford University Press.
Gardner, P. (1976). *The Simplest Game.* Boston: Little, Brown.
_____. (1994, October 10). Soccer talk. *Soccer America* 23, 3.
_____. (1995, October 16). Soccer talk. *Soccer America* 40, 6.
La Gazzeta dello Sport. (1994). New York: Rizzoli.
Gibson, A., and P. William. (1905). *Association Football and the Men Who Made It.* London: Caxton.
Glanville, B. (1979). *A Book of Soccer.* New York: Oxford University Press.
_____. (1999). *Football Memories.* London: Virgin.
_____. (2006). *The Story of the World Cup.* London: Faber.
Goal.com, 2010. http://www.goal.com/en/news/12/spain/2009/09/19/1510122/i-like-pellegrinis-4-2-2-2-formation-real-madrid-star-kaka.html. Retrieved June 20, 2010.
Goldblatt, D. (2007). *The Ball Is Round: A Global History of Football.* London: Penguin.
Goldman, H. (1969). *Soccer.* Boston: Allyn & Bacon.
Golesworthy, M. (1970). *The Encyclopedia of Association Football.* London: Robert Hale.
Gramsci, A. (2008). *Gramsci's Kingdom: Football, Politics, the World.* http://gramscis kingdom.blogspot.com/2008_07_01_archive.html. Retrieved July 12, 2008.
Granville, B. (1969). *Soccer Panorama.* London: Eyre & Spottiswoode.

Greaves, J. (1966). *Soccer Techniques and Tactics*. London: Pelham Books.

Green, G. (1953). *Soccer: The World Game*. London: Pan.

_____. (1960). *The Official History of the FA*. London: Heinemann.

Guttmann, A. (1994). *Games and Empires: Modern Sports and Cultural Imperialism*. New York: Columbia University Press.

_____, and L. Thompson (2001). *Japanese Sports: A History*. Honolulu: University of Hawaii Press.

Halpern, J. (2008, August 4). Balls and Blood. *Sports Illustrated* 109, p. 42.

Hamilton, I. (1992). *The Faber Book of Soccer*. London: Faber.

Harris, H.A. (1973). *Sports in Greece and Rome*. Ithaca, NY: Cornell University Press.

Harris, P. (1976). *Soccer for Americans*. Los Angeles: Pan Books Limited.

Hill, J., and J. William (1996). *Sport and Identity in the North of England*. Keele, UK: Keele University Press.

Hollander, Z. (1980). *American Encyclopedia of Soccer*. New York: Everest House.

Holt, R. (1989). *Sport and the British: A Modern History*. Oxford, UK: Oxford University Press.

Hopcraft, A. (1971). *The Football Man*. London: Collins.

Hornby, H. (2004). *Eyewitness: Football*. London: Dorling Kindersley.

Hornby, N. (1992). *Fever Pitch*. London: Gollancz.

http://www.football-lineups.com/tactic/4-2-2-2, 2010.

http://www.France98.com/english/history/history_of/football.html. Retrieved October 21, 1998.

Hughes, B. (1975). *The Aim of Coaching Soccer*. New York: Kendall Hunt.

Hughes, C. (1966). *Team Tactics*. London: Faber & Faber.

_____. (1975). *Tactics and Teamwork*. London: EP Publishing.

_____. (1990). *The Winning Formula*. London: Collins.

Inglis, I. (1990). *The Football Grounds of Europe*. London: Williow Books.

Janssen, J.L. (1967). *The Legal Position of the Professional Football Player*. Leyden, Netherlands: A.W. Sitthoff.

Jeffery, G. (1963). *European International Football*. London: Nicholas Kaye.

Jones, R., and T. Tranter. *Soccer Strategies: Defensive and Attacking Tactics*. Spring City, PA: Reedswain Books.

Joy, B. (1956). *Soccer Tactics*. London: Phoenix House.

Kane, B. (1970). *Soccer*. London: Barnes.

_____. (1970). *Soccer for American Spectators*. New York: A.S. Barnes.

_____. (1975). *How to Play Soccer*. New York: Grosset & Dunlap.

Keeton, G. (1972). *The Football Revolution*. London: David & Charles.

Kobyashi, M. (1978). *Climate and Sport*. Tokyo: Taishyukan.

Kubota, K. (1978). *A Book of Social Sport*. Tokyo: Taishyukan.

Kuper, S. (2003). *Ajax, the Dutch, the War: Football in Europe During the Second World War*. London: Orion.

Lanfranchi, P., and A. Wahl. (1994). *Moving with the Ball*. Oxford, UK: Berg.

Lever, J. (1983). *Soccer Madness*. Chicago: University of Chicago Press.

Lodziak, C. (1966). *Understanding Soccer Tactics*. London: Faber & Faber.

Longrigg, R. (1977). *The English Squire and His Sport*. London: St. Martin's Press.

Luschen, G., and G.H. Sage (1981). *Handbook of Social Science and Sport*. Champaign, IL: Stipes.

Luxbacher, J. (1981). *Soccer*. Tulsa, OK: Winchester Press.

MacDonald, B. (1972). *Scientific Soccer*. London: Pelham Books.

Maher, A.E. (1983). *Complete Soccer Handbook*. New York: Parker.

The Making of a World Cup Legend. http://www.dw-world.de/dw/article/0,2144,14 86199,00.html. Retrieved June 8, 2008.

Marples, M. (1954). *A History of Football*. London: Secker and Warburg.

Martir de Anglerría. (1964). *Décadas del Nuevo Mundo*. Buenos Aires: Editoría Bajel.

Mason, N. (1974). *Football*. London: Temple Smith.

Mason, T. (1980). *Association Football and the English Society*. Brighton, UK: Harvester Press.

_____. (1995). *Passion of the People? Football in South America*. London: Verso.

Mazunda, W. (1979). *Soccer*. Tokyo: Shyuei.

Meisl, W. (1955). *Soccer Revolution*. London: Phoenix House.

Mencke, F. (1969). *Encyclopedia of Sports*. New York: A.S. Barnes.

Miller, A. (1975). *Winning Soccer*. Chicago: Regency.

Miller, L. (1979). *Mastering Soccer*. New York: Contemporary Books.

Miller, S. (1991). *Arete: Greek Sports from Ancient Sources*. Berkeley: University of California Press.

Moore, M. (2008). Chelsea and Roman Abramovich may be drawn to Luciano Spalletti's style at Roma. *The Daily Telegraph*. http://www.telegraph.co.uk/sport/main. jhtml?xml=/sport/2008/06/05/sfnchel05.xml. Retrieved July 11, 2008.

Morita, R. (1984). *History of Soccer*. Tokyo: Fumi.

Morris, D. (1981). *The Soccer Tribe*. London: Jonathan Cape.

Moynihan, J. (1974) *Soccer*. New York: Thomas Y. Crowell.

Murray, B. (1994). *The World's Game: A History of Soccer*. Urbana: University of Illinois Press.

Pele. (1977). *My Life and the Beautiful Game: The Autobiography of Pele*. New York: Doubleday.

Radnedge, K. (2000). *The World Encyclopedia of Soccer*. N.p.: Seven Oaks.

_____. (2007). *ITV Sport Complete Encyclopedia of Football*. London: Carlton Publishing.

Rosenthal, G. (1979). *Soccer*. New York: Sayre.

_____. (1981). *Everybody's Soccer Book*. New York: Scribner's.

Rote, K. (1975). *Beyond the Goal*. New York: Simon & Schuster.

Rote, K., Jr. (1978). *Complete Book of Soccer*. New York: Simon & Schuster.

Rous, S. (1978). *Football Worlds — A Lifetime in Sports*. London: Faber and Faber.

Russel, D. (1997). *Football and the English*. Preston, UK: Carnegie Publishing.

Santapelota (2009). http://www.santapelota.blogspot.com/2009/05/overview-of-brazilian-football-part-ii.html. May 5, 2009.

SBRnet. (2009). http://sbrnet.com/research.asp?subRID=500&ResCode=soccch1. Retrieved October 21, 2010.

Scarborough, V., and D. Wilcox. (1991). *The Mesoamerican Ballgame*. Tucson: University of Arizona Press.

Sharpe, I. (1952). *Forty Years in Football*. London: Hutchinson.

Signy, D. (1968). *A Pictorial History of Soccer*. London: Spring House.

Silver, Dan. (2008). Real Madrid manager madness: Spurs flop Juande Ramos becomes 10th in 10 years. Mirrorfootball. http://www.mirrorfootball.co.uk/news/Real-Madrid-manager-madness-Spurs-flop-Juande-Ramos-becomes-10th-in-10-years-article34645.html. Retrieved June 28, 2010.

Simpson, P. (2010). Curses, wallies, and the return of the Russian linesman. Fourfourtwo.com. http://fourfourtwo.com/blogs/championsleague/archive/2009/02/20/curses-wallies-amp-the-return-of-the-russian-linesman.aspx. Retrieved June 16, 2010.

Slusher, H.S. (1967). *Man, Sport and Existence*. Philadelphia: Lea & Fabiger.

Smith, S. (1966). *International Coaching Book*. London: Souvenir Press.

Soccer. (1967). London: Gilmour & Dean.

Smyth, R. (2010). *The Joy of Six Counter-Attacking Goals.* http://www.guardian.co.uk/sport/blog/2010/jan/22/joy-of-six-counterattacking-goals. March 21, 2010.

Strutt, J. (1903). *The Sports and Pastimes of the People of England.* London: Methuen.

Taylor, C. (1998). *The Beautiful Game: A Journey through Latin American Football.* London: Victor Gollancz.

Taylor, R., and A. Ward. (1996). *Kicking and Screaming: An Oral History of Football in England.* London: Robson Books.

Thomas, J.R., and J.K. Nelson. (1985). *Introduction to Research in Health, Physical Education, Recreation and Dance.* Champaign, IL: Human Kinetics.

Thompson, B. (1977). *Soccer Coaching Methods.* London: Page-Ficklin.

Tischler, S. (1981). *Footballers and Businessmen.* New York: Holmes & Meir.

Tomlinson, A., and C. Young. (2006). *German Football: History, Culture and Society.* London: Routledge.

Tyler, M. (1967). *The Story of Football.* London: Marshall Cavendish.

USSF Administrative Handbook. (2009). Chicago: United States Soccer Federation.

Vamplew, W. (2004). *Pay Up and Play the Game: Professional Sport in Britain.* Cambridge, UK: Cambridge University Press.

Vasquez, M. (2005). *Fútbol: Una Religión en Busca de un Dios.* Madrid: Debolsillo.

Vogelsinger, H. (1973). *The Challenge of Soccer.* Boston: Allyn & Bacon.

Wade, A. (1967). *The F.A. Guide to Training and Coaching.* London: Heinemann.

Wagg, S. (1984). *The Football World.* Sussex: Harvester Press.

Wahl, A. (1989). *Les Archives de Football.* Paris: Gallimard.

Wall, F. (1935). *Fifty Years in Football.* London: Cleethorpes Soccer Books.

Walvin, J. (1994). *The People's Game: The History of Football Revisited.* Edinburgh: Mainstream.

Weintraub, S. (2002). *Silent Night: The Remarkable Christmas Truce of 1914.* London: Pocket Books.

Wheeler, K. (1967). *Soccer—The English Way.* London: Cassell.

Wilson, J. (2006). *Behind the Curtain: Football in Eastern Europe.* London: Orion.

_____. (2008). "The End of Forward Thinking." *The Guardian.* http://www.blogs.guardian.co.uk/sport/2008/06/08/the_end_of_forward_thinking.html, 2008.

_____. (2008). *The Question: Is 3-5-2 Dead? The Guardian.* http://www.guardian.co.uk/sport/blog/2008/nov/19/argentina-napoli. Retrieved November 19, 2008.

_____. (2008). *Tactics.* http://www.guardian.co.uk/football/blog/2008/dec/18/4231-442-tactics, 2008.

_____. (2009). *Inverting the Pyramid: The History of Football Tactics.* London: Orion House.

_____. (2009). *The Question: How Is Brazil's 4-2-3-1 Different from a European 4-2-3-1?* http://www.guradian.co.uk/sport/blog/2009/jun/24/the-question-brazil-4-2-3-1, 2009.

Winner, D. (200). *Brilliant Orange: The Neurotic Genius of Dutch Football.* London: Bloomsbury.

Winterbottom, W. (1959). *Soccer Coaching.* London: Heinemann.

_____. (1960). *Training for Soccer.* London: Heinemann.

Wittington, E.M. (2001). *The Sport of Life and Death: The Mesoamerican Ballgame.* London: Thames and Hudson.

Woosman, P. (1972). *Soccer.* New York: Lippincott.

Worthington, E. (1977). *Learning and Teaching Soccer Skills.* North Hollywood, CA: Wilshire.

Yallop, D. (1999). *How They Stole the Game.* London: Poetic Publishing.

Young, P. (1968). *A History of British Football.* London: Stanley Paul.

INDEX

245